LIVE
HAPPY

365 Daily Practices for a Happier Life

Dr. Derrick B. Wells

Deep Wells Publishing

This book was printed in the United States of America.

Order additional copies of this book from Amazon.com

Contact info:

the4thletter@aol.com

ACKNOWLEDGEMENTS

While this project has been my labor and my love, I am not the only one responsible for you having it in your hands right now. I am present to my role as the batter, who strolled up to the plate, in the bottom of the ninth inning. Our home team was down a couple runs but there were players on base. We had two outs. The pitch came in and I got to swing away. I connected and knocked it out of the park. I saw my teammates touch home base before I would. Then they turned around, with the rest of the team behind them, to welcome me home. As I triumphantly make my way to the plate, I am reminded that this was a total team effort.

I am celebrated because my name is attached to the home run but just like in the game of life, there are hidden heroes:

To my wife, Sylvia, my mother Felicia, my children—Malika and Mikael, my sisters LaTanya, Pamela, and Stacy, and the newest family member, my granddaughter Mali – words will never truly express what you mean to me. I love you all so much. Nothing compares to you.

To the entire Live Happy team, you all remained committed to our shared vision. You embraced that what we were doing needed to be done. You are making a huge difference. You push yourselves, even when it means taking attention away from your spouses and children. Our work would never be complete without your unwavering dedication. You put in crazy hours working on crazy ideas. Our reward is seeing those ideas help people unleash their potential. I salute each of you!

To my CUT and Temple Talks family, sharing the journey with you is one of the enduring highlights of my life. I continue to learn so much from you all. Your participation and inspiration is immeasurable.

To Darlene Brooks, thank you for refusing to let this idea die. You are a prime example of why we should never stop after one delay. A delay does not equal a denial.

To Paulette Barrett and Gavin Jackson, you made excellent accountability partners. Just knowing you would ask how the book was coming along, kept me moving along.

To Lisa Nichols, Michael Beckwith, and Les Brown. Your coaching, inspiration, and example keeps me reaching for more. I truly value our relationship.

To Shana Kwokenkwo, Shaun Thompson, and Tony Horton, you helped me honor and build my body the way I strive to help others honor and build their soul. Thanks for making me better.

To the giants whose shoulders I stand upon, you are too many to mention. I honor your role in my progress. All I continue to become is impossible without you

Dedication:
This is dedicated to anyone who has ever shared happiness with me!

FOREWORD

23 years ago I longed for life of happiness. I longed for life of fulfillment, execution, joy, and peace of mind. Yet I needed to go get the skill set. I needed to go get the mindset. I needed to understand what people who were operating at their highest level of consciousness, awareness, productivity, and joy. I needed to know what they knew. How do you think believe, act, and execute to the highest level of your possibilities? Live Happy is a book that teaches you how to harness your power. It's a book that teaches you how to shift your mindset.

It's books like this that allowed me to really discover who Lisa was always meant to be. I invite you to not only read this book, I invite you to devour this book. There are action steps, ways of being, and ways of thinking that literally can and will transform who you are becoming every single day.

As I navigate myself through the path of excellence, abundance, and serving the world, I only use books like Live Happy to keep me on path, remind me of who I am, hold me accountable to the woman I am becoming, and most of all, to allow me to show up powerfully. My brother Dr. Derrick B. Wells is an absolute genius in communicating the path, the process, and the necessary action steps to really navigate you to that next best version of yourself...the version that has more joy, more peace, more abundance, better relationships, and greater outcomes.

Very few people have the ability to download, to process, to articulate, and to educate us in our own language. Dr. Derrick has mastered that and he is sharing his mastery with us through this book. So from my mouth, to these pages, to your ears, I say as you begin to designed the next chapter of your life, make it the best chapter of your life, by reading every page of this book.

Lisa Nichols

DAY 1

First Things First

If you want to live a happier life, you must commit to putting the First Things First and you must recognize the power in this commitment to transform your life. Putting First Things First enables you to be in the flow of creation. By doing so, you open yourself to the Mind of the Creator, seeking to express through you. You also open yourself to the seed ideas that are seeking manifestation through you, as well as the inherent good within these ideas. In putting First Things First, you listen attentively for God – the First Cause – who is speaking to you, and your First thought is to move as instructed.

This commitment to First Things First may be new to you but it is not too big for you. In fact, I believe it came to bless you. A baby's first step is always a small one. If you are a baby in putting First Things First, give yourself permission to take small steps and make small adaptations.

Make your relationship with God a First Things First priority. Make paying attention to your breathing a priority; make accepting yourself just as you are a priority; make thinking healthy, productive thoughts a priority; and make speaking empowering words a priority. Taking small actions and putting the First Things First is your first step to living a happier life. ▮

Today's Live Happy Practice

As part of your commitment to putting First Things First, express gratitude. Affirm that you are grateful for a loving God. Affirm that you are grateful for the opportunity to bless and be a blessing. Be grateful for the people in your life. Affirm that you are grateful for your dreams and your disappointments, for they both help sharpen your focus. Affirm that when you put first things first, your steps are ordered and orderly.

DAY 2

What You Listen To

How do you start your day? Does the alarm wake you or is it your internal clock? Do you immediately turn on the television or do you reach for your cell phone? Do you jump right out of bed to get the day going or do you lie there wishing you had more time? We all have a morning routine but the real question is, "Does your routine involve some quiet time alone with God?" If not, instead of going directly to your phone or listening to the morning news with your coffee, consider repurposing that time and managing what you listen to, by allowing yourself to commune with God.

This redistribution of your time could prove to be one of the greatest opportunities for growth and expansion you will have all day. Moreover, doing so when you first wake up gives you the benefit of experiencing something uplifting at the beginning of each and every day. This habit of communion helps condition the soul to not only face the challenges of the day, but also recognize the opportunities each day brings.

When you first wake up in the morning, your mind is operating at 10.5 wave cycles per second. That's when the subconscious mind is most impressionable; your storehouse is most ready to receive; and the dross of doubt is less active. That is when you can most easily shape the mental and emotional tone of your day and when you are most prone to believe that whatever thoughts you are feeding yourself is possible and it can happen for you, to you, and through you. That is also when you are most likely to transfer the wisdom that comes in the sacred silence into action. ■

Today's Live Happy Practice

The next time your alarm clock goes off, commit to taking time to listen to the stillness of the moment and allow yourself to commune with God. Enjoy the silence and prepare your mind to receive what God has to say.

DAY 3

Accessing Your GPS

There is an age-old maxim that says, "If you fail to plan, then you plan to fail." Our plans are a very important part of how we navigate life. In fact, the question I often ask myself when traveling in unfamiliar territory is, "What are the ways in which I can get from point A to point B." Fortunately, rather than attempt to figure it out on my own, I just access my GPS navigation system. My navigation system then does some extraordinary things. It will determine my location and then map out the most effective ways to get to my destination. Once I am underway, it will provide guidance, feedback, and course correction, all accordance with the plan.

Should our plans for how we will navigate and arrive at the desired destinations in our life contain fewer details than random trips in unfamiliar territory? I think not. So let's access our internal navigation system. Where are you presently positioned? Are you happy or content? Are you settling or giving up? Where do you want to be spiritually? Where do you want to go in your health; your relationships; your wealth? How will you get there? Pay close attention to the guidance, feedback, and course-corrections, both internal and external. This is key in arriving at your desired destination. The "Still Small Voice" within you is faithful. It will not fail you or forsake you. Learn to trust this internal guide. Stay flexible, as detours are sometimes necessary in order to arrive at your desired destination. ∎

Today's Live Happy Practice

Planning is part of the work to go from where you are to where you want to be. It's okay if you don't know all the answers or don't know all the steps. Research some how-to. Find someone who has been where you plan to go. Learn from their journey and how they got there. Success always leaves clues. "I don't know" is no longer a sufficient answer. Figure it out and pick a route.

DAY 4

Move Forward With Intention

Too often we allow our circumstances to dictate our actions. The challenge with this approach is that it keeps us in a reactionary mode of operation. What would happen if you shifted out of this behavior and began to assert an intentional design and intentional actions upon your respective circumstances? When I say intentional design, I am referring to specifically selected thoughts and feelings that influence and direct your actions and behaviors. Most of us have had an experience where we were undergoing a disappointment episode and our action was to complain. What was that experience like for you? How long did you carry the unproductive energy of that episode? How many times did you replay it in your mind and relive the emotion and tension? How many people did you talk to about it?

What if, instead of complaining, you exercised the dignity of choice to do better? What if, instead of fixing the blame, you focused on fixing the issue? Remember, one of the best ways to improve your circumstances is to improve yourself. Since complaining is not the same a correcting, consider eliminating complaints. This is particularly important since complaining is a gateway that quenches our receptivity to the Spirit. If you want to be happier, stop complaining; consistently complaining only gives you more to complain about. ▮

Today's Live Happy Practice

When you feel like complaining, as a part of your intentional design and action toolkit, use one of these possibilities instead:

- Be patient
- Focus On Your Desired Outcome
- Be Grateful
- Pray Without Ceasing. To him who has, more shall be given.

DAY 5

Grow, You Must

Now is a wonderful time for you to grow. Growing allows you to have more, do more, be more, and give more, all because growth enables you to become more. How are you growing? Raymond Holliwell offered that, "There can be no progress without change, no growth without renewal." As you begin to see new opportunities and possibilities for yourself, allow yourself to grow into the vision. It's difficult to fit a big dream into a small sense of self and growing gives us confidence.

The size of your growth is in direct correlation to the vision you hold of yourself and the degree to which you are prepared to grow in the areas you already suspect. How have you decided to grow from where you are to where you want to be? What will you need to do, be, and know in order to grow from where you are to where God has destined you to be? What kind of growth work are you prepared to put with your faith?

Abram was living a life of comfort but in order to grow into his potential and become what he was meant to be, he had to leave those familiar things that he identified with. Like Abram, in order to see what is really in store for you, you must grow. Your growth will be a catalyst that enables you to look around and see the opportunities and possibilities that already exist for you. God is ready to expand your territory...are you ready to grow? ■

Today's Live Happy Practice

In the busy world that we live in, it is very tempting to multitask; but if you want to grow – monotask! It is important to be present wherever you are. If you're in a class, don't be on the phone. If you're taking a walk, focus on your present surroundings. Wherever you are, be there. Make a commitment to yourself to be present in every moment throughout this day.

DAY 6

Inspired To Be Tired

American politician Frank Clark said, "What great accomplishments we'd have in the world if everyone had done what they intended to do." So why do we sometimes lack the necessary inspiration to execute and share with the world the beauty and majesty that exists within? As a beautiful piece of graffiti art I once saw while in traveling in Canada suggested, we're "Inspired but too tired."

True inspiration gives us the motivation to push past the mediocre existence or experiences we sometimes find ourselves in. This may come as a surprise but you are not made to be average. Nothing about you is mediocre. You are amazing in more ways than you can imagine. You have been given a unique mixture of worth, talents, skills, gifts, and abilities that make you perfect for your unique opportunities, and ideal for your unique contribution.

The world is deprived and devoid of your unique form of greatness, until you decide to let it out. Your contribution is not insignificant…your contribution is incomparable. Your matchless qualities enable you to express God like no one on this planet ever has. You came as a gift, with a gift…a gift too needed to be wasted in mediocrity. ▮

Today's Live Happy Practice

Try a hobby that you have always wanted to do but secretly thought you might be terrible at.

Trying something new can be fun and inspiring whether you are good at it or not. Also, trying something new actually stimulates parts of the brain that you were not previously accessing. This alone can go a long way towards forming inspiration and letting your creative juices flow.

DAY 7

Your Personal Praise Party

If you are like most people then you have probably had your moments. You know the moments…the ones when your mind was so filled with confusion that you couldn't tell up from down; the times when your body was so consumed with pain that you could hardly determine in from out. Being trapped in those moments can often prompt us to lament or complain because we feel like that is about all we can muster.

Whenever you find yourself trapped in those moments, that is the ideal time for a good praise party. Praise helps facilitate a shift in our mind and emotions because praise helps us move from a problem focus, to a quality of mind that overwhelmingly seeks out the good. All too often we promote our problems when we should be practicing our praise. Praise stimulates and quickens God's will for us, in us. When you praise, you raise your vibration, you raise your awareness, and you raise up the truth to the place where your issues no longer have the same power over you.

Life responds to praise. Gardeners know this. Parents know this. Pet owners know this. Your soul knows this. The purpose of praise is to activate within you an awareness that is in harmony with the presence and power of God working in and through you. Whenever you find yourself having one of those moments, remember, praise is a powerful lever for instantaneous change. Make praise a part of your everyday life by giving thanks always for all things. ■

Today's Live Happy Practice

Praise can literally fill your soul and lift you up. Choose one of the following methods of praise today to put yourself on a natural high.

- Praise Him by lifting your hands.
- Praise Him with singing.
- Praise Him with your words.
- Praise Him with dancing and instruments.

DAY 8

Outperform Yourself

When taking up the critical work involved in modifying the direction in which our lives may be going, one of the most fundamental things we can do is change the way we think about ourselves. Unfortunately, we sometimes overlook this simple, if not so easy step. Whether we realize it or not, the way we think becomes the basis from which we speak and act. Rare is the occasion when we outperform the things we declare about ourselves.

In order to speak life, we must think life. Being responsible for the way we think, speak, and believe gives us the immediate ability to respond when life seems out-of-whack. There are more than enough challenges in the world already and sometimes life can be really difficult. Why add to the difficulties by discouraging yourself every day with negative self-talk. As it has been said, "Don't fill your boat with water. The storm will do that all on its own."

Each of us needs a champion, a coach, and a cheerleader. Become your own encourager. Every time you do a good job, don't just let it pass; give yourself a compliment. When you make a mistake, learn from it and improve. Be patient with yourself. You may not be a finished work just yet. Every constructive thing you can say to yourself will help. Speak life! ■

Today's Live Happy Practice

Make a conscious decision to engage in positive self-talk. Reward yourself when you do something that you are proud of. The reward will help you acknowledge that you did something good.

DAY 9

Your Incredible Internal Drive

When you spend enough time with people, one of the things you might come to realize is that we are naturally wired to strive, grow, and do better. Whether it is in a kindergarten classroom, a hospital examination room, or a family living room, we want to be better, even if we do not quite understand how to become better. This internal drive is part of the eternal beauty that is baked into the incredible way we are made.

Yet in life, there are some things we must work for and there are some things that we must wait for. Either way, we have an obligation to begin each day with dedication, if we want to end each day with satisfaction. It is important to know where and how to direct your dedication. The direction of your dedication will likely influence how you use your internal power. You can remain dedicated to who you used to be and allow your past to be the predictor of your future or you can commit to learning something new every day.

Dedication to improving yourself daily precedes a future filled with possibilities. Dedication helps you grow and when you grow, you expand your vision, you attract more options, you open your opportunities, and you maximize your potential. While you give your daily dedication you will also have to practice patience. New things are usually difficult before they become easy and unfortunately, difficulty often serves as a deterrent for many of us. In fact, most of us never come to realize how close we actually are to achieving our goals and dreams, because we give up too soon. Every achievement we value takes time and dedication. The people who grow and achieve the most are the ones who practice the power of patience and persistence. ■

Today's Live Happy Practice

In order to be persistent, try taking a break and then starting again. After you take a break, you'll be energized and more enthusiastic, giving yourself the wherewithal to keep moving forward.

DAY 10

The Power of Today

Whether it's a new year, a new day, a new hour, or a new season, there's something very liberating about having an opportunity to begin again. New beginnings, like new seasons, represent the insatiable currents of change found in the natural cycles of the rhythm of life. It is a wonderful thing to have an opportunity to turn the page.

The thing we have to remember is that the events of yesterday no longer have any power to influence today, unless we invite them to. The locust of control lies in what you do today. What thoughts are you holding today? What feelings are you entertaining today? Yesterday cannot be modified. It is established and unchangeable in the history of your past moon. No amount of worrying, hoping, praying, or manipulating will adjust this fact.

Here is some more news…the power to mold today is in your hands. The shape of today does not have to be influenced by the past mistakes or failures of yesterday. Today is a brand new opportunity. Do not continue to suffer because you are letting hang-ups from old experiences negatively impact your current possibilities.

The fact that last year, last month, or last season is gone does not mean that it carries no more value. You can make the most of yesterday by learning from it. This is one of the greatest benefits and uses of the past. Learn to tease out the blessings of the past and allow the lessons to be a bridge over troubles waters; that helps you pass over into a bright future, that is more joy-filled and rewarding.

Today's Live Happy Practice

If you have made a mistake, own it. Review what went wrong and reframe it as an opportunity. Think about the lessons you can learn from your mistake and apply it to your future plans.

DAY 11

Abundance of the Stars

Are you committed to living in the abundance that has been promised to you since the beginning of time? Before you answer, let me be clear about the kind of abundance I am referring to. I'm referring to the kind of abundance we see when we consider the grains of sand, on all the beaches in the world. I mean the type of abundance we see when we contemplate all the stars, in all the universe. You know…the abundance that flows from an unlimited source. If you are at, "Yes," but it seems a little intimidating, just remember that the same God that created the aforementioned conditions, placed a similar expansive capacity in you. Also remember that it may take courage to claim that which you are entitled to.

If your answer is, "No," I want to share a saying found in the tribal wisdom of the Dakota Indians, "When you discover that you are riding a dead horse, the best strategy is to dismount." In plane terms, there are perhaps some attitudes that must be adjusted in order to claim the promises of your birthright.

Abundance, whether spiritual or material, is always full, overflowing, and responding to our awareness. Know that there are mental and spiritual laws at work and the purpose of spiritual abundance, as an expression of enduring substance, is to move upon and toward manifestation. When you say, "Yes," you claim abundance as your birthright. Accordingly, an awakened identity breeds optimistic attitudes and confidence in your abilities. Nothing is too hard or too big for God and if you can conceive it and believe it, you can receive it. But you have to get to, "Yes." █

Today's Live Happy Practice

You can live in abundance by taking advantage of every opportunity that presents itself. Don't just let opportunities go half used. Think of other ways to utilize the resources you already have and repurpose them to create something new.

DAY 12

Leading Yourself Well

Leadership is an important quality and we need good leadership like never before. As both good and bad examples of leadership seem to pop-up all around us, many leadership experts will tell you, it is difficult to move a family, community, city, or country above the level of its leader.

I particularly enjoy reading about the leadership challenges and opportunities faced by many of the transformational leaders found in scripture. Now, just as then, transformational leadership remains a valuable commodity. Whether you're leading department, team, company, family or just yourself, when it comes down to people deciding whether you are worth following, remember that people first listen to the words you say, then they watch the things you do. Before you can lead others, you must first be willing to lead yourself exceptionally well. When leaders practice what they preach, people are more willing to trust and trust is one of those invaluable qualities that give leaders the ability to move.

Transformational leaders understand how to use their influence to share their vision and improve their environment. One of the responsibilities of transformational leaders then is to develop the trust that leads to the ability to see into the distant future with clarity and vision. Leadership and vision go hand-in-hand. When we have leadership without vision, we get lost without a place to go. When we have vision without leadership, we get people excited about someplace we can't take them. Leading well leads to people being better. █

Today's Live Happy Practice

If you want to be a great leader, you must do it by example. Be prepared to model the behavior that you want to inspire. Lead with respect and honesty and others will follow.

DAY 13

Allure of the Rear-View Mirror

Have you ever wondered why the front window on your car is so much larger than the rear-view mirror? Perhaps it is so that we can have far greater capacity to see where we are going, as opposed to where we have been. In order to drive forward into the good desires of our heart, we have to focus on what is in front of us. Yet, as in with the experience of driving, we have to occasionally consult the rear-view mirror. Embracing this practice gives us the ability to forge ahead and take close inventory of our surroundings at the same time.

Each of us is experiencing people and conditions that may be impacting us far more than we realize. As we accumulate these myriads of experiences, their cumulative effect can easily drive us places we had not intended to go. How do we prevent this from happening? We remember that progress comes at a price and the price must be paid, if we would arrive at our desired destination. I can distinctly remember each person who questioned or discouraged my ambition, motivation, logic, ability, or common sense, when in a defenseless moment; I shared my plans for profound life change. I can also count on one thumb the number of people in that scenario who still play a significant role in my life.

Life is a delicate maneuver between what we are driving toward and what we are leaving behind. We select what works and we reject what does not. What a blessing it is to be able to guard our minds and hearts as we carefully examine the license and authority of those seeking to drive us to places where the new experiences of our life are formed. ∎

Today's Live Happy Practice

Toxic people are always trying to pull you into their drama. But keep in mind that they are not your responsibility. If they truly need help, direct them towards the appropriate resources.

DAY 14

The Fortitude of Persistence

One of the qualities we must absolutely develop and apply if we intend to live a happy and healthy is the quality of persistence. Our aims and aspirations need constant watching and refinement in order to go from their seed potential to our dream situation; but in order to make it so, we must persist.

Our persistence is demonstrated when we consistently execute the actions that lead to the fulfillment of our aims and aspirations. In studying the law of manifestation, I have learned that persistence overshadows talent as a valuable and effective resource. You would be surprised by the number of talented people who give up a few feet from the goal of creating the quality of life they desire.

This level of resolve can move mountains, even if it's done one pebble at a time. Agricultural scientist George Washington Carver is credited with discovering or developing more than 300 uses for the peanut. What we don't often hear is how many experiments and permutations he ran before arriving at 300! Thomas Edison failed more than 5,000 times, and when asked about it, he replied, "I have not failed at all. I have successfully identified 5,000 ways that will not work. That just puts me 5,000 ways closer to what will." Persistence is one of the most valuable qualities you can possess because it equips you with the fortitude to achieve your dreams and aspirations regardless of any obstacles or setbacks. ∎

Today's Live Happy Practice

In order to be persistent, look for feedback. Gather a sufficient amount of data and determine whether you're on the right track. If what you're doing is leading to the success you want, change your strategy and try again.

DAY 15

The Gift of Greatness

Have you ever been in the headspace where you thought to yourself, "Is this all that life has for me?" If you have or even if you are there right now, you may be ready to get more out of yourself than you ever thought possible? One of the ways we think in alignment is by refusing to justify or rationalize our poor decisions. Don't make excuses, make improvements. Change your mind and open up new possibilities to new experiences.

Paul wrote to the church in Rome, "Do not be conformed to this world, but be transformed by the renewing of your mind, so that you may prove what is the good, acceptable, and perfect will of God." The way we think becomes the process by which we handle ideas and create patterns in our life. Your thoughts become words and your words become actions. Accordingly, if you want to change your actions, begin by changing the way you think and speak. These subtle habits form the foundation upon which you build the new you.

Paul's insights remind us that we must die daily. What old ways of thinking and being do you need to die to? Repetition is a convincing argument. Dying daily to the irrelevant and unproductive gives us license to live more fully into the new. New wine calls for new wine skins. After releasing, we must diligently guard our hearts because this becomes the wellspring of our many issues. God placed His greatness inside of you because you can be trusted to do something great with it. Set your priorities in God then think your thoughts after him. ▮

Today's Live Happy Practice

Work on killing old habits by using sticky notes as reminders. For example, if you want to break the habit of eating sweets after every meal, leave a sticky note on the fridge so that you will see it whenever you go for a sweet desert.

DAY 16

The Power of Yes

Gospel music group Shekinah Glory has so many beautiful songs. One song in particular, "Yes," has lyrics that begin with this melodic question, "Will your heart and soul say yes?" While this question may be intended to prompt us to analyze our receptivity to God, it also brings into focus the power of yes. Your "yes" is an important component to your ability to live a life that works for you. But before we get too carried away, you should know that every "yes" is not equal. According to Chris Voss, there are actually three kinds of "Yes": Counterfeit, Confirmation, and Commitment.

A counterfeit "yes" is one in which our doubts, fears, and unbelief override our faith and sense of fulfillment. It's when the tongue in our mouth and the tongue in our shoe is moving in the opposite direction. It's when we say "yes" but mean "no."

A confirmation "yes" is a reflexive response to the good desires of the heart. You confirm because you are unwilling to reject your good.

A commitment "yes", on the other hand, is the real deal. It is a "yes" that is supported by massive action. This is the "yes" we all want but it is also the "yes" that seems to be the most difficult to exercise.

Your "yes" is like a light switch that turns on the divine flood of light; which was always present in potential. Your "yes" awakens you to the God-potential, which is always present and awaiting your commitment to no longer live marginally; and it all begins with "yes." ∎

Today's Live Happy Practice

To benefit from the power of "yes", you must be in the present moment and make a conscious decision to accept things as they are. Look for the positive in everything and choose a peaceful state of mind.

DAY 17

God's Plan for a Watermelon

Are you ready to get the most out of today? This day holds so much potential for you. We should not only, "rejoice and be glad in it," we should absolutely make the most of it. Dr. Benjamin E. Mayes crystallized the power of a pregnant moment in the timeless poem titled, *I Have Only Just a Minute*. In this self-aware piece, Dr. Mayes penned this proclamation,

I have only just a minute,

Only sixty seconds in it.

Forced upon me, can't refuse it.

Didn't seek it, didn't choose it.

But it's up to me to use it.

I must suffer if I lose it.

Give account if I abuse it.

Just a tiny little minute, but eternity is in it.

Far too many of us miss the target on today's opportunities because our attention is locked onto the mistakes and shortcomings of yesterday. Others of us are so future focused that we miss the importance and power of now as the bridge to tomorrow. Stay focused and make the most of every minute in order to reach your maximum potential. ■

Today's Live Happy Practice

Perhaps we should follow the lead of the tiny watermelon seed. A watermelon seed relentlessly access the potential around it to draw from the ground and through itself 200,000 times its weight to make a watermelon; and each seed in turn, is capable of drawing through itself 200,000 times its weight— to produce God's plan for a watermelon, time and again.

DAY 18

Wired to Enjoy Healthy Relationships

Relationships are an important part of life and truly enrich our experiences in living. Each of us is wired to enjoy healthy, productive, reaffirming relationships. I like to say that when it comes to relationships and human interaction, we all deserve to be in relationships where we are appreciated, celebrated, and not just tolerated. Yet all relationships are not created equally.

Where healthy relationships help us feel valued, seen, heard, and fulfilled, unhealthy relationships have the potential to rob us of the joy, peace, and unity that comes from walking with another. In order to get the most of your relationships, it really helps to be self-aware and self-reflective. Self-awareness and self-reflection enables us to examine the nature of our relationships and potentially better understand who we are involved with.

It's been suggested that each of us has four different types of people in our lives: those who add to us, those who subtract from us, those who divide us, and those who multiply us. Simply put, those who add to us help us do more than the sum of what we could do alone. Those are the people who enrich our lives. The other types of relationships are less desirable; and while you may be able to build meaningful relationships with them if they changed certain characteristics; just remember, changing them is not your responsibility. ∎

Today's Live Happy Practice

We all deserve healthy relationships. But be realistic about your expectations. No one can be everything you might want them to be. Having healthy relationships means accepting people for who they are and not trying to change them to who you wish they were.

DAY 19

Looking for the Benefits

Have you ever heard the saying, "Sometimes bad things happen to good people?" Are you familiar with Murphy's Law? The seemingly infallible law that suggests that anything that can go wrong, will. Living an inspired life does not translate into living an adversity free life. Sometimes it rains on your parade. Sometimes you are the pigeon and sometimes you are the statue.

The question is not whether difficulty will visit. The question is how will you respond when it arrives at your doorstep? Once they enter, challenges can chase you from room to room, tempting you to forget what you have learned. You may be tempted to put your truth on the shelf and deal with the difficulty at the same level of awareness at which the problem is being presented. However, to paraphrase a great thinker, you cannot solve a problem at the same level of awareness that created the problem.

Hardships are not meant to be easy, but they can have the added benefit of sending us to the one room that helps us get over the issues of life, and that is the upper room. The upper room is the place in the house of your soul where you connect with the presence of God. Not only is your time in the closet incredibly transformational, it also helps you reconnect with the aspects of you that is bigger than the adversities. Your upper room experience will enable you to beat back and eliminate the hardship and find the blessing and benefits that are always deeply imbedded in the challenges that present themselves. ■

Today's Live Happy Practice

Prove, beyond the shadow of a doubt, that you are the master of your circumstances. Demonstrate that it is not what happens to you but what happens in you that determine your experience. Think about an adversity that you are currently experiencing. What blessing or benefit can you find in that situation?

DAY 20

Your Capacity for Blessings

Extra! Extra! Read all about it!! It is right now, already, the natural and intuitive will of creation to bless you. However, there are some strings attached:

- You have to be open to it. How many of us go through life turning the faucet of prayer on, only to hold the cup upside down underneath the flow of good. This approach allows us to get just wet enough to know that the possibility for good is real, without ever experiencing any fulfillment. You must be open in order to receive.

- The amount you walk away with is in direct correlation with the capacity of your container. My friend Gaylon McDowell said, "You can go to the ocean with a thimble, a cup, a barrel, or a hose." The ocean will meet the demand of either one, without ever being diminished. Most people are not conscious of the container they take to the source. Here is a secret; you grow the container by growing yourself.

- You attract by right of consciousness. There is absolutely no reason to ever be jealous of what another person has because she or he has attracted it by right of consciousness. We only produce on the outside, that for which we have the blueprint, on the inside. The pint gains nothing by envying the gallon. Even if the pint had the contents of the gallon, the pint would waste most of it. In order for you to receive more, you must stretch and become bigger. ∎

Today's Live Happy Practice

Consider the points above and reflect on how you can apply them to your life now in order to receive your best blessing.

DAY 21

The Rocking Chair Syndrome

It is so easy to get caught up in the busy-ness of life. You know the kind of activity were we are active but not productive; engaged but not advancing; moving but not achieving. I call it the rocking chair syndrome. Sitting in a rocking chair will give you something to do but it will not get you anywhere. Activity and accomplishment is not the same thing. In order to get more out of yourself, you may want to reevaluate whether your activity is leading to productivity.

While I was attending recruit-training boot camp in Great Lakes, Illinois, I learned how to mark time march. For the uninitiated, marking time is a military step in which we would march in place by moving our legs as though we were marching but instead of marching, we remained in place. We learned to master motion without progress. I soon realized that I had been marking time in other areas of my life where I was in motion but not making any progress.

How many of us are exerting energy just to stay in the same place? If you know this is you, it may be time to shake things up and totally reignite yourself so that you can release your God-given capacity to put a stop to what has been stopping you! Sometimes the only thing holding us back is the learned habit of marching and marking time. ∎

Today's Live Happy Practice

You can energize yourself by consuming personal growth content. Consuming growth material can give you an added boost of energy and help you get moving. Reading books and listening to content with growth messages is a great way to rejuvenate yourself.

DAY 22

The Invitation to Pray

Life is meant to be beautiful, sacred, challenging, teachable, and so much more. Which is why we may feel the need to pray for our circumstances at different times. Like the beads of a rosary, there are so many reasons to pray. Regardless of our station in life, something always seems to be pulling us toward prayer. Whether it is the medical diagnosis of a family member, the opportunity of a new business proposal, or a shooting at a school or on the block, there are many things calling us up to the action of prayer.

Yet while many of us feel compelled in the way of prayer, prayer means different things to different people. The English word prayer finds its roots in the Latin word precari, and it means to have intentionality or earnestness in ones asking. It also refers to a form of entreating that easily lends itself to the notion of begging or beseeching God when one finds themselves in a difficult spot.

Interestingly enough, prayer is more invitation than obligation. Prayer is an invitation into spiritual life and soul growth. Prayer is an invitation to change and transformation. The more consistently we accept the invitation, the more thoroughly we will find our lives being transformed. Prayer is the kind of invitation that we all receive but may not necessarily show up for. In fact, our hyperactive culture has convinced us that we should be content with the notion of being so busy that we are too busy to stop and pray. Yet anyone who is serious about transformation and personal growth will take up the spiritual practice of prayer. ∎

Today's Live Happy Practice
Make a commitment to yourself to pray every day. Try doing it as soon as you get out of bed every morning or right before going to bed every night.

DAY 23

Your Unique Purpose in Life

If you want to manifest your greatness, live a more fulfilling life, and experience the success you deserve, it's vital that you learn how to identify and live out your life's purpose. Without the power of our life's purpose to both ground and guide us our goals and aspirations may never be compelling enough to move us to action.

Each and every one of us is born with a specific and unique life purpose. No one else on the planet brings the exact same power of purpose you bring. When we think about creation, there are more stars in the universe than there are grains of sand on all the beaches combined. The same source that so purposefully created that, put the purpose in you. When we consider the different possibilities, obstacles, and random scenarios, the ratio of your being here by chance is something like 400 trillion to 1. This means there is no chance you are here by chance! If you are not here by chance then you must absolutely be here for a purpose.

For many people, their purpose is obvious and clear. It shines through their talents. These people seem to have come upon their life's purpose rather easily. For most people, though, identifying their purpose is a bit more difficult. You have probably even asked yourself at one time or another, "What am I supposed to do with my life?" "What is my life purpose?" Nathaniel Branden, "To live without purpose is to live at the mercy of chance." So why is finding your purpose so important? It's important because it enables you live with the power of intention rather than at the mercy of chance.

■

> ### Today's Live Happy Practice
> Traumatic events can be painful, but they also have the power to change the trajectory of your life. Many times, your pain can lead you to your purpose. Think about how you can use your past experiences to help others. That just may be your purpose.

DAY 24

What You Bring to the Table

Any opportunity to gain deeper insight into one's natural ability, and to optimize those abilities with an end toward greater success, is nothing short of exciting. When Henry David Thoreau observed, "[t]he mass of men lead lives of quiet desperation," it is conceivable that he was not speaking down to anyone. Instead, he may have well been speaking up to the notion of innate strength and how the soul languishes when that strength goes unused and perhaps even undiscovered.

An occasion to become familiar with your strengths presents an interesting opportunity to learn and grow. It is no secret that in a competitive and crowded market place, the difference between winning and losing often "comes down to inches," to borrow a sports analogy. One of the differences between growing your business and losing it could come down to your strengths. The difference between being hired or remaining unemployed may hinge on an individual's knowledge base. The difference between being gainfully employed and being gainfully promoted may be directly correlated to an individual's skill set. The difference between running a successful business, department, or division may rest on how consistently the leaders operate from their talent or strength base. This realization necessitates having clear and concise insight into what you bring to the table of shared experience and what people get when they get you. ∎

Today's Live Happy Practice

If you are negotiating a relationship or a raise, be sure to think about what you bring to the table. Think about your attributes or skills that can benefit the other person and make them known.

DAY 25

Remove All Doubt

We are called to walk by faith and not by sight. Yet somehow in the midst of this lofty charge, doubt seems to be one of the common factors that consistently show up as we walk through life. We all have doubts and whether they originate within or from the opinions of others, when we have doubts, we tend to waver. Every now and again, from some seemingly dark corner of the mind, we seem to be pulled back to doubt.

Doubt manifests in many different ways. It may appear as questions about whether you are adequate or good enough. It may appear as discomfort about your ability to bring forth the vision that God has given you. Doubt makes us look at the circumstances as though everything is stacked against us. Doubt moves us away from the certainty and clarity of a faith-filled walk.

The Apostle Paul wrote in his letter to the Romans that sometimes he did not understand his own actions. According to the letter, the thing he did not want to do, he did; and the very thing he had committed himself to doing, he did not do. Paul is probably not alone. I can imagine that like Paul, all of us, at some point, have had a bout with doubt. But if God is for you, perhaps not even your doubt is strong enough to stand against you. Remember, you have stood still and seen that deliverance of the Lord before, and if God could bring you through at one time, He can bring you through at another. You can get to where God has destined you to be if you can have faith and do not doubt. ∎

Today's Live Happy Practice

Living with doubt can hold you back. You can eliminate doubt by understanding your triggers. Doubt and other negative emotions stem from unhealed parts of who you are. When you honestly access your self-doubt and understand how to deal with it, you will be well on your way to eliminating it all together.

DAY 26

Face Your Trials with Joy

When God guides us, we have within us everything that we need to be laser focused and take radical action in the right direction. However, every time we doubt, we create an alternate path that leads us away from the direction of God's guidance. Double-mindedness makes us unstable in every way. When we doubt, when we hesitate, if we are lucky, we are only second-guessing ourselves. Yet somehow, I get the sense that sometimes when we doubt, we are not only second-guessing ourselves, we are also second-guessing God.

Our doubt means there is some uncertainty or confusion around what we want to do and whether we are able to do it. Of ourselves, we may not be able to do it but in Christ, it is a whole different ball game. When we doubt, we are being of two minds. James 1:2 challenges us to count it nothing but joy when we face the difficulty that comes with doubt. Through this scripture we may consider that when we are going through the difficulty of doubt, we must keep going and discover the ability to consider the doubt and reframe it with faith.

When you are wrestling with a bear, you do not stop when you are tired, you only stop when the bear gets tired. You may question whether you can make it through but the only question is whether or not you will face those trials with joy because joy puts you in a certain mindset, on a certain path, and gives you a certain perspective through which to see your world. ∎

Today's Live Happy Practice

If you want to face your trials with joy, think about the many blessings in your life. Be thankful for the support of your family and friends, and find joy in the sanctity of life.

DAY 27

The Patience to Go Through

For many of us, we are not where we want to be because our endurance does not have its full effect. We have to find the endurance to stand on the faith of the truth that we know. If we cannot find it, what we will find is that we are unstable in all of our ways. We shape our worlds by the way that we think.

Sometimes the very thing that you have been praying for, you can only get it on the other side of your going through it. At this point in your growth, you cannot handle the thing that you see in your head. If you could, you would already have it. Don't get it twisted. Don't ever worry about being where someone else is, if you were supposed to be where they are, you would be where they are. You do not have to compare yourself to anybody or anything. You are where you are by right of consciousness.

The gospel of James says that if any of you is lacking in wisdom, you should ask God who gives to all generously and ungrudgingly, and it will be given to you. Ask in faith, and never doubting, for the one who doubts is like a wave of the sea; driven and tossed by the wind of popular opinion. Being double-minded is unstable in every way. The doubter must not expect to receive anything from the Lord or the law. When you are double-minded, the Lord of the Law does not know what to give you because you are asking in two different directions. ■

Today's Live Happy Practice

When you are anxious about going through something, remember the big picture. Remind yourself that you are putting up with whatever frustration you are facing because it will ultimately help you get where you want to go.

Shoe

There are some basic principles of happy and healthy living. We can only experience true success and enduring happiness as we learn and integrate these principles into our basic beliefs and behavior. These beliefs then become the subconscious source of the solutions. The challenge for many people is that they are not able to generate an adequate level of self-confidence.

Jeff MacNelly, who created the old comic strip, *Shoe*, had one of my favorite pieces on personal belief. Shoe was on the pitches mound, trying to get it together during a shaky performance. As is common in the game of baseball, there was a conference on the mound, when the back catcher suggested to Shoe, "You've got to have faith in your curve ball."

"It's easy for him to say," grumbles Shoe. "When it comes to believing in myself, I'm an agnostic."

It is obvious that Shoe could not see himself or his talents through the lens of his own greatness. He could not separate his performance from the layers of his potential. Sometimes we have to learn to relax and get out of our own way so that our greatness can emerge. Once we begin to see traces of our natural talents, skills, gifts, and abilities, we must begin to affirm and value them. We also have to be conscientious as we work on our motives and cultivate internal sources of safety so that we can be comfortable at home in our skin. ▌

Today's Live Happy Practice

You can gain more self-confidence by acquiring more skills. Sometimes a lack of confidence stems from a lack of preparedness. Access your skill set and take classes, listen to podcasts, or read books to fill any knowledge gaps that you may have. The more knowledge you gain, the more confident you will feel.

DAY 29

Reviewing Your Fav-Five

How do you manage yourself around toxic, energy draining people? Do you have any idea how much energy it takes to carry your doubts as well as the doubts of those who can support you but won't? An old adage says, "Misery loves company." Many of the challenges and struggles we face in life are the result of the baggage we carry when we can't be our authentic self within the context of our relationships.

It has been suggested that, "We are the average of the five people we spend the most time with." If this is a fact, then it's time to take a relationship inventory, particularly if you are someone who is interested in growing and you have toxic people in your favorite-five. So perform your audit. Are the people you're spending lots of time with in the same situation as you? What are the conversations like when you all are together? Do your interactions inspire you or expire you? Toxic people don't help you fly. It is much more likely that they will play into the cause of why you find yourself in a crawl.

Everyone is not healthy enough to have a front row seat in your life and unfortunately, not everyone is interested in helping you get better. When Jesus had someone like this on his team he said, do what you have to do, do it quickly, and keep it moving. It's important to be aware and consciously choose who we spend time with and to insulate ourselves from spending too much time with toxic people. It may be time to change the course of where your relationship is going. It may be time to keep it moving. ■

Today's Live Happy Practice

One of the best ways to deal with toxic people is to set boundaries. If you've made a decision not to respond to toxic people on text or social media, don't! Once you've set your boundaries, stick with them and don't waiver.

DAY 30

Love into Faith

It is the Father's good pleasure to give you the Kingdom and yet it does require a faith citizenship in order to receive that which has been given you. Your credential is simply to have faith and do not doubt. If you doubt that you deserve the Kingdom and counsel of God; that doubt is setting up a mindset that places you outside of the good desires of your heart and bringing you more experiences by which to doubt.

Job is a prime example that doubt on fire is more powerful than faith on ice. We have to turn this around and allow our faith to be more dynamic than our doubt. Faith places us on firm footing with God and helps us get beyond the difficulties. It enables us to shape the substance of potential. Like Job, we sometimes doubt ourselves…and like Job, one of the ways we can tell is in how we talk to ourselves. When we doubt and talk negatively to ourselves, we are overlooking and underestimating our capacity to endure, create, and overcome.

Of all the battles we fight, the greatest ones are often only in our heads. Let there be no doubt about the function of the Holy Spirit in your life. Let there be no doubt about the magnitude out of which you have been created. The Psalmist sang, "I praise you, for I am fearfully and wonderfully made. Wonderful are your works; my soul knows it very well." It is important for us to remember the Holy Spirit and the magnitude out of which we have been made. Show your credential and use your faith, Child of God! ∎

Today's Live Happy Practice

Faith is the complete trust in someone or something. Faith happens when you make a conscious decision to love no matter what the circumstances are; and the more you love, the more your faith will grow. So if you want to grow your faith, chose to express your love.

DAY 31

Life without Limits

In the grand scheme of things, very few people understand or honor their potential for greatness. Because so few people do, many times we limit what we can have, do, be, and experience. Unfortunately, we allow our beliefs to limit how we think because, well, "seeing is believing." But if we continue to believe our apparent limitations, there is a really good chance that we will always live a life with limits. Many of us believe that we are irredeemably flawed, unworthy of greatness, and simply not equipped to manifest the dreams and desires of our heart. These belief systems cause us to either avoid or sabotage our own greatness.

A common misconception is that living from one's own unique form of greatness brings unbearable pressure and stress. When we associate our vast potential with the feelings usually prompted by problems, we are more inclined to shrink back into our limitation shell. We think that by lowering our trajectory we can lower our discomfort and experience more safety. Seeing yourself within the glow up of your innate greatness is critical if you want to produce unlimited results. Results come from our actions and action springs forth from our thoughts. Tennis great Arthur Ashe said, "One important key to success is self-confidence. An important key to self-confidence is preparation." Put another way, your success is determined by what you are prepared to think. The bigger you think and the more massive your actions, the greater your results. ■

Today's Live Happy Practice

One of the best ways to believe in yourself is to develop a growth mindset. A growth mindset means that you learn from your mistakes and improve your performance after mistakes have been made. If you want to live a life without limits, start cultivating a growth mindset today.

DAY 32

The Propensity to Compromise

One of the greatest hindrances to living a happy life is our propensity to tolerate so many undesirable things. It seems like a major part of the human condition and human conditioning, is the instinct to tolerate or settle for a lot of things we don't like. We are cautioned to do things like: go along to get along; hold our tongue; don't complain; and don't rock the boat.

These holes are always possible whenever we make compromises in our standards, values, or expectations. No less an authority than the cynical Larry David said, "A good compromise is when both parties are dissatisfied." Toleration leads to living a dissatisfied life.

Are you ready to shift out of tolerating? If so, goal setting is for you because goals help shift us out of tolerating and settling into accomplishing. Goals are like the gasoline that helps us drive toward our desired experiences and outcomes. We make compromises in order to tolerate undesirable experiences but we are naturally achievement oriented. Whether we are motivated by inspiration or desperation, as goal-getting organisms, we are hardwired to identify, desire, act on, and attain our goals. Because of this hardwiring, we can get virtually any goal we set, if we are clear, committed, persistent, and unwilling to settle. ∎

Today's Live Happy Practice

In order to overcome your need to compromise, you first must identify the source of your desire to please. It could stem from a lack of love or just a general need to please others. Be honest with yourself and tap into the deeper truths that can shift your mindset and set you free from a life of compromise.

DAY 33

The Face of Uncertainty

We all face uncertainty. In fact, uncertainty appears to be a consistent part of life. That's why it's important to have faith. Faith doesn't necessarily eliminate the uncertainty; however, it does give us a confident mental attitude. Ralph Waldo Emerson said, "What lies behind us and what lies before us are but tiny matters compared to what lies within us." This well-known but little understood capacity provides us with tools we need to navigate uncertainty, to become receptive to the answers that come from our inner guidance, and it affords us with the ability to intentionally design our experience.

We live in a world that is largely created through the power of the mind. Here's the good news…you can control what goes on in your mind. This is not to say that it is easy, rather to simply establish that it is possible. You are a living magnet, constantly drawing to you the things, the people, the circumstances, and the experiences that are aligned with your thoughts. Put another way, we are always our own experience. What we have to assess is whether we are on the side of our problem or on the side of our solution. "Choose this day whom you will serve." (Josh. 24:15).

It changes the way we see them and how we relate to them. Perspective is a powerful tool. We have to maintain control of the mind so that it remains open to the power and flow of infinite possibility. Whatever your mind can conceive and believe, you can achieve. That is why it is important to not allow the limitations and restrictions to sabotage you and your desires. As Neville Goddard offered, "Man's faith in God is measured by his confidence in himself." ∎

Today's Live Happy Practice

Deal with uncertainty by focusing on the present. Instead of thinking about the things that you have no control of, refocus your energy on the aspects of the problem that you can control and work on those things.

DAY 34

How to Talk to Yourself

Some of the most consequential conversations you will ever have; will be the conversations you have with yourself. You are probably familiar with the saying, "Mind over matter," but what many of us undervalue and desperately need is mind over chatter. On average, we think some 60,000 thoughts per day and talk to ourselves about 50,000 times a day. However, roughly about 80 of both the thoughts and the talk are negative. This has a powerful impact, as it affects attitude, self-esteem, motivation, actions, and so much more. The problem is that it is incredibly difficult to build self-esteem and self-image and self-confidence when the person who is chiefly responsible for doing that is the same person who is behind the negative chatter.

The conversations we have with ourselves are powerful levers for personal change. In order to make a change, we have to first change our old programming, because it is the old program that ensures we will continue doing things the old way. One of the most powerful ways to rewrite our old programming is to practice conscious self-talk. Watch your thoughts because they become your words. Watch your words because they become your actions. Watch your actions because they become your habits. Watch your habits because they become your character. Watch your character becomes it becomes your destiny. ∎

Today's Live Happy Practice

Much of our thinking is so automatic and happening so rapidly that we barely notice it before we move on to the next thought. Make a conscious effort to slow down and pay closer attention. This will help you catch and correct unproductive self-talk. Also pay close attention to your emotions, as they can cue you when your inner talk has gotten of track.

DAY 35

Becoming Deeply Committed to Your Commitments

What do you want? I mean like really…what do you want? Take some time. Give it some thought. Perhaps it will help if you write it down. Get clear if not concise. What would you like to accomplish? What do you want to achieve? Let your imagination run free. Let it see beyond your present condition. It can be anything at all.

Now ask yourself, "How would I attain it, if you had no limitations?" One of the awesome things about you is that something within you comes alive by desired end states. It's a part of your teleological nature. By the same token, the number of people who get stopped from the life of their dreams, by their perceived limitations, would amaze you. The fact is, as one great thinker put it, "It isn't what you don't know that gets you into trouble. It's what you know for sure that just isn't so." Put another way, your greatest limitations are tied to your inability to recognize how unlimited you really are. A benevolent creator has made you and you have been made of the best stuff.

It will take commitment to unlock your astounding and limitless potential. It will take commitment to love your dreams and live into them. It will take commitment to press forward when your energy, emotions, thoughts, and results all tell you to quit. It will take commitment to "count it all joy." And it will take commitment to learn to honor, support, and love yourself in spite of your fears, failures, disappointments, and difficulties. Oh yeah…it will also take commitment to get clear about what you want. ∎

Today's Live Happy Practice

The best way to become deeply committed to your commitments is to take away the choice. Eliminate the other options as possibilities and don't give yourself a way to opt out. Promise yourself that there is only one option, and that is to follow through on your commitment.

DAY 36

Improving Dedication to Your Goals

In life, there are things that you must work for and there are things that you must wait for. Either way, you have to begin each day with dedication if you want to end each day with satisfaction. But it's important to know where and how to direct your dedication. Dedication to improving yourself daily precedes a future filled with possibilities. Dedication helps you grow and when you grow, you expand your vision, you attract more options, you open your opportunities, and you maximize your potential.

While you give your daily dedication you will also have to practice patience. New things are usually difficult before they become easy and unfortunately, difficulty often serves as a deterrent. In fact, most of us never come to realize how close we actually are to achieving our dreams because we give up too soon. Every achievement we value takes time and dedication. The people who grow and achieve the most are the ones who practice the power of patience and dedication to their cause. ▉

Today's Live Happy Practice

Try improving your dedication to your goal by blocking out a time to work on it. Set a daily routing for yourself that is non-negotiable. Remove all distractions and don't answer calls from your friends and colleagues.

DAY 37

The Power of Love

There is a wonderful congregational song we would sing in church, that goes, "I love myself so much, that I can love you so much, that you can love you so much, that you can start loving me." Those lyrics beautifully capture the transformational power of love. Now imagine what it might be like if we not only sang it, but lived it.

What if the power of love could transform our neighborhoods? What if it could transform our politics? What if it could transform our hospitals and our prisons? What can we do right now? We can love people just as they are. They may need to change but you and I cannot control that, what we can control is the intensity of our cooperation, compassion, kindness, service, and selflessness. Love is among the best medications for the body and the soul. Love alters our chemistry and conditions us for the expression of a happy, healthy attitude.

Love extends the space we occupy in the hearts of others, while also expanding the space others occupy in our hearts. The best way to receive love is to give it. Love has a language and love has some signs. Love is active and it shows up through our intentions. It shows up as our ability to cooperate. It shows up when we have compassion for what someone else might be going through. Love shows up as our ability to be kind, even when kindness may not be warranted; and it shows up when we are unselfish and give our service to others. Remember, when we stay wrapped up in ourselves, we make very small packages. █

Today's Live Happy Practice

Expressing love is not always about words. One of the best ways to show love is by listening. Ask questions and find out what they want. When you show that you care about what's going on in the other person's life, it does wanders for the relationship.

DAY 38

The River of Greatness and the Stream of Adversity

It's no secret that life brings with it a multitude of experiences, some sweet; some bitter. The sweet experiences hardly ever prompt explanation or reconciliation. Sweet experiences are a good representation of how life should be. The bitter experiences, on the other hand, are often times too sour, too uncomfortable, and too unsatisfactory. Or is it? The bitter experience has a purpose and that purpose can enable you to benefit from those experiences which test your resolve. When we understand the foundations of building faith, we can accept each bitter experience as a stepping-stone for self-mastery and personal achievement.

One of my favorite quotes comes from Cavett Robert who said, "If we study the lives of great men and women carefully and unemotionally we find that, invariably, greatness was developed, tested, and revealed through the darker periods of their lives." One of the largest tributaries of the River of Greatness is always the Stream of Adversity. Personal improvement never comes easily. If you find yourself drinking from the cup of difficulty or disappointment, remember, it just may be the fuel that propels you to the next level. ■

Today's Live Happy Practice

Turn your adversity into opportunity by doing the following:

- Seek to understand the challenge
- Identify the lesson to be learned
- Find the opportunity or problem to be solved
- Develop a plan to take advantage of the opportunity
- Enlist any needed resources
- Move forward with your plan

DAY 39

The Kind Universe

Albert Einstein suggested that one of the most important decisions we can make is whether we consider the universe to be friendly or hostile. If you decide that it is friendly then you may also want to embrace that its essence is kindness...a type of tender love and kindness from which you and I can emanate.

Because we originated from the Source of kindness, we are a living, breathing, walking representation of the possibilities of kindness. Put more simply, when you love, trust, and honor yourself, you're loving, trusting, and honoring the Kindness that created you; and when you fail to love, trust, and honor yourself, you are rejecting the eternal presence of kindness. It is important to know that at every single moment of your life, you have the choice to either be a host to kindness or a hostage to hostility. ∎

Today's Live Happy Practice

Today affirm:

- I am worthy of kindness
- I honor the loving kindness that I am.
- I let the activity of kindness flow in my life, world, and affairs and the flow of kindness enriches the respect I have for myself
- I am committed to being kind to myself

DAY 40

Focus and Priority

In order to get the most out of today you will need two things: Focus and Priority. Focus enables you to direct your time, energy, effort, and resources toward the things that allow you to get the most from this amazing day. Focus also helps you avoid doing things that would waste the precious commodity that today is. Establishing your priority helps you be laser focused on the thing that is essential make the most of today. Just like all roads won't efficiently and effectively lead to a given destination, having a priority means accepting that all things cannot be equally important.

Like H2O, both elements are important. If you have a clear focus and no priority, you will have a target, but lack the sense of importance that determines when to pull the trigger. If you have a priority and no focus, you will know what is important but fail to zero in on it. When you put these two elements together, you put yourself in the flow of achieving amazing results. Decide to focus on and make priority only those things that help you tease-out the potential of today.

People who dabble in making the most of today will avoid narrowing their focus and put off prioritizing their activities. The key to sidestepping this outcome is based squarely in the pocket of your decisions. Your decisions give you the ability to determine your future in the now moment. Remember, you are a success the moment you perform the successful act. A decision to focus your attention and prioritize your actions will help you get all this day holds in reserve for you. █

Today's Live Happy Practice

In order to prioritize, make a list of all tasks. Identify the most important items to reach your goal and do those things first.

DAY 41

The Power of Words

Thinking before we speak is a terrific habit to develop. Particularly when we remember that our words have power. The sacred scripture encourages us to remember that, "Life and death are in the power of the tongue." Scripture also reminds us that, "Our words do not return to us void" but rather, our words, "accomplish what they are sent to do." Often times we speak without being conscious or intentional. We forget to stop and think about the gravity, impact, value, or importance of our words. Since our words have power, they can inspire hope or instill fear. Our words can uplift the hearer or deflate the spirit.

As we more consistently speak life, we will enhance the relationship we have with ourselves. Become intentional about speaking words that uplift you, to you. Our minds are very fertile ground and our words become planted seeds. The quality of our words determines the quality of our harvest. You plant a word seed and it grows. The only problem is that too often our words spread seeds of fear. We have to recalibrate and recondition ourselves in order, "Let no corrupt communication proceed out of your mouth, but that which is good to the use of edifying, that it may minister grace unto the hearers." (Eph. 4:29).

Like a rock skipping across the lake, the words we cast forward creates a ripple effect in the world. We may not realize it, but the things we say produces an effect in us and in those we speak it to. We are always creating something with the power of our words. ∎

> ### Today's Live Happy Practice
> Since your words have power, make a commitment to speak only positive words in this day.

DAY 42

Be Willing to Test Your Abilities in the Ring

Many people don't believe in their ability because they define themselves by their capacity to confront their difficulties. You may be familiar with the story of David and Goliath. Goliath was the Philistine giant who openly mocked and intimidated the men of the armies of Israel. Goliath was well versed in war, as he was considered a champion in battle. Goliath had the tools, the armor, the scars, and the pedigree to prevail in the fight before him. So when he shouted to his opponents to get it on, it is because he was combat ready and his shouts struck fear into the hearts of his adversaries. Though he begged to have an Israelite meet him in battle, his pleas fell on frightened ears.

David, on the other hand, was not battle ready. His only involvement with the army was to carry supplies to his older brothers. David was no warrior. He was nobody's champion. He was just a boy and if he was going to get into the ring with Goliath, David had many obstacles to overcome. But David summoned his mettle, called on his experience, shed everything that did not fit him, and ran courageously toward the giant to meet the moment. All while remembering that if God is for him, what challenge could overtake him? David had power, authority, and dominion over the giant in the valley. The giant did not know it and David did not prove it, until it was show time. You and I will not be able to prove it either, unless we buy into our ability to confront and overcome our difficulties. ∎

Today's Live Happy Practice

There are people in the world who need the gifts you have to offer so stop listening to the naysayers and get in the ring. Be willing to fight for what you want before it manifest itself in your life.

DAY 43

The Sum of the Parts

Each and every one of us brings something different and valuable to our collective experiences. Each and every one of us has our own unique form of greatness. When one of us is willing to share our unique gift, we compensate for the gaps or weaknesses of another. The Apostle Paul said, "To each is given the manifestation of the Spirit for the common good."

This common good is really the essence of synergy. We are able to experience synergy when we add our giftedness to create new and better ways of doing things together. There is power in collective consciousness and we experience synergy when we recognize that the whole is greater than the sum of its parts. This level of cooperation and collaboration enables the collective to do more than what an individual would be able to do on their own.

To paraphrase Paul, as he wrote to the church in Corinth, "As it is, there are many of us, but one body. The eye cannot say to the hand, "I have no need of you," nor again the head to the feet, "I have no need of you."

God has so arranged the body, giving the greater honor to those who appear inferior, that there may be no dissension within the body, but the people may have the same care for one another. If one person suffers, all suffer together with it; if one person is honored, all rejoice together with it. This outcome is not automatic and this approach does not just happen. A great deal of intention is necessary for everyone to work together to create new possibilities.

Today's Live Happy Practice

In order to gain the greatest benefits from working together, it is important to focus on each person's strength. The finished product will be that much greater by utilizing the combined skillset of all team members.

DAY 44

The Oneness of God

Alright Jesus, which one is it? Now let me explain the backstory.

I make it a habit to converse with some of the best minds in the history of humanity when I read. When I come across something that intrigues or challenges me, I seek clarity through questions. One gospel writer said, "All authority in heaven and on earth has been given to me." On the other hand, another gospel writer said, "I can do nothing on my own." As these two statements seem to be at odds, I ask again, "Which is it?"

The seeming contradiction may begin to be reconciled when you recognize that, "The Father and I are one." It is a very powerful truth to realize that God is all there is. Knowing that there is One Spirit emanating in, through, and as, all human kind is profound because in this Oneness we live, move, and have our being.

This awareness is both liberating and encouraging. Knowing this helps answer the question we may sometimes ask ourselves when we are uncertain about whether we can trust God. There is authority in a clear understanding of the law.

When, like Jesus, I get God's nature, I see that I am a host to all that is good rather than a Hostage. An abundance of good flows for my spiritual, mental, emotional, and physical well-being. All I do prospers. Even when the answer does not always seem clear, I must affirm the Truth for myself time and again. ▪

Today's Live Happy Practice

Be still and listen for the voice of God. He will give you messages to lift you up like, "You do not need to do anything to please me, I love you already." or "My plans are for your good."

DAY 45

Knock on the Door and It Will Open

When I was writing one of my books I had an opportunity to have the forward written by someone who is internationally known. If I shared her name here, many of you would know who she is. You may have even seen her on daytime television. Short version, I was doing some work with her and she made a commitment to support me, however she could. When the time came to ask her to write the forward, I was reluctant to ask. I decided to save myself from the disappointment I imagined I would feel if she said, "No." Then I was speaking in California and she was there. So I set aside my reluctance and made my ask. What do you think happened? She said, "Yes!" Turns out, I was the only thing keeping me from having what I wanted.

When it comes to being reluctant to ask for things, I was in pretty good company because most people do not know what to ask for or how to ask for it. Either way, we end up doing without what we want. We may have some limiting and negative beliefs that have been programmed into the subconscious and those beliefs now silently control our actions. We may not feel like we deserve it or we may have some underlying baggage around our sense of worthiness.

The master teacher Jesus gave us the formula, "Ask and it will be given to you. Seek and you will find. Knock and the door will be opened to you. For everyone who asks, receives. Everyone who seeks, finds. Everyone who knocks, the door will be opened. ▌

Today's Live Happy Practice

If there is something you desire internally that is not showing up externally, there is something internal blocking it. Begin to eliminate these limiting beliefs by asking yourself right now; "What is the resistance that could be holding me back from asking?"

DAY 46

The Power of Intuition

Intuition is our innate capacity to know spiritual truths and make important decisions, without always having to think about what is right. It is the wisdom of the heart. There are more than 40,000 specialized cells that are organized in such a way as to form neural networks within the heart. These heart cells feel our experiences and store information. It means that at this very moment, you are having two mutually exclusive experiences. One experience is taking place in your brain and the other experience is taking place in your heart. One experience is taking place in your intellect and the other is taking place in your feelings.

Most people are in the practice of relying solely on their reason and logic as a guide for their decisions. While there is nothing wrong with this approach, there are other capacities and abilities available to you. God was highly intentional in how He made you.

Intuition is inherent in all humankind and is among the highest functions of consciousness. The language of the heart is the language of Spirit and it arises from our True Nature. The "little brain in the heart" enables us to come into contact with pure knowing through the feeling nature. The neural networks within the heart translate pure knowing and feeling; which allows your intuition to instinctively know without the use of rational processes.

Today's Live Happy Practice

You would do well to cultivate an awareness of the perpetual activity of intuition in your life. Here is the first step: suspend some of what you think just long enough to remember to count on the heart for what you already know.

DAY 47

A Good Kick of Self-Leadership

You cannot get to where you want to be if you are not moving forward. We sometimes fall into the same trap that legendary basketball coach John Wooden warned of when he cautioned us to "never mistake activity for achievement." Admittedly, life's experiences are sometimes more like laboring through a labyrinth rather than traveling along a clear road. But what does it means to get unstuck so that you can experience the good that is waiting for you?

Whether navigating through the maze of an uncertain journey, or through clarity and vision, moving forward requires some form of change. But many people find change uncomfortable. This sense of un-readiness may be a catalyst for the proverbial tie that binds our resourcefulness and limits our ability to experience the life-giving dichotomy. Sometimes in order to get moving we need a good kick of self-leadership. It is not another person's responsibility to get us moving forward.

Regardless of the aim, if the goal is to get complete, then you must take action. No amount of hoping will produce the desired result if you do not eventually do something. Once you begin to take action, new emergence is the constant companion and you can begin to experience the promise, prospect, and growth that moving forward provides. Your forward movement is what makes things happen. They are the result of a predetermined desire, purpose, focus, priorities, and productivity. These ongoing commitments help you to build momentum for life. ▌

> ### Today's Live Happy Practice
> In order to keep moving forward on your goals, you need to set a vision for yourself. Take some time to visualize what you want and how you will feel when you get it.

DAY 48

The Value of Strategic Alliances

When Jesus was identifying his disciples, it seems like he did so with the framing principle that, "All people are equally important to God, but not all are equally strategic when it comes to the expenditure of their time." Jesus recognized that strategic partnerships are essential to your success as a leader.

The concept of strategic partnerships is not new. Every leader in every age utilized strategic alliances. God encouraged His strategic partners, Adam and Eve, to take an active role in bringing forth certain manner of creation. Moses and Aaron invested wisely in Joshua. Naomi partnered with Ruth who vowed her allegiance, even if it meant she would have to immerse herself in a new culture and embrace a new God. Jesus had many mission critical people then and many mission critical people now.

The Pareto principle suggests that 80% of productivity is a result of 20% of the inputs. It follows that 20% of your strategic relationships are likely producing 80% of your results. An important thing to examine is whether, and to what degree, you are investing in strategic relationships. Greater synergistic outcomes are experienced when we help grow the people who help us go. ∎

Today's Live Happy Practice

When you create strategic partnerships, be sure to assess your own value and ensure it is recognized within the relationship. Strategic partnerships can deliver solid results when both parties add value to the relationship.

DAY 49

The Upside of Fear

Two explorers were on a jungle safari when suddenly they encountered a ferocious lion on the trail in front of them. "Keep calm," the first explorer whispered. "Remember what we read in that book on wild animals? If you stand perfectly still and look the lion in the eye, he will turn and run." "Sure," replied his companion. "You've read the book, and I've read the book. But has the lion read the book?"

Fear is a powerful human emotion. Like the explorers, when we encounter it, fear often stops us in our tracks. It is virtually impossible to accomplish the things we want to achieve in life if we are held back by fear.

Studies have found that people who live in fear die sooner than people who do not. We are inwardly constructed for faith and not for fear. God made us that way. The things that fill us with fear must be overcome if we are to truly live. To consistently live in fear is to consistently live in disharmony with the reality of how we are made. That is why the things we want to experience are often on the other side of fear.

This is not to suggest that all fear is bad. Fear is often informing us that we need more information or more preparation in order to change the course of where an experience is potentially going. Whether real or imagined, fear is an indicator that if something does not change, we might very well be in for an undesirable result. Taking action gives us confidence, courage, and momentum. So if you are experiencing fear, use it to make the appropriate adjustments to propel yourself forward. ■

> ## Today's Live Happy Practice
> If you are experiencing fear, don't deny it; instead, use it for your advantage. Think about what you're afraid of and develop options to resolve the challenges that you face.

DAY 50

How Information Alleviates Fear

If you want to overcome fear; instead of thinking about what makes you afraid, think about what you want to do, and then get busy doing it. Do not forget that it is usually easier to confront the fear than to allow it to control you. When you get more information or make time for more preparation, it gives you the confidence and faith the take more action. Information, preparation, and proper action dis-empowers fear. The more you confront fear, the less power it has.

William Bryan said, "The way to develop self-confidence is to do the thing you fear and get a record of successful experiences behind you." You may have a fear of failure or a fear of success. You may have a fear of losing a great relationship or a fear of being alone. Fear is often unpleasant but you were made to overcome it. Fear is the belief that something is dangerous or threatening and is likely to cause you harm.

Feeling fear is like being at a horror movie, the thrill and suspense are riveting but the threat is not. You are much safer than you realize because God is a present help in times of need. You can unleash your potential if you are willing to identify, face, and challenge your fears. While avoiding the fear may give you some short-term relief, avoidance is hardly a good long-term strategy. Hanging on to fear is a uniquely human experience. Maybe it is time to rise above it. ■

Today's Live Happy Practice

Since fear is largely about the unknown, gaining more information can help to eliminate it. Therefore, one of the best ways to overcome fear is to arm yourself with as much information as you can. That way, you can make smart and informed decisions.

DAY 51

Calm in the Midst of the Storm

We have all encountered experiences in our life that were not only difficult to meet, but difficult to work through. For many of us, these experiences become a sort of dark night of the soul. The walk through the vortex of darkness and uncertainty has led many of us to believe that we could not make it through. Then, low and behold, the storms ceases, the clouds open up, the darkness disappears, and there you stand wet…but on the other side of the storm. Challenges such as these usually bring with them a transformational quality.

Remember Joseph the Dreamer? He had it all: heavenly and patriarchal favor, an attainable vision, confidence, giftedness, and the ability to serve and support others. But Joseph had to go through the storm before he was ready to move into the station that leads from the pit to the palace. So must you and I. Microwaveable mentalities and thirty minute total home remodels would have us believe that the dust will not even settle before we awake fresh, clean, and brand new. While we may be game for a reality makeover, we cannot forget that greatness is often grown, weathered, and discovered through the difficulties of life.

Rushing through the storm increases the likelihood of incident. Keep moving, but take the time to learn about your strength and power. Darkness can draw us closer to the Light if we understand the rhythm of creation. When you are going through a challenging period of uncertainty, remain calm and use that time to gain a closer walk with God.

Today's Live Happy Practice

When you encounter a difficult experience, pray to find and understand scriptures that will be helpful. Read the scripture and then pray about that. The process will become cyclical; pray and read; then read and pray.

DAY 52

Kick Your Faith into Overdrive

Two of the primary factors that influence our lives is how we allow our faith to impact our thinking and how we allow our thinking to reinforce our faith. The intimate relationship between these most important elements continues to shape our lives during all seasons. We have all experienced the harsh winds of disappointment and despair and while such changes in fortune are common, the way each of us responds to these unplanned disruptions may vary.

To paraphrase author Philip Yancey, faith is "trusting in advance what will only make sense [when we think] in reverse." When the challenges of life knock you down, try to fall to your knees or fall on your back. Both positions help you look up and if you can look up, you can get up. Sometimes it requires a greater use of faith to fulfill the destiny that is waiting for you. Hebrews 11:1 tells us that, "Faith is the substance of things hoped for, the evidence of things not seen." Faith is an inherent power we all use to some degree or another. Sometimes we apply faith intelligently and sometimes we do not. True faith gives us the ability to be uncompromising and victorious over adverse conditions, including our own weaknesses and needs. Faith helps us know that nothing is beyond God's power to do. Through faith we realize that there is no condition that can't be changed and no doubt that can't be reversed. "According to your faith, be it done unto you." Don't be afraid to kick your faith factor into overdrive. ▮

Today's Live Happy Practice

In order to increase your faith, you must increase your convictions. You must develop the ability to look beyond your circumstances and believe that God is greater than anything that you are facing or anything that you will encounter.

DAY 53

Mind Readers

Have you ever received a message that was never intended for you? If you are the kind of person who thinks you can read other people's mind, you are probably creating and receiving lots of messages that are not intended for you. Here are some ways you can tell:

- You are jumping to conclusions about what someone else is thinking based on what you would do if you were that person;

- You are drawing conclusions based on your past behaviors;

- You reach your conclusions based on what you expect, overlooking that fact that you wrote the end of the story at the beginning;

- You draw conclusions based on what you want the answer to be;

- You draw conclusions based on incomplete or misinformation.

Mind reading helps us avoid the need to speak up, enables us to avoid putting ourselves on the line, and permits us to avoid the risk of being rejected. As mind readers, most of us are wildly inaccurate. Maybe it's time to stop getting so much exercise jumping to conclusions. ■

> ### Today's Live Happy Practice
> One way to stop making inaccurate assumptions is to take your time before drawing conclusions. Take a deep breath and step back for a moment so that you can regroup your thoughts and make better decisions.

DAY 54

The Challenge of False Comparisons

Have you ever compared yourself to someone else? If you have, you're not alone. It's natural for us to want to know where we rank or how we stack up. Unfortunately, when you compare yourself to others one of two things usually occurs: either you regard the other person as being better than you and you feel discouraged, or you regard yourself as being better than the other person, and you become puffed up.

The challenge is that neither option really supports your spiritual growth. Pointless comparisons do little more than help you take your eye off the prize. Being better today than you were yesterday and being all that God created YOU to be; that's what really matters. You are fearfully and wonderfully made. "Your works are wonderful, I know that full well." Psalm 139:14. Become better by developing what God gave you and growing into what God made you. ∎

Today's Live Happy Practice

Be grateful for what you have and who you are. You will be more appreciative of who you are when you focus on your good fortune instead of worrying about what you may not be getting.

DAY 55

Uncovering Your Purpose

Did you know that you are a sacred gift? You are a sacred gift who has been given a sacred gift...the gift of purpose. Whether you know it or not, you were born with and for a divine purpose. What's more, you are the only one with that purpose, which means you were born an original. Like a treasured work of art, you are bonafide, certified, and qualified as a purpose-filled original – why settle for living as a copy?

There are a number of ways to identify you principal purpose. The thing to remember is to keep it simple. There are two keys to uncovering your purpose. First, you must realize that you are worthy of having one; and second, you must embrace the fact that you were designed with one.

A purposeful life is not something that accidentally happens to touch the lucky few. It is something you must create. Here is the good news; you have what it takes to create it. If you suspect there is more or if you imagine yourself living a bigger life, you can plant and nurture the seed of purpose. You can promote it through the intensity of your focus. Your thoughts have to be directed toward the expression of purpose. Human beings are not random creatures. Everything we do, we do for a reason. We may not be aware of the reason consciously, but there is undoubtedly a single driving force behind all human behavior. It is most consistently, your stream of thought. ■

Today's Live Happy Practice

Take some time to think about your life's purpose. Even if you haven't discovered that purpose yet, it doesn't mean you don't have one. If you need to, go ahead and reinvent yourself.

DAY 56

I Didn't Come Here to Read

"What is my life purpose?" If you have asked this question of yourself, apparently you are in rare air. It's been suggested that only 2% of people even seek to discover their life's purpose. That means 98% of people never truly seek to get clear about why they are here.

Nathaniel Branden said, "To live without purpose is to live at the mercy of chance." That is why identifying, honoring, and living from your principal purpose is one of the most important actions you can take. When you are in alignment with your purpose, the people, resources, and opportunities you need naturally gravitate toward you.

It reminds me of a powerful story involving Hank Aaron, who at that time was the chief power hitter for the Milwaukee Braves. At the time, Yogi Berra, was the catcher for the New York Yankees. The teams were playing in the World Series and Yogi was keeping up his usual, ceaseless chatter. Yogi was known for using his babble to pep up his teammates on the one hand, and distract the opposing team's batters, on the other. As Aaron and his big bat came to the plate, Yogi tried to distract him by saying, "Henry, you're holding the bat wrong. You're supposed to hold it so you can read the trademark." Aaron didn't say anything, but when the next pitch came he socked a home run ball into the left-field bleachers. After rounding the bases and tagging up at home plate, Aaron looked at Yogi Berra and said, "I didn't come up here to read." If you want to make the most of your purpose, you have to know why you are here. ∎

<u>Today's Live Happy Practice</u>

Figuring out your life's purpose is an inside job that only you can do. Take some time to get in a quiet place and do some soul searching. Think about how you can impact the world and consider the things you really care about on an emotional level.

DAY 57

The Importance of Self-Care

I recently met with one of my health care professionals and the recommendation was that I consider doing more exercise and less stress inducing activity. As I began to explain my excuses for why I did not have time for that, my doctor interrupted me and said, "If you are not healthy enough for you, you won't remain healthy enough for anyone else." While my doctor did not use the words "self-care," self-care is exactly what he was recommending. Many people feel as though making themselves a priority is selfish but as my mother used to say to my sisters and me, "You cannot get blood from a turnip."

Self-care is about considering our personal needs and making those needs a priority. Self-care is not a selfish act. It means taking care of your own health in the same selfless manner that you do for others. Caregivers often find themselves being worn down by the challenges that come with caring for other people. Sometimes they even compromise; or worse, neglect themselves.

Whenever you fly on an airplane, one of the instructions they give before taking off is put your oxygen mask on first if there is an emergency. That's because you can't take care of someone else if you don't take care of yourself first. But self-Care can be easily overlooked, particularly if you are responsible for caring for others. As clinical psychologist Agnes Wainman explained, self-care is "something that refuels us, rather than takes from us." ∎

Today's Live Happy Practice

In order to get started on a self-care routine, the first thing to do is determine the activities that bring you joy and restore your energy. Chose one activity and start doing it immediately. Make a commitment to yourself to do it on a regular basis.

DAY 58

The Risk Zone

Are you ready to move from your comfort zone to your risk zone? I am asking because we always act in ways that are consistent with what we believe. Many people incorrectly believe that this transition from the comfort zone to the risk zone happens naturally and as a result, they end up not making the move. As Dr. Abraham Maslow, wrote, "One can choose to go back toward safety or forward toward growth. But growth must be chosen again and again." Are you ready to choose growth and the risk that comes along with it?

In order to move into your risk zone and live better, you will have to develop a better quality of thinking, better emotional states, better behaviors, better attitudes, and better habits. You have so much intelligence, ability, and talent that you may never be able to use it all. But you certainly do not want to waste it in the comfort zone. Your actions are the true indication of what you really believe and the best way to predict the future is to create it. If your comfort zone is not allowing you to grow as you desire to, it may be time to take a risk. ■

Today's Live Happy Practice

In order to move out of your comfort zone, you must put your ego in check. Your ego is always concerned about how things will make you look. This makes it difficult to take risks. When you keep your ego in check, it allows you to luxury of trial and error.

DAY 59

You Gotta Be In It to Win It

I played baseball in high school along with many of my guys but I was not among the better players. As a matter of fact, I barely made the squad while some of my guys were among the best players in the city. So how did a marginal ball player get to run at one of the best programs, with some of the best players around?

Well, I started with two things: 1) a clear assessment of my abilities and what it would take in order to get better; and 2) an unrelenting desire to get better. What these two elements gave me was a starting point and an accurate map. With no clear direction we are prone to be lost and frustrated. Life can be challenging enough so who needs more of that? Besides, even when we have good directions, there will still be plenty of twists and turns.

People who are committed to getting better cannot afford to remain paralyzed by the fixed conditions of current experiences. In order to get better you must be willing and determined to continue driving forward because old patterns grow deeper roots the longer they remain unchanged. You may not be *the* best, but you can certainly be *your* best.

I never became one of the best but I did get better. I struck out plenty but I did it swinging. I made some errors but I also made some good plays. I got some hits. With my limited skill, I still balled out and I was victorious, if only over my own fears and doubts. In the game of life you get to decide if you're ready to play ball. But like the old marketing slogan, "you gotta be in it to win it." ∎

Today's Live Happy Practice

In order to be engaged in life, try the following tips:

- Be Spontaneous.
- Embrace Who You Are.
- Open Your Mind to the World.
- Listen more and talk less.

DAY 60

Faith

Faith is one of the most important elements in life. But for too long, we have been conditioned to think of faith as some sort of magic catalyst that prompts God to work for us. Faith doesn't actually work this way. Faith is like connecting to the right frequency on the radio; it tunes into the divine flow that has always been present. Our perception gives us access to the creative flow.

Many people go through life holding a coffee cup under the mighty Niagara-like flow of God's plenty, having learned to accept that this is all they deserve to have. Faith helps us change how we relate to the potential of plenty because it helps us see that there is an all-sufficiency even if our container will only hold so much.

It requires a greater use of faith to fulfill the destiny that is waiting for you. Hebrews 11:1 tells us that, "Faith is the substance of things hoped for, the evidence of things not seen." Faith empowers us with the ability to be uncompromising and victorious. Neville Goddard offered that, "Man's Faith in God is measured by his confidence in himself." In faith we realize that there is no condition that can't be changed and no doubt that can't be reversed. "According to your faith, be it done unto you." ▮

Today's Live Happy Practice

Read the Word and head the word. Reading or hearing God's Word is like planting a garden. If you want to grow or "build" a garden, you must first plant the seeds. God's Word is the seed that grows the faith. If you fail to heed what you're reading and ignore what God is telling you then your faith will grow stagnant.

DAY 61

Diamonds Need Pressure to Sparkle

Among the many wonderful things about life are the occasional peaks and valleys, the ebbs and flows, the highs and lows, the thrills and the chills. Old Blue Eyes, Frank Sinatra, called it, "Riding high in April...shot down in May." Most of us know how to celebrate and enjoy the peaks, but we often overlook how to make the most of the valleys.

In the moments that we go from the peak to the valley, we invariably learn lessons about ourselves. Such moments push us then pull us. They fill us with fear before we activate our faith. These times help us grow through the resistance of the challenge.

The problem is that many of us approach life like Jesus' disciples in the Gospel of John. When the disciples encountered a man who had been blind from birth, they asked Jesus whether the man had sinned, or his parents. Jesus told them that neither the man nor his parents sinned; instead, he was born blind so that God's works might be revealed in him.

Very often, when people experience the valleys of life, they assume that they have done something wrong. But what if we were to recalibrate this perspective and approach the lows of life as if they happen so that God's work may be revealed in us? Remember, when we change the way we see things, the things we see change. The lows in life can be valuable even though they may require us to recalibrate a bit. You are built to grow during the valley lows. Diamonds only reveal their potential after a little pressure. ∎

Today's Live Happy Practice

In order to take advantage of challenges in your life, don't react to the problems, instead, focus on the improvements. Reflect on how things will be better after you take the appropriate action to deal with the situation at hand.

DAY 62

How to Win the Game of Life

My career playing organized football was short lived. So short in fact, that it lasted an entire total of two whole practices. It almost took me longer to write the two previous sentences as it took me to realize that the game of football was not what I thought it would be. When I went to my first practice with the Washington Park Redskins, the coach said, "Some of you boys aren't going to make it. Look at the kid to your right and look at the kid to your left; two of you won't be here in a week." I had no way of knowing that I would fall into that category.

Many people show up for life the same way. They are not able to win the game of life because they do not understand the game they are playing. They do not know the rules that govern the law of Mind in action. They are unaware of how to use their emotions so that their feelings can be a blessing. In order to win in the game of life, you must know the rules of the game.

Here are a few things you need to know about the rules in order to be successful in the arena of life: You are made to accomplish amazing things. You will win when you amaze yourself. You are designed for success. You will win when you realize that success is not something that comes to you, you must go to it. You can make yourself more attractive to draw to you the things that will support you. Every time you perform an action that feeds into your victory, you are winning. ∎

Today's Live Happy Practice

One of the best things you can do to win in the game of life is to create a supportive network. Evaluate your circle of friends. Is it a supportive group? Are they takers or givers? Do you have each other's backs? If things are not productive, it may be time to get another group.

DAY 63

Success Comes When You Work It

If you have ever thought that "things" could be better, you are absolutely right! Not only that, whether you realize it or not, you absolutely deserve a better life. Even if everything in your life is great, you still deserve better. Yet most people never experience life at the design level.

People are generally motivated to change by inspiration or by desperation. While inspiration pulls us forward, desperation makes us run from difficulty. Believe it or not, many people develop an emotional addiction to their difficulties. When this happens, we can have a tendency to get entrenched in the patterns that enable us to confirm our excuses and sabotage our success. Too many of us have become content with our own limitations. Do not fall into this behavior. Instead, I want to encourage you to continue stretching beyond the borders and barriers of what seems possible. And here is a little-known secret, with enough inspiration; you can easily tap into your deeper capacity to succeed.

What if you could design your way out of difficulty and disappointment? What if you could give yourself new patterns of behavior that helps you achieve greater success? What if you could literally design the life you deserve? Success does not come from knowledge alone; rather, as my teacher Johnnie Colemon taught me, success comes from knowing how to work it and then working it. As a fundamental rule, we are constantly designing our life with the decisions we make. As the architect, you are responsible for directing your way into your highest design. ▌

> ### Today's Live Happy Practice
> If you want to be more productive, do the hardest tasks first. When you get the tough things out of the way first, the rest of your day will be a piece of cake.

DAY 64

The Gateway to New Benefits

When was the last time you showered yourself with affirmations and encouraging statements that instantly let you feel better? This is important because you deserve love, encouragement, and affirmation. Affirm to yourself that "I am beautiful;" or "I forgive myself." One of the fringe benefits of being intentional about what you say to yourself is that it is a remarkable way to reprogram your negative conditioning and change the course of where your moment, day, week, or life is going.

Conversely, when you are consistently discouraging in your self-talk, it adversely affects your attitude. It is difficult to have confidence when you are discouraging yourself. It is in this way that the dichotomy between the encouraging and discouraging statements become manifest and most obvious. You have to remember that the things you say to yourself reflect how you see yourself.

Become highly intentional about increasing your encouraging conversations. Your self-talk will be the gateway to the new beliefs that enable you to more consistently talk to yourself in ways that support a bigger vision of yourself. Your past is not prologue. It is time to give yourself a way to make all of the adjustments you would like to make, regardless of whether you have been able to successfully do it before now. Your new self-talk will help you move yourself beyond who you used to be, as you use your internal conversations to paint a new picture of who you desire to be. These conversations will help you, as you start to become a new, better version of yourself. ■

Today's Live Happy Practice

Don't compare yourself to others. When you do this, you can easily get down on yourself and the negative self-talk will begin to flow. Focus on your own good qualities instead.

DAY 65

Be Sure to Read the Signs

Each and every one of us carries the DNA of the Divine. This divine design is always pulling us toward a greater expression of the potential that has been placed within. However, potential needs attention if it will ever become something more. This same potential lies at the core of what powers our dreams, goals, and desires.

I will let you in on another secret…you already possess the tools and raw materials needed to design the life you deserve but you have to know how to read the blueprint.

One day two priests got together and erected a sign which said: "THE END IS NEAR. TURN YOURSELF AROUND NOW, BEFORE IT IS TOO LATE." As cars sped past them, the drivers would leans out the window and yell, "Leave people alone, you religious nuts. We don't need your lectures." From around the next curve they would hear screeching tires and then a big splash. Shaking their heads, Father Patrick said, "Dat's da therd one dis mornin.'" "Yaa," Sean agrees, then added, "Do ya tink maybe da sign should just say: "BRIDGE CLOSED"?

The problem is that these tools, materials, and blueprints can do you no good if you do not possess the discipline to use them. As Nansen said, "The difficult is what takes a little time; the impossible is what takes a little longer."

It is never too late to begin designing the life you deserve; you just need to be able to read the signs! ■

> ### Today's Live Happy Practice
> Work on your time management skills. Develop the ability to split your time between your projects for maximum productivity. The more efficient you are, the more successful you will be.

DAY 66

Choosing the Right Windows

We all face uncertainty sometimes. Whether it's financial uncertainty or health concerns. That's why it's important to have faith. Faith doesn't necessarily eliminate the uncertainty but it does give us a confident mental attitude with which to approach the unknown.

We live in a world that's largely created through the power of our mind. Here's the good news…you and I can control what goes on in our mind. It reminds me of the story of the father who stood back as he watched his young daughter stare out of the window of their home. Though the sun was shining on that beautiful day, the child was overcome with sadness. Her father walked over to comfort her and as he put his arm and hand across her shoulders, he turned the young child around and led her to another window looking out into the garden. In short order the little girl was soon screaming with delight as she noticed new blossoms on a small bush she had recently helped to plant. Patting her shoulder lovingly, the father said, "You see, dear, you were looking out the wrong window."

How many of us are looking out the wrong window? Looking through the wrong lens? Looking at our experience the wrong way? Faith is your awareness of the universal powers. The thing is that we are not to simply have faith; we must use it.

We have to maintain control of the mind so that it remains open to the power and flow of infinite possibility. Whatever your mind can conceive and believe, you can achieve. That's why it's important to not allow the limitations and restrictions to sabotage us and our desires. ■

Today's Live Happy Practice

If you have limiting beliefs, recognize that they are based on falsities. It is just a belief, not a fact. Challenge yourself and think of ways to think outside the box.

DAY 67

The Process of Healing Relationships

People are naturally relational; accordingly, relationships are an important part of our everyday lives. When it comes to our relationships, we attract people who are similar to us. People are also different and our differences can sometimes manifest themselves through issues and disagreements. The interactions and exchanges we have with them can cause some unresolved issues to emerge and prompt responses that have little to do with the person we are having an exchange with.

Within each of us are patterns created by the experiences of a lifetime. Some patterns are faint and hardly noticeable. Others are well grooved and coded in pain, hurt, disappointment, and dissatisfaction. If you have ever experienced a severe snowstorm, where the elements produce a bed of ice beneath your car tire, then you have probably had the experience of having the friction from your wheel create a groove in the ice. These groves work themselves into a deep pattern of slick inescapability. Generally, your only way of escape is to get help from some understanding soul. This process mirrors the conditions we sometimes work through to heal our relationships.

If you find that your relationship is in trouble, it is okay to get help. When your issues are not addressed and for whatever reasons go unresolved, these same issues can have a harmful impact and become a breeding ground for conflict and hidden resentment. While knowing how to successfully manage these conflicts may be difficult, you have to determine if your relationship is worth it. Sometimes you may not even realize how important the relationship is. ∎

Today's Live Happy Practice

If you are involved in a relationship that is in need of repair, don't blame yourself. Learning not to blame yourself is a critical step in healing a poor relationship.

DAY 68

The Willingness to Forgive

Once when talking about forgiveness, Oprah Winfrey said, "Forgiveness is giving up the hope that the past could have been any different; it's accepting the past for what it was; and using this moment and this time to help yourself move forward." The willingness to forgive is often rooted in our right thinking. Thinking is the gateway to emotion, and emotion is the gateway to action. You can enjoy the freedom that comes with forgiveness as long as you are willing to stop holding on to an experience from the past.

Other people may have been at the root of your pain, but you are the one who controls whether you allow that pain to go on. You don't have to be held captive by what was done to you in the past and you don't have to feel compelled to punish them in order to get better.

Today's Live Happy Practice

Here are some things you can do to help you forgive:

- Change how you see the person who was part of the pain.
- Accept and embrace yourself completely.
- Recognize that you make mistakes too.
- Uncompromisingly holding on to the truth.
- Honor that you are responsible for what you do with the pain.

DAY 69

The Liminal Space

As Joshua was preparing to lead the children of Israel from the wilderness into the Promised Land, a word of reassurance was delivered to him. The word was reassurance that just as God had been with Moses, God would also be with him. He was also encouraged to be strong and courageous and not be afraid or dismayed. Sometimes it is in the place of our greatest uncertainty that God will speak and helps us to see the potential to our greatest improvement.

What we often miss is that during these seasons of uncertainty, we are in a liminal space. The word "liminal" comes from the Latin word limens, which means "threshold." In essence, a liminal space is a place of transition. It is here that we wait, and quite possibly, not know. It is the intermediate time, the in-between, the transitional state where we cannot go back to where we were because a threshold has been crossed, and we have yet to arrive where we are going because it is not yet available. We enter a liminal space when we leave from one door but the new door has not opened or appeared yet. It is when one season ends and the new season has not yet begun.

The most common question individuals ask in this place is: "What do you do when one door has closed and another has not yet opened?" The answer is, "You make the most of the liminal space…you produce." ■

> ## Today's Live Happy Practice
> When you reach your limits, that's the time when you need to find meaning in what you do. What is your purpose? What brings you joy? Why do you do what you do? Answer these questions to get in touch with your motivations and renew yourself from one season to the next.

DAY 70

Committing to Good Habits

Everyone is interested in a good future, but the fact of the matter is, we don't necessarily decide our future. What we do decide; however is our habits. Our habits serve as the framework, reference point, and criterion by which everything else is examined and evaluated. Each habit has the potential to lead us to, or away from our desired future. If we build good habits, we can build good behavior, because our habits influence nearly 50% of our behaviors.

You cannot effectively design the life we desire if you have poor habits. Make sure that the things you say and do are consistent. Avoid sabotaging yourself. Once you have decided what you want, go about applying the behaviors that help you achieve it.

Eventually, people who are not committed to being better will find themselves giving up on the hope for their future. What follows quitting is a string of excuses, tolerances, and settling for a life that is less than what you desire. You can set yourself apart and enjoy the kind of lifestyle that most people cannot, if you have the kind of habits that enable you to do the kind of things that most people won't. No one drifts to the top of the mountain. It requires planning, attention, commitment, discipline, and showing up every day to move closer to your desires. You can be happy or you can be content. You can be rich or you can be poor. You can be purposeful or you can drift. The fact of the matter is that if you want to be healthy and make meaningful contributions for the future, you have to make good decisions today. Your habits will decide the outcome.

Today's Live Happy Practice

In order to develop good habits, think about the triggers and obstacles you face. For example, if you can't resist sugary snacks, eliminate them from your kitchen. This can help you develop good eating habits.

DAY 71

Kick Your Faith into Overdrive

Problems are to the mind, what pain is to the body. They are warning symbols. They are different indications that something creative must be done with what God has given you. So what have you been called to create? Know that your new creation will require a new mindset and new behaviors. "No one puts new wine into old wines skins. For the old skins would burst from the pressure..." Matt. 9:17.

The African Impala can jump to a height of over 10 feet and cover a distance of greater than 30 feet. Yet these magnificent creatures can be kept in an enclosure in any zoo with a 3-foot tall wall. The animals will not jump if they cannot see where their feet will fall. Like the impala, we sometimes do not leap if we do not know where our feet will land. Faith is the ability to trust what we cannot see, and with faith we are freed from the flimsy enclosures of life. Faith without works is dead.

Sometimes it requires a greater use of faith to fulfill the destiny that is waiting for you. Hebrews 11:1 tells us that, "Faith is the substance of things hoped for, the evidence of things not seen." Faith is an inherent power we all use to some degree or another. Sometimes we apply faith intelligently and sometimes we do not. True faith gives us the ability to be uncompromising and victorious over adverse conditions. Faith helps us know that nothing is beyond God's power to do. Through faith we realize that there is no condition that can't be changed and no doubt that can't be reversed. "According to your faith, be it done unto you." Don't be afraid to kick your faith factor into overdrive. ▌

Today's Live Happy Practice

You can increase your faith when you encourage and build up others. When you are spreading joy to other people and encouraging them in their faith, your faith will be increasing at the same time.

DAY 72

Dedication to the Daily Improvement of Self

In life, there are things that we must work for and there are things that we must wait for. Either way, we can still give ourselves a greater degree of personalized service if we begin each day with dedication. When we begin the day with dedication, we are better positioned to end the day with satisfaction. It is, however, important to know how you will direct your dedication and in what areas you will take action.

Dedication to the daily improvement of self, precedes a future filled with greater possibilities. When we are dedicated to being better in the simple things, like being a better parent or a better spouse, our dedication facilitates and supports our growth in the big things.

Dedication helps us grow and when we grow, we expand our vision, we attract more options, we open more opportunities, and we optimize our potential. We must remember that the law of increase is subjective. The soil will willingly accept the seed and do its part of helping the seed transform into a plant; it does not, however, determine if it is making a tomato or potato. No matter where you find yourself planted, it is your dedication to remain true to the potential of what you can become that determines what you will produce.

New things are usually difficult before they become easy, and too often, our difficulties become a deterrent that prevents us from becoming better. Every worthwhile experience of growth and achievement requires dedication and determination. The people who grow the most are the ones who most consistently practice and prepare to grow day after day. ∎

Today's Live Happy Practice

You can embrace bigger challenges by seeking growth. Don't just chase what you know, get out of your comfort zone and pursue new challenges daily.

DAY 73

To Thine Own Self Be True

We all have those moments when our lives are so filled with confusion that we can't tell up from down; so bereft with pain that we can't see in from out; and so full of frustration and hopelessness that we can't see the light at the end of the tunnel. Theologian Martin Luther recommended that we, "Pray as if everything depended upon God and work as if everything depended upon you."

It is obvious that some people bounce back to overcome their challenges and some don't. The problem is that some people don't know how to bounce back.

When your car malfunctions and the cause is not immediately apparent, the mechanic will seek to determine the cause of the trouble by hooking their equipment up to the car and doing a diagnostic test. The same is true when you encounter problems in your life. Sometimes the work that needs to be done during these moments is a reflective diagnostic. As Shakespeare admonished us, "This above all: to thine own self be true."

In order to make the most of your reflective time, it is necessary to be honest with yourself. Like looking in a mirror, if your reflection makes you uncomfortable, it means there is some inner work to do. Many people go through life never coming to this realization. █

> ### Today's Live Happy Practice
> In order to get clearer, remembered to stop and pray. Prayer helps you in those reflective moments. It gives you the strength to go forward. Prayer helps you adjust and prepare your mind and heart to receive

DAY 74

Focus on Your Success

You are uniquely crafted and divinely designed! Not only that, but you have the amazing ability to align with and use your spiritual identity and spiritual power to live a bigger life, regardless of any appearance to the contrary. One of the primary things that interrupt our ability to live full out and in accord with what God placed within us is the notion that we are not good enough.

In 2017, the Barna Group took a close look at the segment of the American population who consider themselves to be "spiritual but not religious." They looked at who they are! What they believe! How they live out their spirituality daily! What they found was that a number of people equated being religious with being institutional—and practicing one's spirituality in accordance with an external authority. The idea that you compare yourself to some external authority is the primary cause of the thought that you are not good enough.

This type of thinking implies that there is some arbitrary standard that you don't measure up to, but no individual can set parameters for your life. In order to change your mindset, you should give up the habit of comparing yourself to others. Free yourself by recognize that life is not a competition between you and everyone else. ■

Today's Live Happy Practice

One way you can stop feeling like you're not good enough is to recall past achievements. If you find yourself thinking about times when you failed, take a deep breath and recall previous successes. Undoubtable, you have had more successes than failures in your life, so focus on those times.

DAY 75

When You Want to Go Far, Go with Others

When Jesus began his ministry, one of the first things he did was recruit a support system. It is worth noting that the people who would become part of his support system were not random. They were sought out, observed, selected, and suited for the mission. Even when team members had discrepancies with one another, or jockeyed for position, or expressed doubts, or did not have all the answers, or could not perform, they remained anointed for their respective role in the group.

The saying goes, "When you want to go fast, go alone. When you want to go far, go with others." Throughout all history, solo actors have achieved very few great accomplishments. In order to go as far as God wants to go through you, you may need a support system as well. You may need some people who can help support you in one instance and serve as guides to how you might navigate the many opportunities coming your way, in the next instance. Having a trusted circle can be invaluable when you're trying to get to the next level.

A solid support system is one of the environments we cannot afford to neglect. A good network can be empowering and provide the compass many of us need in order to navigate in the world. Working with your support system may also help you further build out your emotional intelligence. Your support system can become an invaluable resource as you face the tests and trials as well as the opportunities and possibilities. ■

Today's Live Happy Practice

When you want to build a sustainable support system, it is imperative that you stay in touch. It is also important to show your appreciation. Let them know that they are appreciated and say thank you often.

DAY 76

Your Decisions Determine Your Destiny

Life is decision driven. Raymond Charles Barker, who was one of the great minds on the power of decision wrote, "If today's thinking is not exciting, tomorrows experience won't be either." We have to remember that decisions determine our destiny. Decide to develop a non-critical, non-judging attitude toward yourself. If you are not able to develop this sort of generous attitude to give to yourself, you probably won't have it to give to others!

I see people hold on to negative attitudes about themselves, regardless of how miserable they consider their situation to be. Here's the thing, when you do this, it comes at the expense of your self-respect. Your attitude is a major part of what you use to determine what a thing is worth to you. If your attitude is for or against something, that will go a long way in terms of your acceptance or rejection of that particular thing. These same attitudes become learned tendencies and predispositions that influence your behavior.

Criticisms are often a form of subtle rejection. You are not your unmet expectation. You can choose to stop being critical of yourself. You can choose to avoid judging yourself, but if you do decide to continue your self-judgement, you may want to err on the side of overestimating your potential. ■

Today's Live Happy Practice

In order to develop a positive attitude, don't do anything passively. Whatever you do should matter. You time is incredibly valuable so don't waste it on anything that you cannot actively engage in.

DAY 77

Have Gratitude for all You Have

One of the easiest ways to become a vibrational match to the better life you desire is to focus on generating positive emotions throughout the day. What do I mean by positive emotions? I mean emotions such as love, joy, appreciation, and gratitude. Believe it or not, generating these types of emotions gives you the feeling of already having what you want. You can create and experience these emotions by being highly intentional about the thoughts you think. In fact, your thoughts are creating feelings all the time.

Albert Einstein said, "There are only two ways to live your life. One is as though nothing is a miracle. The other is as though everything is a miracle." If everything is a miracle then gratitude has to be a given. Though gratitude is a given, it is also a choice. When you choose to develop the mental and emotional habits of gratefulness, you unlock the uncanny power to instantaneously transform yourself, by transforming your emotional state.

Happiness is a benefit of gratitude. When you make a commitment to express your gratefulness, your practice will immediately begin to recondition your belief about whether you have a right to be happy. Here's the great news, your belief dictates your effort, enterprise, and action, so gratitude impacts the creativity you bring to what you do and how you do it. Just by choosing to be grateful, you will become happier. As one writer put it, "Have gratitude for all you have and you can be happy exactly as you are."

> ### Today's Live Happy Practice
> Show your gratitude to someone by calling to say hello. Just hearing your voice can make a world of difference in someone's life and it's a quick and easy way to show your appreciation.

DAY 78

Forward Motion Leads to Success

Want shows up in conversation. Expectation shows up in action. Whenever you apply the power of faith, you have to also be ready to apply the law of action because faith without work is ineffective and unable to produce the desired result. You do not get better by chance, you get better by change. Why is it important to put your faith in the action of your dream? Because an object at rest stays at rest and an object in motion stays in motion with the same speed and in the same direction unless acted upon by an unbalanced force. Here's the thing: It takes the same amount of force to stay at rest as it does to stay in motion.

Inaction produces doubt and fear and erodes your confidence, but taking action gives you confidence and courage. If you want to use your faith to conquer your fear, think about how you might do it and then go do it. Go out and get busy. Believe it or not, human beings are hard wired for caution. This can prevent us from taking action. Most people steer clear of situations that expose them to the possibility of failing or might cause them to lose face or feel foolish.

Remember, you are what you are and where you are because of the dominating thoughts in your mind. Taking action leads to change, so get yourself in motion and your forward momentum will propel you to the success you desire. ∎

> ### Today's Live Happy Practice
> Keep moving forward by taking a step back. Think about where you are, what got you here, and where you want to be. Evaluate and make adjustments as necessary.

DAY 79

Adjust Yourself

You and I are not equipped for mediocrity. In order to live an average life, you have to shrink back from your potential and stay satisfied in your comfort zones. You are so wonderfully made that what you think, you can experience. The time, energy, and effort you put into developing yourself can be the springboard that helps you manifest those imaginings in your life.

Your prize for making the effort and choosing a new design is to change your life for the better. It is all up to you. No one else can live your life for you. No matter how well intentioned they are, no one can do your push-ups and sit-ups for you. No one else can design and execute your success habits for you! Just remember that even a good start can be wasted if we cannot generate and sustain the motivation to keep going. As Raymond Charles Barker observed, "Those whose enthusiasm wanes, soon return again to their old complaints."

What if you have not been able to do it up to this point? You did what you could with what you had. One suggestion: do not judge yourself—adjust yourself! When you resist changing, it brings you face-to-face with the one who is holding your success hostage. When you make up your mind, nothing can stop you from changing your life for the better; not even your opinions about yourself. You are more resourceful than you realize. Design it! Get after it! Give it another go! It is your life and it is your choice. ∎

> ### Today's Live Happy Practice
> Be specific about what it is you really want and develop a plan to get you there. Try to understand the things that are getting in your way and think of things you can do to work around your obstacles.

DAY 80

Respecting Boundaries

One of the best-kept secrets is that establishing healthy boundaries is a form of self-care. Having boundaries is a critical part of establishing healthy relationships and facilitating a healthy life style. Unfortunately, setting boundaries is a skill that many of us don't intentionally deploy and our self-esteem and quality of life may be suffering as a result.

It reminds me of the story of a man who found a cocoon of a butterfly. One day a small opening appeared. He sat and watched the butterfly for several hours as it struggled to force its body through that little hole. Until it suddenly stopped making any progress and looked like it was stuck. So, the man decided to help the butterfly. He took a pair of scissors and snipped off the remaining bit of the cocoon. The butterfly then emerged easily, although it had a swollen body and small, shriveled wings.

The man didn't think anything of it and sat there waiting for the wings to enlarge to support the butterfly. But that didn't happen. The butterfly spent the rest of its life unable to fly, crawling around with tiny wings and a swollen body. Despite the kind heart of the man, he didn't understand that the restricting cocoon and the struggle needed by the butterfly to get itself through the small opening; were God's way of forcing fluid from the body of the butterfly into its wings. As Gina Greenlee observed, "Honoring your own boundaries is the clearest message to others to honor them, too." ■

Today's Live Happy Practice

It is important to communicate your boundaries with respect. Healthy relationships require respect on both sides. Be open and honest with the other party and communicate your desires in a respectful manner.

DAY 81

An Attitude of Gratitude

Scientists have been discovering and documenting, for some time now, that there are health benefits related to the practice of gratitude. I do not know about you, but I would be willing to trade my anger, stress, and frustration, to thank someone for their contribution if it made me feel better. It certainly seems like that would be an awesome trade for me!

An attitude of gratitude helps to reduce your stress level and jump start your mood; and, as an additional advantage, those around you will enjoy the same positive benefits. A lesser known fact is that being in a state of gratitude puts you in a mindset of abundance. We know that like-energy attracts like-energy. If you are someone who desires to experience more abundance in your relationships, finances, peace of mind, overall level of joy, and sense of purpose, then gratitude is the gift you must absolutely give to yourself.

It is commonly held that the way you begin your day goes a long way in shaping the tone and tenor of the entire day; so make gratitude a part of your morning daily routine. Research shows that practicing gratitude before going to bed helps us have longer and more refreshing rest. By simply recounting the things you are grateful for, helps you receive the benefits of gratitude. That's why I love the quote from Brian Tracy who said: "Develop an attitude of gratitude, and give thanks for everything that happens to you, knowing that every step forward is a step toward achieving something."

Today's Live Happy Practice

For three minutes in the morning and for three minutes before bed, take time to contemplate the things that you are grateful for. Allow yourself to feel it and don't be afraid to express it.

DAY 82

The Law of Mind in Action

Are you finding it more difficult to get through your days? Is life presenting you with what seems like an unfair share of tough situations? This may not be the best time to spring this on you but it may help to know that your outer experiences are usually the result of your inner patterns. As the soul legend Teddy Pendergrass sang, "You can't hide from yourself. Everywhere you go, there you are." The good news is you have the power and the ability to address the causes that create the experiences. It requires a change in the way you see things.

Proverbs 23:7 reminds us that, "As a man thinks in his heart, so is he." The wisdom of these words calls to the forefront the fact that, the end or what we experience, begins with the seeds of thought. The challenge is that so many of us are focused on what we do not want, and then we are surprised when it shows up over and over again. But the law of Mind in Action is as reliable and impersonal as the law of gravity.

The law of Mind in Action is a creative law. It states that you create your life based upon the thoughts you think. It has always been working in your life. The only question is whether you have been consciously and intentionally directing it. When you become more aware of how the law works, you give yourself more leverage to design the life you deserve and turn obstacles into opportunities. As one enlightened person shared, "I used to resent obstacles along the path, thinking, if only that hadn't happened life would be so good. Then I suddenly realized, life is the obstacles. There is no underlying path." ■

Today's Live Happy Practice

Focus on the good things in your life no matter how small they may seem. Always look for the silver lining in every situation.

DAY 83

Activate Your Design Setting

When living the inspired life, you must decide whether the inspiration God gave you will be nurtured by your design or ignored by default. If you do not develop your own design and become responsible for how your inspiration will be used, you will, by default, empower other people to direct and benefit from your inspiration.

Your design setting directs inspiration according to your vision; while your default setting directs inspiration according to your script. Your design setting gives clarity to your pattern; while your default setting gives you back the baggage of past failings. Get in sync with the divine design of your inspiration. It will help you better understand the unique gifts that reinforce your unique contribution to the world. ■

Today's Live Happy Practice

Sometimes you can get inspired by simply disconnecting from your current environment. Set aside your electronic devices and go for a peaceful walk. Taking a walk in nature or around the block may do wonders to help inspire and rejuvenate you.

DAY 84

A Delay Is Not a Denial

We live in a fast paced society. Instant access to connections and information has fueled our microwave mentalities. Programs highlighting thirty-minute makeovers and quick-fast remodels have helped create the false expectation that most things, if not everything, should come quickly and easily. Yet, things do not always happen within our expected time frame. Things do not always go the way we want them to. Sometimes plans do not unfold the way we expected. When the winds do not blow your way, it is best to know how to adjust your sails.

When encountering interruptions, it is critical to remember that a delay is not a denial. A delay is an opportunity to grow more patient and invest more time developing the additional skills, relationships, and experiences necessary to support attaining the things you want, which will come in due time. Ecclesiastes 3 reads, "For everything there is a season, and a time for every matter under the heavens." You must be willing to invest the appropriate amount of time, energy, and effort if you want to develop the ability to properly handle the blessings that are set before you.

When life hits the pause button on you, remember to take a couple of steps back from the immediacy and intensity of the moment. Allowing some space will give you a chance to take a long, hard look at the experience, without the emotional attachment. This distance will also give you time to do some introspection and take another look at yourself. Everything will go okay in the end. If it is not okay, it is not the end. ■

Today's Live Happy Practice

Sometimes a delay can mean that what you are doing is not important. When you face a delay, take some time to evaluate whether your activity is important or not. Then stop doing anything that is not essential to reaching your goal.

DAY 85

A View from the Top

Do you give yourself the benefit of a view from the top? Do you use your imagination to contemplate all the changing, challenging experiences from the highest possible point of view? Regardless of the appearances of conflicts or limitations, your imagination helps you to see realities in their mental and spiritual form before they are transmuted into physical form.

A view from the top gives you the opportunity to see things creatively and with an attitude that is constructive and optimistic. But nature does not give you an abundance of anything without demanding that you use it. Use your imagination to visualize the uncreated worlds of potential that lie within you. Awaken your imagination and see the abundance attached to the sacred promise, "I came that they might have life and have it more abundantly." If you are unable to see this abundance in your imagination, you will never see it in your life, world, and affairs.

It probably was not easy for Noah to build the arc as people mocked him. But Noah kept holding the thought firmly in his imagination. It may not be easy for you to be the first person in your family to do something no one else has ever done. But keep holding the thought firmly in the imagination. Use your imagination to visualize the uncreated worlds of potential. Use your imagination to get out of your comfort zone. Use your imagination to give form to the formless. Live from your imagination and give yourself a view from the top. ∎

Today's Live Happy Practice

Daydreaming can help you improve your imagination. Take time out of your busy day to stop and just observe the things around you. Let you mind wander. Do plants feel? Are extraterrestrials out there? Routinely speculate on things until it becomes a habit. Your imagination may eventually lead you to write a bestselling book or invent a new product.

DAY 86

The Power of Perseverance

In order to be successful, you have to be willing to do whatever it takes to get the job done. But what do you do when it does not go well? According to Napoleon Hill, "Before success comes in someone's life, they are sure to meet with much temporary defeat, and perhaps, some failure. When defeat overtakes them, the easiest and most logical thing to do is to quit. That is exactly what the majority of people do." What these people miss is that it is not any one single push on the flywheel, but the cumulative total of all their sequential, unfailingly consistent effort that eventually creates movement and generates the momentum for good to breakthrough and flow in their lives.

Successful people persevere and form habits that feed their success. They understand that life is a dance between selection and rejection. Every decision you make touches your penchant to persevere. Simply by making those right decisions, or making more of them—one at a time, over and over again—you will have enlisted the awesome power of perseverance on your behalf. The unwanted circumstances and poor results produced can become a thing of the past. By putting the power of perseverance on your side, you can marshal the divine forces and your success becomes inevitable. ∎

> ### Today's Live Happy Practice
> One of the best things you can do to continue to persevere is to maintain optimism. Expect good things to happen. Try keeping a daily diary and record all of your good experiences.

DAY 87

Unnecessary Comparisons

One of the greatest ironies in life is that people are so amazingly unique and uncannily similar at the same time. While it may not be wise to overgeneralize about what people want, it is safe to say that people generally want to be happy. We all have a unique perspective of what happiness is. We all have certain habits, some of which may support our desire for happiness and others that do not. Becoming aware of the habits that negatively affect your happiness will give you the ability to immediately correct them.

Have you ever compared yourself to someone else? If you have, you are not alone. One of the habits that may impact your happiness is comparing yourself to other people. It can sometimes be intimidating to be in the presence of people you perceive as smarter, more successful, or otherwise better than you. Unfortunately, when you compare yourself to others, you may begin to feel discouraged. Pointless comparisons do little more than help you take your eye off the prize...being all that God created *you* to be.

Ridding yourself of the need to be compared against others can be incredibly difficult, but it can be done. ▮

Today's Live Happy Practice

Pegging a specific instance in your life in order to correct a behavior makes the behavior a bit easier to manage. Think about a time when you compared yourself with someone else. Ask yourself if the comparison was worth the attention you invested and the negative tension it caused you? If not, take this into consideration the next time you feel inclined to compare yourself to someone.

DAY 88

Stretch Beyond Where You Are

There is an enormous power inherent in the thoughts you think, the beliefs you hold, and your willingness to stretch beyond where you are. These three points of potential are major keys in exercising the levers that help you grow.

- Thought catalyzes experience. The thoughts you think are seeds of your creative capacity; and the power to think, choose, and make decisions is an incredible tool. With this tool, you can reconfigure your life, repair your family, rebuild your community, and reconstruct your self-determination.

- It is done as you believe. The accepted notions that make up your belief system can act as chains that keep you stuck or as wings to help you fly. If you do not believe that you can accomplish or overcome whatever is before you, you will not have the passion and determination to get it done. Therefore, if you are serious about changing a behavior, start by changing some of what you believe.

- Outgrow your comfort zone. The desire to become the very best version of yourself will require you to take some risks and get outside your comfort zone. As a Bateke proverb states, "We learn to cut down trees by cutting down trees." Many of us want something different, yet we may not be willing to grow from the place that makes us the most comfortable. Getting out of your comfort zone will help you circumvent repeating the same behaviors and give birth to new and amazing potential. ■

Today's Live Happy Practice

Take another look at the three keys to growth and use them to help you stretch.

DAY 89

Your Body is the Temple of God

Your body is an amazing temple and it is endowed with the vast intelligence that stands underneath all of creation. The order with which it works is so incredible that the simple act of breaking a fingernail will send the signal that deploys and directs the healing agent to begin sending the cells that generate into porcelain.

Your body is the temple of the Life Giving One. The more fully your concept of your wholeness is in harmony with the Life Giving One, the more fully your mind, emotions, and body will allow the radiant health and vitality of God's goodness to flow in, through, and as you. The goal is to ensure that every aspect of your being is attuned to the Spirit of God.

The most important healing is found in the transition from those negative, incongruent thoughts and beliefs that become the mental equivalents that produce disease. You must understand that the foundation principle upon which God created is, "It was good," then work to ensure that your thoughts and beliefs are grounded in this simple Truth. You are a child of God and knowing this Truth shall set you free from those things that might otherwise limit the expression of your good.

Unfortunately, God does not compel you to claim your birthright. Just like your luggage will ride on the carousel until you remove it, you will have to step up and claim what is yours. You can never truly be separated from your good, so have faith in the Holy Spirit (God's Spirit of wholeness). God is life and that life animates and emanates from within you. ∎

Today's Live Happy Practice

In order to be the best you can be; keep your body in the best shape possible; and achieve the happiness you desire; be sure to eat a healthy, balanced diet with lots of fruits and vegetables.

DAY 90

The Valuable Ability of Transformation.

Your habits have an incredible and important influence on how you live your life. Moreover, interrupting and unlearning your patterns can be more difficult than developing them. That is why it is more important to develop good, productive habits, rather than using that creative energy to undo unproductive habits. In order to get the most from yourself, you will want to develop habits that lead to self-mastery, self-control, and self-dominion.

Each of these aspects might better be considered as a tool in your toolbox. In order to be effective in life, you will need to be intentional about personal development, for when you neglect to develop yourself in the areas of self-mastery, self-control, and self-dominion; you do so at the risk of surrendering the valuable ability of transformation. The Apostle Paul wrote that we are to, "Be transformed by the renewing of the mind so that you may prove what is the good, acceptable, and perfect will of God."

Awareness and self-facilitation helps you see the blind spots that sometimes conceal your internal conflicts. Being proactive allows you to continue progressing forward to reach those possibilities that are not always easily brought forth. The ability to overcome difficulty and improve your situation, condition, and circumstance in this way, is always available to you, but you must know how to access and use the resources you have. When you work it, it can help you improve every area of your life. ■

Today's Live Happy Practice

You can engage in transformative learning to change how you think and change your perspective to one that is new, and more empowering. One great way to engage in transformative learning is to allow continued discussion and debate on the issues that matter.

DAY 91

The Power Within

Success in dealing with the challenges you face is often dependent upon your ability to actively develop the mental and emotional states that allow you to access the power within. The strength needed to withstand conflict, be courageous in the face of controversy, or overcome the odds is at hand. If the persistent effort of a drip of water can cut through a rock, why should it not follow that your persistent efforts can cut through the hard places in your life? You are more powerful than you think for you have been filled with the fullness of God.

Like an iceberg, there is so much more beneath the surface. Also, the mountain of what you are capable of is vast and mostly frozen. Fortunately, there is something operating through you that can dissolve any difficulty, overcome any obstruction, and renew any relationship that has been broken.

"Now to [those] who are able to do exceedingly and abundantly above all that we can ask or think according to the power that is working within us." Be strengthened with power in your inner being. Be rooted and established in love and you will come to know this power. Finally, let Christ dwell in your heart. You will be glad you did. ■

Today's Live Happy Practice

You can strengthen your inner power by strengthening you brain. One way to strengthen your brain and have fun at the same time is with jigsaw puzzles. Whether you work on a hundred piece or a thousand piece, jigsaw puzzles are an excellent way to strengthen your brain.

DAY 92

Enthusiasm is Like Gasoline

It's important that you not let your enthusiasm find expression in the wrong things. While I won't attempt to define those things for you, I will offer that there are things that support your sense of health, happiness, and overall wellbeing and there are things that do not. Be clear on where those lines are for you so that you can commit your enthusiasm to accomplishing those things that support your ability to live a healthy, happy, and prosperous life.

Why is that important? When you pour all your enthusiasm into things that don't enrich your life, you have less available for working on the things that inspire and leave you fulfilled. If you avoid spilling and splashing your enthusiasm, you may find that you can:

- Increase the intensity of your thinking and imagination

- Reduce the grind in your work

- Gain confidence

- Build your personal initiative and motivation

- More easily overcome mental, emotional, and physical fatigue

Enthusiasm is like the gas you put in your car. Properly employed, it can help you do magnificent things and reach marvelous places. But if you spill and splash it about carelessly, you run the risk of having an explosion in your life. ■

Today's Live Happy Practice

Negativity is contagious, so if you want to stay enthusiastic, spend time with enthusiastic people. Evaluate those around you. If you feel drained, or if you feel bad about yourself after an interaction, you know that you should stay away from that person.

DAY 93

What You Think About, You Bring About

The creative capacity within you is able to manifest anything you contemplate. It has been said that what you think about, you bring about. This being the case, you are the result of your contemplations. In order to make the most of this incredible ability, you will want to condition yourself to only entertain those thoughts that most consistently reflect the life you want to live. Once you are able to hold these kinds of thoughts, allow yourself to be excited about the seed thought and the future harvest. When you have an emotional reaction that enlivens your passion, nothing can hold you back.

James Baldwin once wrote that "fires can't be made with dead embers, nor can enthusiasm be stirred by spiritless men." Passion can ebb and flow so you find it necessary to continue fueling your passion to keep it alive. One way to do this is to focus on your relationship with the Source. Commit to being in a state of readiness with the Oneness and let the Divine find communion with you. ■

Today's Live Happy Practice

Keep your mind thinking about positive things by starting your day off with a ritual of uplifting thoughts. Listen to happy and positive music to get you going and maintain that uplifting mood all day.

DAY 94

The Power of Decision Making

The power to make decisions is an incredible tool. With this tool, you can reconfigure your life, repair your family, rebuild your community, and reconstruct your self-determination. When you make decisions that are in alignment with where you say you want to go, those decisions become the power that drives you forward and propels you toward the destination to which you have set your intention.

The wisdom writer in Proverbs counseled that we should, "Trust the Lord with all your heart; lean not on your own understanding; acknowledge him in all of your ways, and he will direct your path." Whenever you find yourself confused or unclear, perhaps, it is because you have disconnected your process of decision making from the Source. If you want to make better decisions and live by divine design, include these steps in your decision making process:

- Trust God to participate in the process. It does not matter whether the issue is heavy or light; invite God to weigh-in. The more you do, the more your faith and trust will grow.

- Refuse to lean solely on your own understanding. If you share the weight of your burden with the Lord, you will find that the yoke is easier and the burden is lighter.

- Admit that you can use some help getting to the destination.

- Accept His direction and allow it to illuminate your path. ∎

Today's Live Happy Practice

When you are faced with an important decision, be sure to weigh the pros and cons before you act. Make a list and compare the upside and downside before developing your plan.

DAY 95

Create a Vision Board

Accomplishing your goal is about getting from where you are to where you are to be. If you are going to achieve it, you have to put in the work and pay the price for success. Are you committed to planning your work and working your plan? One way to stay committed is to identify someone who is successful, resourceful, and highly effective at what they do and what you want to accomplish. Use that person as inspiration. Let them be a model to help you implement your own plans.

Surround yourself with books, pictures, recordings, and anything else that represent your goals. You may even want to create a vision board for yourself. You can use anything for your vision board. You can make one by cutting out and displaying photos that represent and remind you of your dreams. Use the board to help you concentrate and maintain focus on your goals. Be sure to keep your collection fresh and inspiring.

My wife and I were doing some remodeling in our primary residence. We painted different swatches on the wall as we were trying to choose colors. Then we put the decision off for some time. So long, in fact, that we stopped noticing blotches of different color paints all over the wall. Similarly, you may find it necessary to rearrange things so that you are consistently seeing your vision board with fresh eyes.

Finally, recognize that anything worth having is worth paying for. Make a commitment to work for what you want. If you are willing the pay the price, the power you will have at your disposal will be unlimited...as will be the rewards. ■

> ### Today's Live Happy Practice
> Think about your goals for the coming year. Then grab a poster board, some old magazines or computer printouts, scissors, and glue and start your vision board today.

DAY 96

Be Intentional About Adding to Others

In Julius Caesar, playwright William Shakespeare's Cassius asserts, "A friend should bear his friend's infirmities, but Brutus makes mine greater than they are." In a nutshell, that describes why everyone is not healthy enough to have a front row seat in your life. When psychologists Cliff Notarius and Howard Markman studied newlyweds over the first decade of marriage, they found a subtle, but significant difference at the beginning of the relationships.

Among couples who would ultimately stay together, 5 out of every 100 comments made about each other were putdowns. Among couples that would later separate, 10 of every 100 comments were offensive. That gap intensified over the following decade, until couples that were growing apart were expressing five times as many harsh and undermining comments at each other as happy couples. "Hostile putdowns act as cancerous cells that, if unchecked, erode the relationship over time," said Notarius. "In the end, relentless unremitting negativity takes control and the couple can't get through a week without major blowups."

Unhealthy people do not bear the burdens of those they are in relationships with. In fact, they often make those burdens heavier. If you are not someone who is intentional about adding to others in your relationships, it is possible that you are the cancerous cell. But if you commit to it, you may be able to turn your relationships around and be the person who lifts the relationship to higher heights.

Today's Live Happy Practice

Internality means doing something on purpose. Be intentional about adding to others can be as simple as saying "thank you". This is an effective way to appreciate someone else for something they did, no matter how big or small it was.

DAY 97

You Are Strong in the Lord

From the day we are born, there is within each of us a durable, persuasive, and exciting will to live. We are hardwired in this way. As we come of age, mature, and go through the peaks and valleys of life, we sometimes become weathered; perhaps even jaded by experience. The storms of change, challenge, difficulty, and hardship seem to erode our wires and interrupt our connections.

As we allow these happenings to serve as the experiences that educate and condition our soul, we sometimes lose sight of the durable, compelling, and exciting source of life. Yet, every breath we take is a literal and figurative affirmation of life. Every heartbeat is a harbinger for the forward pull of life that reminds us of all that is in store.

Nothing can override Life in you, for in Him you live, move, and have your being. Your life is the very life of God, Alpha and Omega, beginning and end. The challenges you go through, in whatever form, do not impede or impair the life of God expressing in, through, and as you. You are divinely designed, by the Life Giving One, with the purpose to promote life. All within you and about you is the strength you need for you are, "strong in the Lord and in the power of His might." ∎

Today's Live Happy Practice

Affirm life, affirm that you are strong in the Lord, and affirm that your body is the temple of the living God. You are a new creation in Christ, who makes all things new. You have a durable, persuasive, and exciting will to live. You did not give it to yourself. Rather, it was the gift you received in the beginning. The past is behind you and all of God is before you. Refresh your wires, reclaim your connection, and live victoriously.

DAY 98

Tough People Last

Taking a clear look at life and where we need to grow can be uncomfortable. In fact, if you're like most people, you may experience great internal resistance. This resistance pushes you to avoid rather than face the facts. Avoiding however, leads to endless cycles of distraction, excuses, cop-outs, and procrastination. Instead, stand up, lead on and summon the strength to deal consciously. It is not enough to start inspired. You have to stay inspired.

When you decide to breakthrough and pursue your dreams and goals, you sometimes have to withstand your own internal controversy and opposition in order to overcome the burden of what would limit you. There is an African proverb that says, "If there is no enemy within, the enemy outside can do us no harm." Many people are simply unwilling to pay the price of overcoming. Robert Schuller said, "Tough times don't last but tough people do."

Remember, you are strong in the Lord and in the power of His might. I pray that you will stand up for good; stand in for someone needing a breakthrough; stand back for a larger perspective; stand down on mess and nonsense; stand out from the crowd; stand against injustice, and stand tall in the word with truth and principle. You have to stretch beyond your comfort zone before you can scratch the surface of your greatness. ■

Today's Live Happy Practice

Build tenacity in your life by changing your expectations to intentions. Don't just expect something to happen, instead, make it an intention and then develop a plan to make it happen.

DAY 99

Remain Firm in Who You Are

The Gospel of John shares a narrative where we get to experience an exchange between Jesus and his brother. In this exchange Jesus' brother is urging him to let the world know about the great things he is capable of, yet oddly enough, the brother does not really believe in Jesus. What do you do when the people who are supposed to be close and supportive of you don't really believe in you?

Use your intelligence, wisdom, and freedom to exercise agency and release yourself from other's opinions about you. Do not become bogged down contemplating what others think about you. Do not ingest the negative words directed at you. Take full advantage of the occasion to rid yourself of the opinions of those around you that are full of worry, doubt, or pessimism. Remain firm in who you are and whose you are.

You have been called by God with and for a definite purpose. Do not be moved by their disbelief. Only be moved by God's divine directive. It is done unto you as you believe," not as others believe in you. Their belief is not a prerequisite for what God is doing in your life. Stay committed and let the Father be glorified! As the Psalmist sang, "My soul waits only upon God for my expectation is in Him." ▮

> ### Today's Live Happy Practice
> It can be tempting to overthink things. Overthinking can cause you to judge your own actions and result in procrastination or paralysis. If you are an over-thinker, learn to recognize this tendency and replace it with positive thoughts and actions.

DAY 100

Making Little Changes to Overcome Inertia

When it comes to aspirations, there are two types of people: People who are willing to work for what they want, and people who aspire to something more but make an excuse. If you find yourself in the former category, it is well earned. If you find yourself among the latter group, you may want to consider whether or not you have an expiration date on your excuses. In order to achieve your aspirations, you have to be committed to doing the work. That is why success is not something you just achieve, it is something you must create.

One of the most difficult mental obstacles to achieving your aspirations is overcoming your own inertia! According to the law of inertia, an object that is at rest will stay at rest unless something intervenes to put it in motion again. If, for example, you are in the habit of coming home from work and binge watching TV, you have to overcome your inertia in order to force yourself to get moving on your goals. Essentially, it means that you have to find a way to shock yourself into action.

You may not have to make an earthshaking change. Sometimes just changing one little thing will be enough to get you out of your rut. You might try a new hairstyle or wear something that you've never worn before. You might try a new hobby or learn a new skill. One small change in routine may lead to another one and it could give you that snowball effect that you need to get things rolling again. █

Today's Live Happy Practice

When it comes to achieving your aspirations, one of the very first things you must do is give yourself a blueprint of what you want. Study the blueprint of your desires. Develop a plan so that your aspirations can become powerful enough to overcome the inertia.

DAY 101

Slow Motion Beats No Motion

In studying the law of manifestation, it is clear that determination overshadows talent. Determination is one of the most important characteristics an ambitious person can possess because it is the ability to be persistent, to do or achieve something regardless of any setbacks.

Life consistently tests our level of commitment and life's greatest rewards are reserved for those who demonstrate the determination to act until they achieve what they have set out to accomplish. Yet, you would likely be surprised at the number of people who give up just a few feet short of their goal! This level of resolve can move mountains, even if it's done one pebble at a time. A consistent, determined drop of water can cut through a rock, but only if it is followed by another drop that is just as determined, and so on. Slow motion beats no motion; and the determined keep making small progress toward their ambitions until they are done!

Agricultural scientist George Washington Carver is credited with discovering or developing more than 300 uses for the peanut. What we don't often hear is how many experiments and permutations he ran before arriving at 300! It's said that a young journalist came to Thomas Edison and asked why he persisted in his experiments after having failed more than 5,000 times. Edison replied, "Young man, you don't understand how the world works. I have not failed at all. I have successfully identified 5,000 ways that will not work. That just puts me 5,000 ways closer to the way that will." It took great determination for both George Washington Carver and Thomas Edison to achieve such amazing feats. ∎

Today's Live Happy Practice

Breaking your goals down into a series of simple and practical steps will make it easier to achieve them. This makes your goals more manageable and gives you a constant reference point for your progress.

DAY 102

Understanding Productive Habits

It is not really a secret that the habits you employ today are the predictors of your experiences tomorrow. Therefore, the gateway to a preferred future lies in your ability to modify your habitual patterns of behavior and ensure that your thinking, feeling, and actions are more consistently aligned with the good desires of your heart.

This is not to suggest that every habit you have needs to be changed. In fact, most of your habits are useful. We all learn to write and develop the complex skill of writing through habit.

But what happens when you develop what might be considered a bad habit? When you develop bad habits, you establish ways of thinking and behaving that produce undesirable and unproductive experiences. These undesirable experiences collide with the better versions of yourself and you have difficulty reconciling why your new wine inspiration seems to keep getting lost in the wine skins of your former thinking. A bad habit never goes away on its own. As Jim Rohn suggested, "You don't get better by chance, you get better by change."

Fortunately, if you have learned the habits, then you can unlearn them. If you have ever seen a stream run across a rock over a period of time, you know that the stream can cut right through the rock because of its consistency and persistency. Similarly, you overcome unproductive habits by consistently and persistently reconditioning the thoughts you think, the words you speak, and the actions you take. In order to do something you have never done, you have to become someone you have never been, but then, that is not really a secret. ■

Today's Live Happy Practice

Identify one habit unproductive habit to release and one new habit to support your desire to live happy.

DAY 103

The Road to Success

The road to success is difficult, that is why so many people never really experience or enjoy the success that is possible for them. They don't realize that part of their daily success is linked to their attitude. In order to eventually succeed in your endeavor, it helps to be able to develop and maintain a positive attitude, regardless of the challenges you may be facing.

The road to success requires that there be testing times. These are the times when you come face to face with defeat and difficulty, doubt and fear, lack of conviction and lack of motivation. It is during these times when you do not quit, you persist. Maya Angelou suggested that "There is no greater agony than bearing an untold story inside you." The law of diminishing intent suggests the longer you wait to do something you should do now, the greater the odds that you will never actually do it. Don't let this law be your undoing and don't make any more excuses.

God knows what you have need of and the perfect time will never find you unless you get started. "Now is the acceptable time" 2 Cor. 6:2. Trust the power that God has placed inside of you. That is why I like the exercise that encourages us to consider being on our death bed and standing around the bed are the dreams given to you by life. The ideas that you never acted on; the talents, the gifts, the abilities that you never used; and there they are, standing around your bed, looking at you with large angry eyes saying: "We came to you! And only YOU could have given us life. And now we must die with you forever!" Don't let this example become your reality. ∎

> ### Today's Live Happy Practice
> Use humor to develop and maintain a positive attitude, regardless of the challenges you may be facing. Watch funny movies, read funny books, and above all, lighten up and don't take yourself too seriously.

DAY 104

The Law of Action

Whenever we apply the power of faith, we have to also be ready to apply the law of action because faith without work is ineffective and unable to produce the desired result. That is why want shows up in conversation and expectation shows up in action. Why is it important to put your faith in the action of your dream? An object at rest stays at rest and an object in motion stays in motion with the same speed and in the same direction unless acted upon by an unbalanced force. Here's the thing: It takes the same amount of force to stay at rest as it does to stay in motion

Inaction produces doubt and fear and erodes our confidence. Taking action gives you confidence and courage. If you want to use your faith to conquer your fear, think about how you might do it and then go do it. Go out and get busy. It's been said that, "Those who want to, make a way. Those who don't, make an excuse." Making progress helps our confidence and self-esteem. Believe it or not, human beings are hard wired for caution. This can prevent us from taking action. Most people steer clear of situations that expose them to the possibility of failing.

Remember, you are what you are and where you are because of the dominating thoughts in your mind. Procrastination in dealing with these thoughts only sentences you to further limitation and frustration. ■

Today's Live Happy Practice

Do three things today that put you in the action of achieving your desired result.

DAY 105

The Fruits You Produce

One afternoon, after doing something pretty miraculous, Jesus and his disciples were traveling to another village. Between the steps of their journey, Jesus initiated what seemed to be a fairly innocuous conversation, which he began innocently enough by asking the question, "Who do people say that I am?" The disciples answered according to what the people had been saying about this man of mystery. Then Jesus raised the stakes and asked, "But who do you say that I am?" to which one of the disciples replied, "You are the Messiah."

What would happen if you would ask the same questions of the people in your circle of influence? Note, it is not that you should be overly consumed with what other people think about you. However, there is something to be learned from the conversations being generated based upon the fruits you produce and how you are perceived.

As a child of God, you have been given authority over what you can produce. You have the ability to determine what you think, how you feel, what you do, and how you respond. This also means that you must take complete and total responsibility for everything in your life. As a divine being, you are responsible and accountable for what you create. God lives in you as your true spiritual nature and desires to express through you as love, joy, peace, patience, kindness, generosity, faithfulness, gentleness, and self-control. No excuses, just the execution that comes with being true to who you are and whose you are. You will be known by your fruit, so get at it and really give them something to talk about. ∎

Today's Live Happy Practice

Take complete responsibility for making the most of today. Don't blame others for your failures. Taking responsibility for your actions will help you take control of your life.

DAY 106

The Closet of Prayer

One of the best daily practices you can have is spending some time each and every day in silence. This is the time you spend in your true home…the house not made with hands. This is your time to release the tension, the stress, the blocks, and the negative build up in the soul, as you reconnect with the source of your being. It is your opportunity to be in contemplation and concentration. The silence is where you clear out the debris and ground yourself in purpose, as you transform your mind.

Charles Fillmore wrote, "When one goes into the silence, [they] enter the secret place of the Most High, the closet of prayer within." Prayer pulls you into the core of your spirituality. The closet of prayer is the place where God lovingly transforms you. If you are willing to change, you will make entering your prayer closet a regular occurrence, regardless of the ebb and flow of your day. Mother Teresa taught that, "Prayer is putting oneself in the hands of God, at His disposition, and listening to His voice in the depth of our hearts." ■

Today's Live Happy Practice

Go into your prayer closet and trust God to empower you. Go into your prayer closet and recognize God as the Source of your supply. Go into your prayer closet and be grateful for all the good things in your life. Go into your prayer closet and let your soul to be fortified with the energy of God. Go into your prayer closet and enjoy unmerited grace and mercy. Go into your prayer closet and allow the presence of God to nurture you. Go into your prayer closet and let your praises ring out. Go into your prayer closet and fellowship with the Father.

DAY 107

Honoring Differences in Perspectives

Have you noticed that people sometimes see things differently than you do? This difference in perspective does not mean that one party is right and the other is wrong. It means that we each live from our own consciousness and we see our experiences through our own lens. Your unique worldview is valuable. You must honor it. However, balance recognizes that the same honor must be extended to those who see things differently than you do.

It is not a good idea to hold on to the feelings that are generated when you need to be right. It is easy to become angry, frustrated, or resentful because someone sees things differently than you. To state the obvious, for as much as people are alike, people are different. Different is not right or wrong. It is simply how we are. ■

Today's Live Happy Practice

Ask yourself, "What would I see if I treated those with whom I see things differently the same way I treated those whom I honor, love, and respect?" When attempting to honor the perspective of others you can:

- Deal with differences in ways that are healthy and constructive
- Honor your perspective without having to win the argument or discussion
- Explore what is right rather than who is right
- Be willing to deescalate the situation in favor of the solution.

DAY 108

Focus on Results

Tim Ferris calls time wasters, "Those things that can be ignored with little or no consequence." It may be time to do an inventory and identify whether there are some time-wasters you can drop? We all tend to have some behaviors, events, activities, people, and unproductive conversations taking up the precious commodity called time. Many times our top priorities go unaddressed because, as the saying goes, we are majoring in minors.

What would happen if you focused your time, effort, energy, and resources primarily on those things that get you the results you want? You may be familiar with the Pareto Principle, which tells you that 80% of your results come from 20% of what you do. When it comes to this principle, there are two questions I want you to ask yourself: (1) What are the 20% activities that produces 80% of your results, and (2) What are your time and energy wasters?

If you are like most people, some of your least obvious time and energy wasters are comparing yourself to others; continuing to hold on to things you cannot control; not making myself a priority; and focusing on opinions that do not enhance your life. What would happen if you focused your time, effort, energy, and resources primarily on those things that get you the results you want? ■

Today's Live Happy Practice

Think about the question: What are the 20% activities that produces 80% of your results? Now think about what are your time and energy wasters? When you find the answer, increase the activities that get you results and eliminate the time and energy wasters.

DAY 109

The Importance of Self-care

Have you decided to indulge in self-care? Admittedly, the way the question is presented makes self-care seem like a luxury but in fact, self-care is a necessity. Self-care is any state of being or behaving wherein you deliberately engage in order to take care of yourself in any of these four primary areas:

- Spiritually. Your level of self-care comes from knowing that you have a divine connection. Self-care means letting nothing and no one shake this foundation.

- Mentally/Psychologically. Self-care is a personal choice. You can always choose in favor of it because you have agency and you always have a choice. Other things may influence your choices but your agency has nothing to do with external factors.

- Emotionally. Self-care involves being able to recognize when you are experiencing emotional distress.

- Physically. Self-care means that you recognize the importance of getting enough rest, enough water, sufficient exercise, and food fuel.

In a few words, self-care is key in living a balanced life.

> ### Today's Live Happy Practice
>
> I encourage you to adopt a mindful attitude in which you deliberately pay attention to your inner experience so that you can notice when you are beginning to shift into a different state (be it positive or negative). The minute you realize that you are feeling emotionally unsettled in your body, stop and remind yourself that, "Something is occurring in me and it is attached to this moment."

DAY 110

Attitude Determines Altitude

For most everyone, attitude determines altitude. That is why having the right attitude toward yourself is important. There is an interesting story I heard that amplifies the power of attitude. As the story goes: A lady moved into a retirement home. On her very first day at lunch, she was seated across the table from a gentleman who was visiting someone else at the home. After some time had passed, things began to get a little uncomfortable for gentleman. Without being sure, he felt as though the woman was watching him. Looking out the side of his eye, his suspicions were confirmed, he then became concerned about the fact that the woman was focused like a laser as she stared at him! Finally he turned toward her and said, "Ma'am, I don't understand. Why are you staring at me?"

She said, "I can't believe it."

"You can't believe what?" he said.

"I can't believe that you look exactly like my third husband. The color of your eyes, your mannerisms, the way you talk, your age, your size! I mean, you look exactly like my third husband!" she casually offered.

"Third husband! How many times have you been married?" He finally asked.

"Oh twice!!"

Attitude is a learned tendency through which we evaluate things in a certain way. If your attitudes are for or against something, that will go a long way in terms of your acceptance or rejection of that particular thing. ■

Today's Live Happy Practice

You can foster a winning attitude by being proactive. Being proactive means that you decide how you feel regardless of your circumstances.

DAY 111

The Importance of Boundaries

Boundaries are amazing things. They give you the ability to be emotionally connected to others, without losing your agency or giving up your sense of self. Boundaries enable you to live a healthy, happy, high-functioning life with mindful limits. Gina Greenlee suggested that "Honoring your own boundaries is the clearest message to others to honor them, too." However, it is difficult to honor boundaries that have not been defined.

Each and every one of us carries the responsibility to define and communicate our boundaries. Why? Poorly defined boundaries can lead to unnecessary suffering. But defining your boundaries is not something you wake up one morning and have all ironed out. It is often a steady process that involves intentionality, mindfulness, releasing tolerations, prioritizing, and implementation. The work is worth the effort as it leads to a more genuine and formidable version of self. ■

> ### Today's Live Happy Practice
>
> Begin to define your boundaries by asking and answering these questions (stop and do this now):
>
> 1.   What do I want to experience in my life?
>
> 2.   How do I want to involve others?
>
> 3.   How do I want others to experience me?
>
> 4.   What kind of access will I give to my heart?
>
> 5.   How will I share my brilliance?

DAY 112

Write It Down

How many of us have a legitimate excuse attached to our tendency to stay in the comfort zone and forgo forward momentum? Marianne Williamson said, "There is nothing enlightened about shrinking," That is why the motivation and ability to continue working to manifest your aspirations is so important. Before you can activate persistence and eventually accomplish your objectives, you have to first clarify your wants or desires. You can do this by simply jotting down what you intend to do. Writing it down will reinforce your subconscious nature and put some additional faculties to work on your behalf.

In deciding to clarify your desires, you are beginning to give yourself permission to have them. That is why writing down what you want and committing to having it is the starting point of all great achievement. Whatever you focus on grows and intensifies your desire. When you write your goals down, it helps to intensify your desires and it allows you to gain greater focus and intensity.

There are two words that can super-charge your ability to stay focused on your written goals. Keep them top of mind when attempting to be fulfilled as you commit to experiencing the good desires of your soul. Those words are, "I can!" Remember, you will have obstacles and barriers but the only limitations are the ones you have established in your own mind. "I can" will activate your faith and enthusiasm and enable you to climb higher in altitude and free yourself of the limitations. You can do it. It may not be easy but you will have to remind yourself, "I can." ■

Today's Live Happy Practice

Take some time to reflect and think about what you want out of life. Write it down and make a commitment to yourself to put in the work to make your dreams a reality.

DAY 113

Keep Your Eyes on the Target

Is there a chance that you can lose your enthusiasm to change your life for the better? The answer, unfortunately, is "Yes!" Therefore, it is critical that you know how to rekindle the flames of focus and constantly refuel yourself to keep the drive of attention burning inside you. You are probably familiar with the old adages, "Use it or lose it" and "Out of sight, out of mind."

It reminds me of the story of when the Zen master wanted to show his students a new technique of shooting an arrow. The master covered his eyes with a cloth and then pulled his bow back and released the arrow. When he opened his eyes, he saw the target with no arrow in it and when he looked at his students, they were embarrassed because their teacher had missed. The Zen master asked them, "What lesson do you think I intend to teach you all today?" They answered, "We thought you would show us how to shoot at the target without looking." The Zen master said, "No, I taught you that if you want to be successful in life, you have to keep an eye on the target; otherwise you are likely to miss the opportunity in front of you."

The moral of the story is you need to consistently focus on what you want. The more worthy and desirable your target; the more dedicated and enthusiastically you need to focus on it. ■

Today's Live Happy Practice

Try these techniques to help stay focused:

- Put it on your bathroom, bedroom, and rearview mirror
- Carry it in your wallet or purse
- Put post-its on your computer
- Make it the screen saver on your phone

DAY 114

Eliminating Distractions

Achievers can easily get distracted and discouraged when they think about all it will take in order to overcome the uncertainty of the future. When you cast yourself into the future and begin to project ahead, doubt can sometimes creep in. This is especially true when you begin to imagine issues, problems, obstacles, and barriers that do not exist. In order to override the distraction of your imagination, ask yourself empowering questions. Arnold Schwarzenegger dropped some wisdom when he said that it is better to do an exercise movement once with awareness, than it is to do it ten times while distracted.

In order to allow yourself to be fully present and more aware, ask yourself, "What is the next immediate action I can take to fulfill my plan?" The answer to this question has the potential to place you squarely in the present moment. Not only that, it enables you to experience some micro-success by taking actions that are consistent with your plan. When you engage your present opportunity more fully and strategically participate in making your situation better, you bring out the best in yourself.

This approach will enable you to be a force in your own life, as you are active in your own rescue. Having the life you want is something you create and attract based on the awareness you develop and the person you are committed to becoming. You can make massive progress toward that commitment when you eliminate distractions and focus on the task at hand. ▌

Today's Live Happy Practice

One way to eliminate distractions is to clarify your priorities. Take a few minutes each morning to set your priorities for the day. Determine what is most important and commit to doing those things without interruption.

DAY 115

You Are Not Your Circumstances

One of the most critical mistakes you can make is collapsing your identity into your experiences. You are not your finances; you are not your profession; and you are not your relationships. You are an undeniable, unrepeatable, uniquely gifted expression of God's goodness. You are a spiritual being.

It is said that the ant and the eagle do not share the same worldview. This is largely so because they are often surrounded by different circumstances; which can have a profound impact on their individual experiences. But while your circumstances and experiences may influence your identity, they are only an indication of your past. Today's circumstances are built on yesterday's thinking; so if you want to change your circumstances tomorrow, you must change your thinking today.

When you let go of the belief that you are a product of your external conditions, you will immediately benefit from your power to choose. It is important to remember that your circumstances may change, but your worth does not. When you insist on remaining rooted to the truth of your being, you will realize that you are more powerful than what happens to you. You have the strength to withstand. You can love yourself regardless because you are not limited by the circumstance surrounding you. On the contrary, you are the limitless, unrestricted, persistent expression of the Omni-active essence. ■

Today's Live Happy Practice

One of the things you can do to prevent your circumstances from controlling your future is to learn to forgive. When you learn to let go of the past, your future can be as bright as you want it to be.

DAY 116

Rewiring Your Tolerations for Progress

When you tolerate certain things in your life, it costs you. The things you are tolerating are easy to identify but it does require a level of self-awareness and self-reflection. It requires identifying those things that pester you and are not fulfilling. It means identifying the things that rob you of your energy. When will you stop tolerating the things that keep you denying yourself, denying your feelings and denying your potential?

Tolerations impact your ability to become more, because tolerations are holes in your personal success cup. Settling for less than you deserve eats away at your happiness and your peace of mind. Tolerating unhealthy relationships means experiencing more than your share of people who subtract from you. In fact one statistic suggests that every adult is at least 75% responsible for how others treat them.

The good news is that no matter how engrained you have become at settling; you can begin to stand for something so that you are no longer falling for tolerating. Rewiring your tolerations is about examination, elimination, and recreation. You can perform a diagnostic and start recalibrating yourself and what you will accept. Progress is possible and you can stop settling. Life is moving and so can you. We are all creatures of habit and patterns. Most times we slip into patterns solely because we have failed to develop and give ourselves other response choices. Change the patterns of what you will tolerate and you will radically change your life. ∎

Today's Live Happy Practice

Examine what you have been tolerating. Eliminate the toleration. Recreate experiences that feed your happiness.

DAY 117

No Strings Attached

Relationships represent one of your primary environments. Your relationships are either supporting you or draining you. Your relationships are one of the fundamental ways you experience love; however, all relationships are not created equally. You have primary relationships and you have secondary relationships. Primary relationships are those that are characterized by close intimate interactions. They generally involve the exchange of love and support. Most people will have an opportunity to enjoy six primary relationships:

- Relationship with God
- Relationship with Self
- Relationship with Significant Other
- Relationship with Parents
- Relationship with Children
- Relationship with Friends

Your interactions in your primary relationships should pour into your emotional tank. However, sometimes the people who are closest to you don't live up to your expectations. If that's the case, don't worry, just focus on those who make you feel loved and cared for. The key thing to remember is that you do not have to tolerate an unhealthy relationship. ■

Today's Live Happy Practice

One of the things you can do to minimize disappointments is to throw your expectations and assumptions out the window. Instead of attaching expectations to your loved ones, simply accept them for who they are with no strings attached.

DAY 118

Staying in Perfect Peace

The Prophet Isaiah wrote, "I will keep you in perfect peace, if you will keep your mind on me." Let's share some gateways to staying in peace:

- Reclaim control of your mind at the start of each day. Develop and maintain a positive mental attitude throughout the day. Remember that thoughts have producing power and every thought you release comes back to you multiplied in its effect. Monitor your thoughts, and make sure you send out only those thoughts whose fruits you are willing to receive.

- Ignore trivial circumstances in your interactions with others; avoid allowing them to become controversies. Big people look past small slights. Adjust yourself so that other people's states of mind don't disrupt the calm peace of your soul. Making this adjustment will position you to get along peacefully with them.

- Identify the seed of good in each and every circumstance. Instead of complaining, turn all unpleasant circumstances into opportunities for learning and positive action. Make this an automatic habit. Look at life through the lens of what you want to create and not from what you think is missing.

- Focus on what you can control and concentrate on what you can do. Don't spend time worrying about what might go wrong. Remember, worrying is like sitting in a rocking, it will give you something to do but you won't be getting anywhere. ■

Today's Live Happy Practice

Re-read the tips above and put them into practice in your life. They will help you stay in peace.

DAY 119

Practice Your Way to Greatness

God always meets us where we are and slowly moves us along into deeper things. There is a change that takes place when we enter into and experience practicing the presence of God. Just as it takes concert pianist years of practice before they develop the necessary skill and proficiency to perform before their audiences, we slowly but consistently become more proficient as we practice the presence of God. Michelangelo said, "If people knew how hard I had to work to gain my mastery, it would not seem so wonderful at all."

Practice starts in different places for different people. For one it begins with being discontent, for another it starts with being inspired. For one it begins in the valley, for another, it starts with a vision. One person begins practicing the presence to release the guilt and someone else begins practicing the presence to release the growth. However you arrive at your practice, it is an opportunity to be awakened by something profoundly true.

Your practice can enable you to become more loving, open, stronger, clearer, more genuine, and truer to the purpose you are here to release. Your practice is a powerful choice to both live in the true place where your soul resides, and live from an authentic place that genuinely nourishes and fulfills your spirit, soul, and body. ∎

Today's Live Happy Practice

Practice enriching your relationship with God through prayer. Try keeping a prayer journal where you write down specific things that you have prayed for. Review the journal from time to time and give praise for the blessings that you have received.

DAY 120

Prayer with the Holy Spirit

Everything that concerns you can benefit from being bathed in the full flow of the Holy Spirit. There is nothing so insignificant that you cannot bathe it in the flow. Saturate your health, spirituality, growth, relationships, finances, family, work, business, and contribution to humanity with this habitual uplift. See each of these lifted up and being filled with the effluence of the Holy Spirit.

This is a way of ordering your mental life on more than one level at once. On one level, you may be thinking, discussing, seeing, calculating, and meeting all the demands of external affairs. But deep within, beyond the surface, at a more profound level, you can be in prayer with the Holy Spirit. █

Today's Live Happy Practice

Pray about these things when you enter into prayer:

- Committing to a life of excellence
- Awakening your creativity
- Recognizing you are worthy of and owning your purpose
- Making a greater contribution
- Honoring your needs
- How to overcome your pain, hurt, and suffering
- Permission to love yourself.

DAY 121

Saving the Receipts of Success

Lessons are being presented to us all the time, from expected and unexpected places. Take for instance the lesson taught to us from electrical utility companies. One of the most consistent lessons they share with us is that you can have access to the power but they will not be giving it away. Meaning, you can use the power as an accommodation in your life but it will come at a cost.

When you are considering the idea of self-concept, it may help to first recognize that you hold a very compelling concept of self. This self-concept is both formed and informed by what you see, hear, and do. Arthur Ashe said, "One important key to success is self-confidence. An important key to self-confidence is preparation."

You develop self-confidence by confronting your fears, making the necessary adjustments, doing the things you fear, and saving the receipts from the times you were successful.

Self-confidence is not time bound. Sometimes it may be up and at another time it may be down. The thing to remember is that it may fluctuate, depending upon your experience and expectations. When you review your past experiences, you will recognize how many things you are good at, and your self-confidence will skyrocket! Once you master self-confidence, many things will begin to improve for you. ■

Today's Live Happy Practice

Make a list of the things that you have accomplished and that you're good at. Whenever you experience a drop in self-confidence, take a look at the list to remind yourself of how awesome you are.

DAY 122

Your Success Is Not Influenced By Whims

When you walk by faith, you come to understand that nothing is too hard for God. Nothing is immovable, incurable, or beyond help. All things are possible.

The healing you have been praying for, the overcoming you have been believing for, the prosperity and success you have been persistently striving toward —even though you may be facing incredible odds —these things are all possible through the disciplined application of divine law and the steady effort to know God.

Your life is not unfolding by chance and your success is not influenced by whims. It is determined by the shape of your consciousness. In the words of the medieval mystic Brother Angelus, "That thou seest, man, become too thou must; God, if thou seest God, dust, if thou seest dust." Once you see things through the lens of faith, you think, feel, and act differently. If you want to make minor changes in your life, work on your behavior, but if you want to make major changes, work on the way you see things.

All your striving must be directed toward manifesting your unique form of greatness, rather than toward littleness. It requires vigilance to protect your miracle working power. To hold your miracle working power in perfect awareness in a world of settling is not a task for the faint of heart. The small minded rarely undertake it. This is offered to you, from you, as a tribute to your greatness and not your littleness. ▌

> ### Today's Live Happy Practice
> Affirm throughout the day, "My faith is on fire."

DAY 123

The Upside of Building a Positive Experience

One of the methods that Jesus employed as a leader, teacher, and healer was to challenge people to do things they doubted they were able to do. This was done in part to help them know the potential of their divinity, and in part to help them build a positive experience. There is miracle working power in you. Miracles are natural, corrective, healing, and universal. There is nothing good that miracles cannot do, but they cannot be performed in the spirit of doubt. Let your faith be on fire and your doubt out on ice.

It is hard to build a positive experience with negative people. Not even Jesus could perform miracles with these kinds to people. See things as you desire them to be. Protect the miracle working power within you and clear your atmosphere of doubts, doubters, and double-mindedness. ■

Today's Live Happy Practice

To help with the process of building a positive experience:

- Be mindful about being with people and in environments where doubt prevails. It's difficult to do great things in environments filled with doubters.
- Notice what or who you may have to put out.
- Recognize the people who can find a cloud in every silver lining.

DAY 124

Your Opinion Matters

During the first century, one of the technologies that was used for communication was the written letter. This is the mode the Apostle Paul employed to communicate with the church in Ephesus. In one of his letters he encouraged them to, "Be strong in the Lord..." but strength is not only demonstrated through physical displays.

Get clear on where you are strongest. Own your strengths and lean into those as you play from your greatness. A specific and concerted focus on your strengths during a difficult task produces the best results. It reminds me of a story about a young nurse who was completing her first full day of responsibilities in the operating room of a large hospital. She noticed something was missing and said, "You've only removed 11 sponges, doctor," she said to the surgeon. "We used 12."

"I removed them all," the doctor declared. "We'll close the incision now."

"No," the nurse objected. "We used 12 sponges."

"I'll take full responsibility," the surgeon said grimly. "Suture!"

"You can't do that!" blazed the nurse. "Think of the patient."

The surgeon smiled, lifted his foot, and showed the nurse the 12th sponge. "You'll do," he said.

It is important to stick to your guns when things do look quite right, the world may just depend on it. ■

Today's Live Happy Practice

You have an expertise and a perspective that no one else has so it matters. When you see something, say something.

DAY 125

Your Words Become Your Actions

Your thoughts become words and your words become actions. Accordingly, if you want to change your actions begin by changing the way you think and speak. These subtle habits form the foundation of your creative ability.

What old ways of thinking and speaking might you need to be strong enough to die to? What unproductive relationships is it time to change your thinking on so that you're strong enough to live beyond? What habits and behaviors have outlived their usefulness to you? Dying to the irrelevant and unproductive makes you strong enough to live into the new. God placed His greatness inside of you because you can be trusted to do something great with it. ▌

> ### Today's Live Happy Practice
> Commit to no negative thoughts for 24 hours. If you catch yourself having a negative thought, start the clock over.

DAY 126

Forgiveness Makes Room for Happiness

For many of us, our happiness is interrupted when we find that we have been offended. If you are like most people, when you have taken offense, the overriding desire is to get some level of revenge. But taking offense is a choice and holding on to grudges is a mistake. In order to reclaim your happiness, it is important to forgive.

Forgiveness makes room for more happiness. When you forgive, it gives you mastery over your wound. Forgiveness is a habit of the heart that allows you to release the chance that you can make yesterday better. Where forgiveness opens the door to your own freedom, retaliation is an unproductive companion on the road to reconciliation. Buddha put it this way, "Holding on to anger is like grasping a hot coal with the intent of throwing it at someone else; you are the one getting burned."

Sometimes forgiveness is defined as the feeling of peace that emerges as you take your hurt less personal. In order to experience your happiness zone, you must forgive those who have offended you. Forgiveness is your opportunity to experience significant healing. In the book of Matthew, Jesus said, "For if you forgive others their trespasses, your Heavenly Father will also forgive you your trespasses." Forgiveness does not mean that you have to excuse anyone's bad behavior. While it is true that forgiveness does not excuse negative behavior, it does prevent their behavior from turning out the light in your heart. █

Today's Live Happy Practice

Forgive anyone who has offended you. Instead of trying to control the person's behavior, just let it go.

DAY 127

Affirmations

You are worthy of your love, just as you are.

You are valuable enough to make yourself a priority.

You get to honor yourself because of who you are.

You do not have to justify enjoying your own respect.

You will always be greater than the roles you fill.

You are generous, because you have so much to offer.

You do not need anyone's permission to go after what you desire.

You are more than what happens to you.

You deserve to have your needs met.

You can give yourself permission to unhook from negativity.

You are so much more than anyone's opinion about you.

You are God's unique gift. ▋

Today's Live Happy Practice

Read the affirmations for today and internalize them. Now read them again, but this time, replace "You" with "I."

DAY 128

The Law Was Established For Your Benefit

The grace and mercy of God is always sufficient in every need and we truly have so much to be thankful for. Everything God made is good. As we think this through a bit further, we might also begin to rethink the notion of law as this hard and unrelenting aspect of God. For if the law was established for your benefit, the law is therefore a product of grace and mercy.

Did I mention that I am not necessarily talking about the Mosaic Law, but rather the mental and spiritual laws that are always at work in your life? I am referring to the laws by which you are shaping your experiences, attitudes, and opinions. These laws of mind are objective and exact in the same ways that the laws of gravity are objective and exact. The challenge; better yet, the opportunity; is for you to approach these mental and spiritual laws with the level of mindfulness that gives you the opportunity to design the type of experiences you want to have.

God is so merciful that you have inherited a system through which to intentionally and consistently approach life. The Omniscience of God within you presumes that you will use what you have to create what you want. You are always using what you have. When you use it rightly, you consistently experience the grace and mercy of God, just without the drama. ■

Today's Live Happy Practice

Allow yourself to enjoy the love and grace of goodness today. Monitor and adjust your thoughts if they are not producing the results that you desire.

DAY 129

The Law Works

There are mental and spiritual laws and these laws work. These laws are just as consistent as the laws we see at work in the natural. Water will boil at 212° on your stove and on your neighbor's stove. It is as specific as it is unbiased. All things being equal, it works the same every time. It is the law. The law will freeze the water at 32° regardless of whether you are in the world or of the world.

The law is specific, intentional, and consistent. The law of gravity says that what goes up must come down. So, you can count on it. That's why it is important that you be careful about who you offend on your way up because you will encounter those same people on the way down. You can count on it. The law is consistent and mathematical and always on point. And so, the law of thermodynamics says that the only thing you can get out of a thing is what you put in that thing. When you look at your life, you don't have to look at it with judgment, guilt, and shame. All you have to do is look at it through the lens of the law and say, "What I am getting out is the byproduct of what I am putting in."

The law is established for your benefit. The prophet Jeremiah wrote, "Before I formed you in the womb, I knew you. Before you were born, I consecrated you." Meaning, that the omniscient God established a system, then equipped you to move intelligently and successfully in that system. The law works. ∎

Today's Live Happy Practice

Remind yourself of the mental and spiritual laws working on your behalf throughout the day. Guard your mental images because your subconscious mind will respond to them.

DAY 130

You Deserve to Have Your Needs Met

Are your personal needs being met? Are they being met in the way you care for yourself? How about from the people you are in relationships with? Your needs are important and one of the primary things that interrupts your ability to be all you are made to be is not consistently getting your needs met. Unfortunately, learning to settle for unmet needs develops into a voracious feedback loop. When that happens, most people make the mistake of settling for what seems to be available rather than committing to getting what they need. Many people forget that if you do not expect much – you will not get much. Regrettably, not getting what you need often leads to being unsatisfied and unfulfilled.

Without consistently having your needs met, it becomes increasingly difficult to make the most of your God-given potential. We see this illustrated when Jesus encountered a fig tree. The Gospel of Matthew offers that he had spent some part of his days traveling to Bethany, had been traveling that morning, and had likely grown hungry from his journey. Jesus came upon a fig tree but it had no fruit, only leaves. So what did he do? He recognized it as perpetually unproductive and insufficient to be counted on to meet any future needs. Jesus was clear about what he needed. The tree was unproductive so he moved on. Like Jesus, you should be clear about what you need and you should not settle for anything less. If your circumstances are unproductive, move on to something better. ∎

Today's Live Happy Practice

Do not apologize for consistently having your needs met. Until your needs are met. Get clear about what you need and act on getting it.

DAY 131

Unlock the Power within You

You are made by God, which means that you were made by the best. God created you in His image, and everything that He made works. This means that you were not made to fear or to fail. You have 206 bones and 634 muscles, all of them working together. You have billions of neurons and trillions of synaptic connections, all firing at the same time. You can use your mind to think one thing, use your mouth to say something else, move your hand to do something different, and use your imagination to reflect on something else entirely. You were created for success.

Among the unlimited number of things your brain can do exceptionally well, it is most proficient at enabling you to survive and thrive. This is the prevailing, principal function your brain seeks to help you do. If you were able to get a print out of your brain activity, you would discover that what it does all day, every day is support you in progressing in life. This activity is so important, that it also helps you do this for the people you care about. That is why you can sometimes see the answer for how someone you care about can get ahead, even when you do not yet see the way ahead for yourself.

Your brain will get to work on anything you could ever want or any factor that you would consider important to your happiness. Regardless of what it is, it can be designed by your brain. All you have to do is give your brain a target to shoot for. ∎

> ### Today's Live Happy Practice
> Remind yourself about your greatness. Remember, if you cannot see it, you will never be able to achieve the wonderful things that are possible for your life, from Get clear, be serious, and unlock the God given power within you.

DAY 132

Learn the Lessons and Get the Blessings

You have so much to be grateful for, yet you may not always recognize your blessings; especially when they appear through unexpected people and unanticipated places. The decision to accept your blessings is an invitation that also attracts new experiences of good. Some of those experiences may not be comfortable so remember that short-term discomfort is better than long-term regret. It may not look like it, but you are too close to give up now.

When identifying your blessings, do not get distracted by people who do not understand your why! Building your ship before there is any evidence of a flood may seem odd to some people, but like Noah, it can be a blessing for you.

Living in the memory of failure is a choice, but so is getting the blessing that is the invaluable lesson, which can only come with getting it wrong. Learn the lessons and get the blessings! ■

Today's Live Happy Practice

Stop right now, look around, and identify 10 things you are grateful for.

DAY 133

It's Time to Pay it Forward

There is a saying, "You might be the only bible some people will ever read." This is not to suggest that you have to be super religious or extra spiritual. It is simply to recognize that some people may glean their example or truth from you. Your impact and influence are truly amazing. As an example, someone is looking to you to uphold the framework of what is possible, as they view you as the model.

That means you are the road map for someone else's sense of safety when it comes to sharing love, giving support, coaching up, and teaching how. You make up someone's sphere of influence and the example and information you share helps them to optimize their abilities.

Just think back on some of the people you have been blessed with, who served as your unofficial role models. It may have been a single-parent family who showed you what patience looked like; or a teacher who taught you how to instill confidence in others. It could have been King, Jesus Christ, who showed you service and courage. The point is simply that you may have also benefitted from having role models you could point to, lean on, learn from, and emulate, regardless of whether they ever knew the reverence and esteem with which you held them. It may just be your turn to pay it forward. ∎

Today's Live Happy Practice

Be an example today. Try these ways to pay it forward.

- Offer to help someone for free.
- Give something without expecting anything in return.
- Spend some time with the elderly.
- Read a story to a child.
- Visit someone in the hospital.

DAY 134

You Are Equipped to Serve Others

You have a unique purpose. One that is perfectly suited for who you are and what you bring to the table of life. This purpose is as tailor made for you as is your fingerprint. You are the only person on the planet who can execute your purpose, in your distinguished way. However, your unique purpose is not your only purpose. There is also the purpose you share with others. That purpose is to demonstrate the goodness and grace of God and to help others identify their innate value, capacity, goodness, and potential for growth.

You may have sensed or experienced this latter purpose already. For it springs forth from your most authentic self. If you have ever found yourself contemplating how to help someone else, you were prompted from this latter purpose. You are designed to execute this purpose. In fact, your brain is wired to help the people you care about get ahead in life as well. As you unpack, unfold, and evolve your individual value, you will carry with you the key to the divine expression of Christ and universal harmony. This experience will help you feel connected to the uplift of the whole of God's creation.

As you commit to living from the purpose for which God created you, you are able to live a life rooted in love. You are equipped to satisfy your passions and become more influential in the lives of those you support and serve. You will experience a greater sense of value, fulfillment, and synergy in your collaborations with others, and you will build your confidence and self-esteem as you continue to live on purpose. ■

Today's Live Happy Practice

You can make a big difference in someone's life by sending them an encouraging note. Find someone that you can encourage and send them a note letting them know how proud you are of them.

DAY 135

Listening to Your Intuition

What is your approach to your spirituality? How have you decided to demonstrate the presence of God in your life? How do you live out your Truth? Not in a Pollyanna or naïve way, but rather through an acute understanding of how you have been created and how it is that you intend to choose and craft new experiences through the power of your transformed mind.

What is your formula for forgiving? What do you say to yourself to shift you out of the rut of stinking thinking? How do you honor people from whom you stand to gain nothing; and how do you uplift, encourage, and empower people, even if it means they will outshine you?

One of the best ways to live out your truth is to follow your intuition. Intuition is the feeling that you get inside when you instinctively know that something is right or wrong. The truth is that you already know what to do based on your internal GPS. When you are true to yourself, you will realize that you have the power to make the right decisions in any situation. Don't fight it. Allow yourself to listen to that still, small inner voice and be instructed by it. ▮

> ### Today's Live Happy Practice
> Pay attention to your surroundings. The more information you have about your environment, the more you can rely on your intuition to make good and informed decisions.

DAY 136

The Power of Expectation

There are a number of clever quotes about the power of expectation. For instance, "Want shows up in conversation but expectation shows up in action." Also, "You must inspect what you expect." Then there are the ones that tend to cut in the other direction or reflect a different schools of thought on the power of expectation…like, "Expecting the world to treat you fairly just because you're a nice person is a little like being in the middle of an amphitheater, waving a red cape but expecting the bull not to charge you because you're a vegetarian."

So what do you expect? Is it your best thinking? Do you expect better living and better experiences; better health and better circumstances?

Regardless of the angle, the take away is that there is something to having sustained expectations. When you expect the best, you activate the subconscious power of attraction. Unlocking this power often results in facilitating having the best come to you. As in the examples above, the power of expectation cuts both ways. When you expect the worst, the subconscious mind cannot judge or discriminate against your adverse expectation. It will simply accommodate your expectation and deliver your mail to you. ▍

Today's Live Happy Practice

Determine what you expect from life. Whatever your expectations are, be sure to elevate them because, "In life you do not get what you deserve. You get what you believe, plan, and expect."

DAY 137

You Have No Competitors

Congratulations!! You are the original! The first and only one made from your specific pattern. You are not just the result of your parent's blissful interaction. You are an urge prompted from the impulse of the Divine. You have no competitors because you have no competition. You are the only game in town.

You are the successful demonstration of what can be created from the dynamic seed of possibilities.

What you have to offer is different from everyone else on the planet. As you begin to look around at others, it's easy to start to analyze how you stack up. But this trail can only lead you down the path of false equivalency. Because you are here to complement creation, not compete with it. You are here to affirm greatness. You are here to be all that you are to be. ▌

> ### Today's Live Happy Practice
> Celebrate your uniqueness. Stay true to yourself by embracing who you are and not worrying about what other people think of you.

DAY 138

The Essence of Radical Passion

What are you head-over heels excited about? What gets your blood pumping enough to make you take action? I am presenting this question to you because, if you are like most people, not only have you stopped asking yourself this question, you have also put your excitement to sleep. Also, if you are not excited about it, it is unlikely that you will be able to recruit the support you need in order to help you manifest it.

It often requires a level of radical passion in order to move excitement into experience. This radical passion often spills over into the things you think, say, and do. You interject your radicalized excitement into conversations. Your mail carrier probably knows it is your passion because of how often you have mentioned it. Your radical passion carries the potential seed of excitement for others. It has been said, "If you set yourself on fire, others will come from miles around to watch you burn." That captures the essence of radical passion.

A word of caution: do not be intimidated by whether others seem to share your excitement and certainly do not allow that to convince you that your excitement is insignificant. In academic circles, it is determined that a result is significant when it has not occurred by chance. That which you are excited about exists beyond chance. Your radical passions are not incidental so you must be intentional. ▪

Today's Live Happy Practice

Answer this question: What am I head-over heels excited about? Once you determine that, be intentional by being prepared and getting organized. The more organized you are, the less stress you will have and the closer you will be to reaching your goals.

DAY 139

Take Time to Be Still

How do you react when it's time to come apart? Hopefully you welcome this most important time. But if you are someone who resists rest, know that you can benefit from your period of quiet and rest. You need an opportunity to recalibrate, center, and consciously establish yourself in the presence of God.

In our busy society, many people cannot see the benefits of coming apart. They believe it is unproductive and that it prevents them from reaching their goals, but this is a fallacy. In fact, taking time to come apart can rejuvenate you and help you become more productive. That's why your journey to becoming the best version of your illustrious self requires you to be less busy and be attuned to the Holy Spirit.

Remember, it becomes increasingly more difficult to listen to God while your attention is given to external things. The only thing to be gained from ruminating is more of the same. But when you come apart and turn within, you can gain clear insights on how to maneuver the outer appearances.

So when you turn to the secret place, allow yourself the freedom to get away and bring your mind into perfect harmony with the Christ ideal. The more you accept the Christ within, the stronger will grow your consciousness of the Divine Presence. Take time to be still! ■

> ### Today's Live Happy Practice
> Take a moment to recalibrate, center, and consciously establish yourself in the presence of God

DAY 140

The Grace of Rest

In our western mindset and approach to life, rest for many people means doing nothing. We are masters of multi-tasking. In coaching some of my high-achievers, they often tell me that they do not have time to rest. However, you should recognize that rest is not a waste of time; on the contrary, it is a form of grace. It is a biological need—a process for restoration and rebuilding. Rest is a major pathway to your renewal and survival.

Rest facilitates the grace for healing and rebuilding life itself. When you learn to rest using the inner wisdom of your body, you find that what had been impossible becomes possible. Rest is the original transformative technology, the capacity of which you always have within you. Rest helps you think creatively and get into the process of putting flow in your life and balance in your activity.

There is a rhythm to life. Everything you do follows cycles of activity and rest. So be sure to take advantage of the grace that is rest. ■

Today's Live Happy Practice

Rest requires you to be intentional. Treat rest the same as you do any other important goal in your life. Plan it and put it on your calendar.

DAY 141

What's Your Motivation?

The soft drink *Sprite* had an interesting commercial in 1988. What made it interesting was a question one of the actors asked. The question was, "What's my motivation?" This is an important question. What is your motivation for doing what you are doing? Why are you putting yourself through the ringer? Why do you keep showing up?

If you know your motivation, you will also be equipped to silence your dissenting voice when things do not go as you have planned. Knowing your motivation will give you something to ponder with power, emotion, and conviction.

Being clear about your motivation will give you some insight into what the thing means to you and why it is important that you follow through. It will place top of mind the benefits and value of why you will not give up, even though you feel like you should throw in the towel. It will be a reminder of why you deserve it, even if it requires you to stretch yourself a little more. Knowing your motivation can be your rod and your staff to help you make it through all that you will invariably go through. You deserve it but you may have to remind yourself from time to time why you are motivated to get it. ∎

Today's Live Happy Practice

If you want to stay motivated, it is important to understand why you do what you do. Being clear about your reason for wanting something will give you that boost you need to keep going and stay the course.

DAY 142

Things Improve By Change

What are you waiting for? Is it when you are debt-free? Is it when your children graduate? How about when you retire? Regardless of what you are waiting for, here is what you have to remember; things do not improve by chance, they improve by change; and in order to change, you have to take a chance. The chance I am referring to is the chance of massive action.

Believe it or not, most people do not take nearly enough of the right kind of chances and as a result, they end up living less than fulfilling lives. You have to be willing to take a chance and do what you can, with what you have, from where you are.

But don't worry. While it may not be easy, you can make any changes you like if you stay focused. Stay positive and make a list of your strengths. Understanding and recognizing your good qualities will make it a lot easier to change your unwanted behavior and undesirable habits. ∎

Today's Live Happy Practice

In order to learn how to change, you must think about the behavior that you want to change. Be sure to take ownership of the behavior. Once you acknowledge the behavior and take ownership of it, you will be in a better position to do something about it.

DAY 143

Manifest What You Want

In order to manifest something in your physical existence, it must first be created in your mind. Someone called it "as within, so without." Someone else said, "Begin with the end in mind." Another said, "As man thinks in his heart, so is he." Each version is basically saying that manifestation begins in the mind.

In order to manifest more of the things in your life that will amaze you, you must remain in charge of your mind. If you do not keep your mind, what you manifest will be mostly unintentional and quite possibly, undesirable. Why? Because a haphazard mind can only manifest haphazard experiences. Therefore remaining in charge of your mind is the most consistent way to manifest what you want. In life you have choices. You can either choose to focus on what you think is missing or you can choose to focus on what you intend to manifest!

When you manifest something, it means that you intentionally think or act in a way that ultimately leads to what you want. You can literally manifest anything that you desire. The best way to manifest something in your life is to visualize and focus your thoughts on it. The key is that you don't want to wait for things to happen to you. Instead, you will want to actively pursue what you want by staying positive and making your desires known to the universe. ∎

> ### Today's Live Happy Practice
> In order to manifest the things you want, you must first be clear about what that is. Think about your desires and be very specific. Visualize your goal and include as much detail as you can.

DAY 144

Imagination Is the Eyes of Your Consciousness

According to the Psalmist, the link between what you desire and what manifest in your life is found in your willingness to delight in the Lord. Psalm 37:4 (NRSV). But how do you delight in the Lord? One way to do it is by using the power of your imagination, as your porthole through which you form your good. Someone once said, "Imagination operates at a threshold where invisible and visible come together." William Warch proposed that, "Imagination is the eyes of your consciousness. It is the ability to perceive the limitless possibilities of your good."

The way you use your imagination has a profound impact on your life. Imagination allows you to see yourself already in possession of the fulfilling life you desire. Your potential is really only limited by your imagination.

Using your imagination provides you with a wonderful opportunity to test drive your good. The beauty of this opportunity is that there is no physical limitation to how frequently you can use your imagination to see yourself experiencing your good. No project is beyond your ability to imagine yourself performing it effectively and productively. No price tag is beyond your means to imagine yourself covering the outlay of cash. You cannot hear "no" enough times to force you to relinquish your imaginations capacity to continue seeing the perfect "yes" coming your way. Nature never gives you an abundance of anything without demanding that you use it, and using your imagination is a renewable source. ■

Today's Live Happy Practice

Use your imagination to test drive your good. If at any time this begins to feel uncomfortable, remind yourself that you are only playing with your imagination...then continue the test drive.

DAY 145

Control Your Emotions

You are not at the mercy of your emotions and you do not have to be held hostage to your mood. You did not inherit being quick-tempered. The challenge is that you may be too easily excusing yourself when your feelings go into overdrive and do not sync up with who you consider yourself to be. One of the primary reasons you have a mind of your own is so that you can control yourself and not abdicate the responsibility of regulating your emotions. Your emotions are an important characteristic of your well-being; however, they can be problematic if they start to make you feel out of control.

Also, it has been determined that your emotions play a part in your financial success, so putting in a little work can literally pay off. But it is not a good idea to try to suppress your emotions. The idea is to regulate, not suppress. Don't try to suppress your emotions. Instead, aim for regulating them. Suppressing your emotions means that you prevent yourself from experiencing your feelings. On the other hand, regulating your emotions means that you adjust your behavior and act responsibly when things happen.

Today's Live Happy Practice
Make an effort to consciously control and direct your emotions by perceiving, understanding, using, and managing your emotions in ways that support your progress.

DAY 146

Respect Yourself

There is a saying that, "Those who live in harmony with themselves live in harmony with the universe." Harmony is often experienced when we make an internal commitment to respect yourself and to feel worthy of all life has to offer.

Self-respect should be a natural state for you, just as it is for all of the animal kingdom. A grazing deer will never behave as though it is unworthy of what it wants to have. The deer will simply walk up and begin to eat what was naturally provided.

Your sense of worth and level of harmonious self-regard must come from knowing that you have a sacred connection. When you live in harmony with this truth, you do not allow anything to shake you loose from the divine foundation. Your sense of harmony comes from the self in connection to the divine. Respect yourself and you will be able to generate harmony with one of God's greatest creations...you!

The genius in you knows how to support you. There is power in your thoughts, feelings, words, actions, and reactions. You are so amazing that you are designed to achieve, to strive, to build and to attract. You simply have to live in harmony with the fulfillment of your good. ■

Today's Live Happy Practice

Command your mind and emotions so that there is no room left to think or feel as though you are unworthy of your good.

DAY 147

Focus Your Thoughts on What You Want

You are a powerful overcomer. You have proven it so many times before but do you truly realize it? Will you give yourself permission to let your own unique form of greatness unfold? When Jesus said, "All things are possible to them that believe," what was He saying? He was saying what you believe on the inside can become manifest on the outside. He was saying that "how" is not your business. He was saying you can have more because you can believe more.

When you become aligned with the truth about yourself, your thoughts are no longer focused on what you do not want, but rather, on what you do want. The best way to begin reconditioning your mind is to consciously think in aligned ways, so consider the following:

- Your Source never thinks in terms of what is missing.

- Your Source never thinks in terms of what it cannot have or do.

- Your Source never thinks in terms of what has never happened before.

- Your Source never thinks in terms of what others will think, say, or do.

- Your Source never thinks in terms of bad luck. Do you? █

Today's Live Happy Practice

Distractions are always lurking just around the corner. Learn to differentiate between the things that get in your way and the things that really matter. Make a commitment to focusing your attention on the things that really matter.

DAY 148

Opportunity from Adversity

If you are like most people, changes generated by adversity catch you completely by surprise. This unpreparedness may be what sparks the feeling of instability that stymie your creativity and limit your ability to maximize the moment of change. That is why you have to know how to tap into your reserve strength so that you can be relentless and continue moving forward through the storms of adversity. You can fix the experience, if you can face the challenge.

It is said that luck is what happens when preparation meets opportunity. Part of the preparation is in changing your mind so that you can move beyond the perception that you live in anything other than an orderly universe. Changes that appear to be random are not even remotely so. In an orderly universe, "Order and creativity are complementary" as Lewis Mumford observed. That is why a change in perception is required in order to get the most from the seeds of opportunity that are embedded in every adversity.

Whatever your adversity may be, regardless of how much it shakes your foundation, there is a seed of opportunity within it. You will easily miss it if you do not look for it. You have the wisdom to discern it. God never puts more on you than you can bear. Though the pain is intense and the fear does not seem to relent, you will get the seed of opportunity from the adversity. ∎

Today's Live Happy Practice

Look for the seed of opportunity in today's adversity. The best way to attract new opportunities in your life is to let people know what you're up to. Network and connect with other people in your field and make sure they know that you're available.

DAY 149

Patience of the Chinese Bamboo Tree

When a Chinese Bamboo tree is planted, someone must be responsible for regularly watering and fertilizing the tree. The interesting thing is that there are no visible results for many years. In the fifth year however, as the caregiver continues to water and fertilizer as they did during the previous four years, the tree grows 95 feet tall in a span of five weeks.

Like the Chinese Bamboo tree, you sometimes undergo a more gradual change or shift. It is this kind of transcendence of the mind that produces transformation in your results. Your evolution produces the emergence of those latent qualities and aptitudes that are waiting to be brought forth by you. For what is seeking to be birthed through you may require patience! Particularly when the results you desire are not yet showing up.

If you were to identify and put a percentage to the amount of spiritual, mental, and physical resources you are using right now, and your commitment to watering and nurturing them, what would the number be? By psychologists William James' estimate, most people are using less than 10% of their ability. If you were to use just five percent more of your spiritual, mental, and physical resources, what could you achieve? Begin right now watering and fertilizing your tree. ∎

Today's Live Happy Practice

Answer this question: If I were to use just five percent more of my spiritual, mental, and physical resources, what would I be able to do?

DAY 150

Be Courageous In the Face Of Adversity

Two explorers were on a jungle safari when suddenly a lion jumped in front of them. "Keep calm," the first explorer whispered. "Remember what we read in that book on wild animals? If you stand perfectly still and look the lion in the eye, he will turn and run."

"Sure," replied his companion. "You've read the book, and I've read the book. But has the lion read the book?"

The strength you need to withstand conflict and be courageous in the face of adversity is always at hand. You are more powerful than you think. You have been filled with the all-ness of God. The sacred scripture says, "Now to him who is able to do exceedingly and abundantly above all that we can ask or think according to the power that is working within us." This verse encourages you to be strengthened with power of your inner being.

When you are courageous in the face of adversity, you are more likely to reach your goals. One thing you can do to live a more courageous life is assist other people who need help. As you might imagine, there are tremendous benefits in living a life filled with bravery. In fact, being courageous in the face of adversity is the quickest way to succeed because it helps you build self-confidence and gives you a different perspective on life. ∎

Today's Live Happy Practice

It is a good idea to face your fears if you want to live a courageous life. Maintain a positive attitude in the face of adversity.

DAY 151

Be In the Moment

In order to live fully present, in the moment, you have to release the past and forego the future. It means your body and your mind have to be together instead of one being present, without the other. Remember, your mind is a canvas upon which you can draw whatever you want. Thought is such a powerful agent that it allows you to position your mind, behind or beyond your now moment. You can think about your childhood, or your retirement, or anything in between.

The challenge is that you cannot experience all the blessings this moment holds for you if you are not fully present. You cannot completely enjoy the manna of this moment, if you are unable to be with what is here right now. Though your cerebral ability and your creative imagination are respectively suitable to help you revisit your past or form your future, it does not mean you are always best served by reliving yesterday's highlights or diving into tomorrow's creation.

Here is a little secret for you; the possibility for peace exist in the now moment. The prophet Isaiah signaled that, "Those of steadfast mind, you keep in peace." This steadfast, present moment focus enables you to avoid the suffering of past pains from 20 years ago and the future fears of assumed perils. Being in the present moment enhances your performance because it ensures that your attention is focused on the details that matter. ▮

Today's Live Happy Practice

Be present and grateful for this moment and this day, just as they are. You can make the most of this moment and experience a peace that passes all human understanding by steadfastly recognizing that moment is exactly as it should be.

DAY 152

Searching For the Seed of Good

Sometimes in order to accomplish what is on your greater to-do list, it requires relentlessly searching for the seed of good in the season of difficulty. One of the tricks of opportunity is that it has a sly habit of coming disguised in the form of challenges. This may be why you sometimes fail to recognize opportunity.

It is important to search for the seed of good for many reasons: first, it is really easy to get swept away in the currents of difficulty. Second, suffering setback is not usually easy on the mind, emotions, or body. Third, since the seed is not always easy to find, it is often easy to assume that it does not exist. So when you realize that there is some hope in your hardship, you will be able to accept the experience as a breakdown that is leading to a breakthrough. The best blessings sometimes come wrapped in sandpaper.

Difficulty is simply one of the languages by which intelligence communicates its feedback. You do not know for certain that fire is hot to the touch until you make the mistake of touching it. The turning point at which you make the most of your new feedback is not only when you no longer put your hand to the fire, but also move into successful action of using the fire for something beneficial. ∎

Today's Live Happy Practice

Create opportunities for yourself by giving back. Give away e-books, videos, or other resources that help people do what they do. When you give your knowledge to other people, you will win because you are establishing yourself as a resource.

DAY 153

A Prayer Mindset Makes the Difference

Throughout scripture you will see different attitudes of mind in relation to prayer. You may be told to pray in the spirit, to pray in understanding, or to pray without ceasing.

You are incredibly bright so you may be wondering; can't I just go to God in prayer? The answer is unequivocally, "Yes." You can just go to God in prayer; particularly when you don't know what else to do. But I would be remiss if I didn't point out that Jesus taught his disciples, when you pray; pray this way...!!! Having the system, attitude, and mindset makes a difference. You can go to the faucet with a spoon; or you can go with a sponge; or you can go with a glass. But if your aim is to drink of the living water, one of these is best suited for the application. ▮

Today's Live Happy Practice

If you feel that your prayer life has stalled, try changing your prayer routine. If prayer feels like a chore, you might benefit from switching up how you do it. For example, you could try going on a prayer walk, praying on the phone with a prayer partner, or listening to worship music while you pray.

DAY 154

Empowering Yourself

If you intend to design your life, you must give yourself permission to create your own good and refuse to be dependent upon having your good determined by others. Determining your unique design means taking total responsibility for your mental patterns and massive actions. You empower yourself when you do not succumb to your excuses and give in to your lesser inclinations. You have the amazing ability to not only face what is not working in your life, but also correct the interference of an inconsistent consciousness.

Decide to live out your ideal design and cut off all options that are inconsistent with this objective. Making a decision means that you will not give yourself the easy out of suspending action. You are a creative force and it is time to use it to your advantage by recalibrating your thoughts, feelings, words, and actions. This process of recalibration will help you avoid the powerless act of blaming others for what is showing up in your life.

Remember, if anyone else on the planet can live the life of their dreams, then so can you. You can enjoy success in the areas of your health, wealth, relationships, sense of fulfillment, and sense of purpose. Design it. You deserve it. ∎

Today's Live Happy Practice

Throughout the day, remind yourself that you are responsible for the tone and tenor of your day. Establish new beliefs that are in alignment with your new design.

DAY 155

Learn and Grow From Within Your Own Consciousness

Are you comfortable counting on yourself for the right direction, the right thing to do, or the right answer? If the answer is no, you are not alone. Far too many people believe that the answer to life's most basic and most treasured questions lies outside themselves. Unfortunately, this causes many people to overlook that there is an all-knowing source within them. The master teacher Jesus instructed that you should seek first the kingdom and all the other things would be added to you. The interesting thing is that he located the kingdom in familiar proximity.

Nearly every mystic and teacher, every religion and philosophy, have explained with care that the factual world should always be questioned. Just because a thing is a fact does not mean it is a reality. The search for ideas from within your own consciousness brings satisfaction. It keeps you evolving in consciousness and unfolds the new, the fresh, and the different. It is progress. ■

Today's Live Happy Practice

Renew your commitment to learning and growing. The repetition of that which is known is not progress. What you know indicates what is still to be known. No person has ever known enough so the best way to a happy, healthy, and successful life is to continue to search for understanding within your own consciousness.

DAY 156

Grace

Emmett Fox once said that if a person could not get along with other people, they should make a sign and hang it where they would see it every day. This sign was to read, "Like attracts like." Have you ever thought about what kind of attitude and reactions you have? Are you loving and kind? Are they tolerant and encouraging? How do you feel inside most of the time? Are you resentful and jealous, or full of love and grace?

The best way to change you, is to gracefully reconnect to who you are and what you are. If you try to change your attitude and feelings by determination or willpower alone, you may not get very far. The secret of transformation is to begin with grace; which is the undeserved, unmerited favor of God. The changes you want to bring about are not of the outer but of the inner, and the potential to experience this change is powered by grace.

How can you change your feelings and your thoughts into those that make you feel right inside; happy and satisfied with yourself? You can center yourself in the loving Christ presence by bringing every thought and feeling into alignment with God's grace. Let grace guide you as you apply these words from the Apostle Paul, "When reviled, we bless; when persecuted, we endure; when slandered, we speak kindly."

For the grace we freely receive is the same grace we must freely give. ■

Today's Live Happy Practice

Bless, endure, and speak kindly of those who do not deserve your grace.

DAY 157

Your Words Are Filled With Life

It's time to recondition your thinking. One of the ways you can do this is by reminding yourself that good things are supposed to happen to you. It is time to stop being amazed when good things happen to you. Unfortunately, too many people walk around like they have some sort of black cloud hanging over them, as they are expecting bad things to happen. Stop waiting for the other shoe to drop because eventually it will. Stop thinking your outcome is too good to be true. Instead, give thanks and learn to expect good to flow abundantly into your life.

Be highly intentional about how you describe your life because your words are powerful. Your words are filled with life. Your words touch and accomplish the ends towards which they are directed. Watch what you say about yourself. There is a statement in the Bible that says, "Let the weak say I am strong." Your words carry within them a transformational power and vibration. That's why it is critical that you claim what you want, not what you do not want ▊

Today's Live Happy Practice
Expect good things to happen to you.

DAY 158

Do the Work and Success Will Come

Do you expect to be successful? Are you currently doing all that is necessary in order to achieve your aims and objectives? Are you doing the things that others will not do so that you can have the things that others will not have? You can catapult yourself and accelerate your process if you will make a commitment to be disciplined when it comes to your success. Wanting success without the work is like wanting water without the wet.

Unfortunately, most people are content to settle for assuming that they do not have what is needed in order to make the most out of their life. They have given up, quit, surrendered, thrown in the towel, and put their life in park. No mission. No purpose. No meaning. No plan. Failure is not final. Do the work and success will come. ■

Today's Live Happy Practice

Writing your goals down gives them life. When you write your goals, be sure to make them specific. It means that you attach time frames when things should be done, as well as establish details about what the final product should look like.

DAY 159

Overnight Success Requires Hard Work

If you want something new from life, know that getting it may not be as simple as it appears to be. One of my all-time favorite myths is the "overnight success." You probably know the people. They burst onto the scene with talent, charisma, skill, and expertise that seemed to just develop overnight. Yet, here they are, no names one moment, and world conquerors the next. The things that are often undersold and undervalued when it comes to the overnight success is the years it invariably took to become one.

Like so many others, many things have conditioned you against your success. Those things have become barriers and obstacles that must be overcome. Someone said that, "You are either in a storm, coming out of a storm, or heading into a storm." While the observation is not all that appealing, you may have found it to be so, as it does capture the crux of the resistance that must be met in order to be a success.

People who appear to be overnight successes know how to overcome the storms they face. They take responsibility for developing themselves and they learn that they have the ability to accomplish their dreams. You can do the same thing. Be forward-looking and be ready to face the storms as they arise. Make decisions based on what you want and where you want to be, and after lots of hard work, you too, may just be an overnight success. ■

Today's Live Happy Practice

Be careful about making decisions based on the advice of people who will not have to live with the results. Recognize that your success can not become what you want it to be without your persistence, willpower, and hard work.

DAY 160

Guard Your Self-talk

Are you sometimes tempted to speak recklessly to yourself? If so, you will want to begin to guard your self-talk. If you are like most people, nearly 80% of your thoughts and internal dialogue is negative. This has a powerful impact on you and is a very important part of how you build self-esteem. The problem is that it is really difficult to build self-esteem when you have too much internal negative chatter.

The prophetic writer of Isaiah shared that just as the rain and snow fulfill the purpose for which each is sent, so shall the word that goes out of your mouth; it shall not return to you empty, but it shall accomplish that which you purpose, and succeed in the thing for which you sent it. Likewise, your innermost words do not return to you void because whether you realize it or not, you will never outperform our internal conversation.

Beneath the surface, you have an inner voice on a loud speaker trying to tempt you into believing something negative about yourself. The boost you have been looking for might be found in the things you say to yourself! Speak life, especially to yourself! If you need help overcoming temptation try praying consistently and guarding your self-talk. This will help you go from temptation to triumph. ∎

Today's Live Happy Practice

A great way to implement positive self-talk is to get in the habit of collecting all of the data of a situation before you make any judgements. When you get all the facts, you can take a look at both sides of the issue. Considering the good and bad can give you a more balanced perspective, thereby making a great difference in your perspective.

DAY 161

You Are Designed to Achieve

Are you ready to live the life you have been dreaming about? In order to manifest, experience, and enjoy dream, it is important to get a larger vision of yourself because you cannot fit a big dream into a small vision. In the book, *Think and Grow Rich*, Napoleon Hill writes, "Whatever the mind can conceive and believe, we can achieve."

You would not be equipped with the ability to even imagine prosperous conditions if you were not equipped with the ability to turn those imaginings into reality. The thing that makes you want to experience prosperity is the same thing that transforms a tiny acorn into a mighty oak tree. It is life seeking fuller expression.

Every life form seems to content to strive for its optimum expression except human beings. Once that acorn becomes an oak tree, that tree will grow as tall as it possibly can. The thing that catapults you is the same thing that limits you, the dignity of choice. You can choose to express it all or you can choose to play small. There is greatness in you and your job is to let it out. You are designed to achieve, to strive, to build, and to climb. Say yes to your dream assignment. It is a gift from God. ∎

Today's Live Happy Practice

If you want to achieve more, seek knowledge, not results. When you focus on discovering and improving, you will automatically keep learning. This will help you improve and obtain the success you desire.

DAY 162

Humility Is the Mother of Giants

It's been said that humility is the mother of giants. But what is humility? Humility is an attitude that truly frees you. It frees you of your ego's need to be overbearing and it also frees you from the need to be right. Humility frees you by helping you reconnect to the power of God within. Humility recognizes that you may not be able to control what happens to you. You may not be able to control what happens around you but can control what happens in you.

You have the freedom and power to focus and your focus creates your reality. So humility is not about being less or allowing others to walk over you. Instead, true humility is the recognition that you are a child of God and all that God is, you are. Pick yourself up. Dust yourself off and remember to live empowered and you can do it humbly. █

Today's Live Happy Practice

If you want to practice humility, seek feedback from others on a regular basis. Be open to what they have to say. Many times, honest feedback can be hard to swallow, but when you listen to feedback and receive it gracefully, you will not only learn and grow, but your humility will increase along the way.

DAY 163

Discipline Is a Confidence Builder

Practicing discipline in your everyday life is not urgent but it is important. There may be an area in your life that seems overwhelming to you and you may be experiencing some breakdown in your health, your work, your family, or something else. You may have also noticed that the breakdown is causing a slow erosion of your self-esteem.

The erosion likely happened in small, bite-sized, barely recognizable increments; a little bit every day instead of all at once. But with a healthy dose of discipline, you can turn it around.

Since your self-worth is based on the positive habits, actions, and decisions you practice every day, why not build your self-esteem and tackle your biggest problems at the same time? This is the time to sweat the small stuff. Discipline is a confidence builder. Boost yours by taking small steps that will move you in your desired direction. ▮

Today's Live Happy Practice

Removing temptations from your environment is a great way to increase your discipline. For example, if you want to eat healthier foods, remove the snacks and junk food. The fewer distractions you have around you, the more discipline you will have to accomplish your goals.

DAY 164

Practice the Power to Forgive

Human beings have an innate proclivity to reciprocate negative behavior with more negative behavior. But when you resolve yourself to forgive someone of a transgression, you should not bring up the transgression every time a new argument arises. You should not remind the person of their offense against you every time they make a mistake. If you have let it go and you have gotten over it, then there is no need to remind them about what they have done. Just practice your power to forgive consistently. If you truly let it go, then let it go and move on. Don't keep bringing it up.

Forgiveness helps you move past the situations, conditions, and circumstances that are not healthy enough to have a front row seat in your life. Forgiveness does not excuse the behavior. It prevents the behavior from destroying your heart. Whether insulted by a friend, forsaken by a lover, attacked by an enemy, or wronged by any other means, it is vitally important that you consistently forgive. ▌

Today's Live Happy Practice

Whenever you need to forgive someone, you must first embrace your feelings about that person. Try putting your feelings into words. Write them down or talk about it with someone you trust. This will put you on a sure path to forgiveness.

DAY 165

The Habit of Reviewing Your Day

The way you start your morning can impact the tone and tenor of your day. So what would happen if you were to begin each day by aligning your thoughts and actions with divine order? If an orderly morning leads to an orderly day, how much could you accomplish? Going from one day to the next without considering the day's events is like taking a lecture course without ever testing your knowledge of the course material.

The best way to get the most out of your day is to plan your spiritual practices ahead of time. Order and willpower work like a muscle, by setting your intention ahead of time, you are preparing the atmosphere of your soul and setting the expectation for your good. Set aside your prayer time, devotional reading time, inspirational listening time, and time for how you will put into practice the juicy stuff you got that morning.

Look for the seeds of good throughout the day. Jesus told the crowd that if they would seek, they would find. Why spend time looking at problems like there is a reward for it. Instead, reinforce your thoughts and feelings with good. █

> ### Today's Live Happy Practice
>
> At the end of your day, take time to answer the following questions:
>
> - Did you accomplish what you set out to accomplish today? Why or why not?
> - What worked?
> - What do you need to change? What did you do right? How can you do more of this?
> - What didn't go well? How could you handle things differently?

DAY 166

Adjust Your Thoughts to Live a Bigger Life

It has been said that a mule can carry a heavy load of precious gold on its back and never know its preciousness; only its weight. Life can be full of feeling only the weight of circumstances, while never being able to appreciate the true value of the system of thought that created those circumstances. Research suggests that the majority of your thoughts are negative and repetitive. That means the precious system of thought that is creating your life is most likely counterproductive and working against you. Put another way, your thoughts may be at the core of your self-sabotage.

How do you break the repetition of your past conditioning so that your current consciousness is not creating more chaos? First, you do it by first embracing a new belief about the importance of your thinking. Belief dictates your effort, your energy, and your enterprise. What you believe determines your attitudes, motivates, and feelings; and informs your actions. It will be very difficult to obtain success if your thoughts do not support your desire to live a bigger life. ■

Today's Live Happy Practice

You can adjust your thoughts by starting every day on a positive note. Try creating a ritual where you listen to happy music or share something positive with the first person you meet.

DAY 167

Small Steps Lead to Big Leaps

Sacred scripture instructs you to avoid despising the day of small beginnings. Most of the things you have come to know and accept as great, likely began very small. Yet, those who do not take the small steps never make the big leaps. In order to operate inside your opportunity, you have to be willing to grow through the small beginnings. A small beginning could involve overcoming personal doubt, excavating negative thoughts, or learning to better function under pressure.

Wherever there is an opportunity, there is an opposition. Sometimes the opposition is your own inertia and unwillingness to sweat the small stuff. Identify the opportunities and get moving on the small things. If you want to improve your health, you will not be able to stay glued to your couch and transform your health at the same time. Put your body in motion. Eat that which is consistent with the new you, and drink plenty of water. Each of these actions could be a small step, depending upon you.

Do not be intimidated by the unfamiliar journey of small steps. The journey of a million miles begins with a single step. Take one step, then take another, and another. Before you know it, you will be at the point of no return. By taking advantage of small beginnings, you will gradually move toward your goals of fulfillment and happiness. ■

Today's Live Happy Practice

If you want to take big leaps and reach big goals, it is a good idea to break them down into small steps. But after you break your goals down, it is equally important to track your progress and modify as needed. There is no need to feel that you cannot adjust as you go.

DAY 168

Change Your Life and Become Better

My minister, mentor, and teacher, the Reverend Dr. Johnnie Colemon would often say, "Change...we must." She knew that dealing with the disruption of change is often one of the pressures that compel us to take action in our own lives. If you are someone who lives a life of desire, hope, promise, expectation, and achievement, then you should recognize that change is inevitable.

You would be amazed at the number of people have become content studying the limits of humankind. They settle for the status quo, forgetting that the status quo always wants to maintain itself. In order to change your life and become better, you must break through this resistance. You can do this by either changing what you see or changing what you do.

Remember, you can experience better because you can become better. The flip side is; unless you change how you are, you won't be able to move past what you have.

Don't wish things were simpler; make changes for the better. Don't wish for fewer challenges; develop more skills. Don't wish for less fear; use more faith.

Both tears and sweat are salty, but they get us different results. Tears might get you sympathy; but sweat will get you change. Don't miss your opportunity!!! ■

Today's Live Happy Practice

If you want to change your life for the better, be ready to make sacrifices. Don't expect everything to come easy. Making great strides forward involve letting go of old habits and developing new ones, no matter how difficult it may be.

DAY 169

Your Beliefs about Money

A report that came out in 2018 indicated that the average American has approximately $40,000 in debt and this is excluding mortgages. Debt is often a major obstacle to saving and eventually enjoying financial freedom. The obstacle is made larger by the fact that many people have developed the habit of spending more than they earn and investing whatever is left over, if they invest at all. While amassing debt may be so easy that it seems intuitive, it is a counterproductive habit. It is the kind of habit that starts in a small way and continues to grow until the molehill becomes a mountain of such enormous stature that it eventually troubles your soul.

These conditions are enough to rob you of your aspiration, erode your sense of hope, and eat away at your self-confidence. Being tied to excessive debt is like being in chains of your own making. If you have encountered this, it may be time to reevaluate your belief around money, debt, desire, and deservingness. It is time to release the limitations in your mind and overcome the debt and unlock your desires. The error is not in your supply. The error is in your programming. We all have a blueprint of belief about money! Your blueprint of belief consists of what you were taught about money. It may be time to overwrite those beliefs. ■

Today's Live Happy Practice

Reevaluate: your beliefs about money by considering:

- How much income or profit you want and what you want to do with it?
- How much money will you set aside to retire your debt?
- What amount do you want to have in your savings?
- What amount do you want to have to invest with?
- What amount do you need to fund your dream?

DAY 170

Be Sure to Trust Yourself

You can be a good person and still be a bad judge of character. Imagine you have decided that someone is trustworthy only to have their behavior later prove that you have missed the mark in your assessment of them. Now go a little deeper down the rabbit hole and imagine that missing the mark in this way has probably caused you to experience some confusion, regret, disappointment, and hurt. Perhaps even more damaging is that it caused you to question or mistrust yourself.

When you extend trust to someone, it comes with certain expectations. Whether those expectations are communicated or not, they still exist; and having your expectations violated often generates feelings of betrayal, disappointment, and maybe even outrage. In fact, one of the toughest parts of trusting is managing your disappointed expectations.

Somewhere along the way you will have to cope with the unanticipated and unwelcome damage of broken trust. Yet, as with most things, the real key is to not lose yourself when you extend trust to others and they are unable to honor it. ∎

Today's Live Happy Practice

Use these tips to trust yourself when someone else proves untrustworthy:

- Don't ignore the signs
- Don't silence your intuition
- Don't go against what feels right to you
- Don't make excuses for suspicious behavior
- Be sure to communicate your expectations
- Don't make the same mistake over and over again

DAY 171

Add Value like The Bumblebee

It is impossible to consistently behave in a manner that is inconsistent with the way you see yourself. Likewise, it is difficult to add value to others, when you see yourself as worthless. Nathaniel Braden, a psychiatrist and expert in the area of self-esteem, wrote, "No factor is more important in people's psychological development and motivation than the value judgments they make about themselves. Every aspect of their lives is impacted by the way they see themselves."

Some people show up dripping in self-confidence, others are able to develop it early on; still others work on developing self-confidence well into adulthood. According to Barrie Davenport, "Low self-confidence isn't a life sentence. Self-confidence can be learned, practiced, and mastered just like any other skill. Once you master it, everything in your life will change for the better."

You can learn a lot from a bumblebee. Bees go from flower to flower, gathering and distributing pollen as they go. Since bees are in the business of making honey to support themselves and other members of the hive; through pollination of the trees and flowers, they add value to the rest of the world. This process produces benefits that radiate out to practically every living thing on the planet. If a bumblebee has enough confidence in its ability to do what it can do, just imagine what you can do. ■

Today's Live Happy Practice

In order to ground your self-confidence, recognize that it is difficult to feel bad about yourself when you are doing something good for someone else. So continue to grow yourself and continue adding value to others. It creates a cycle of positive feeling from one person to another.

Your Life Is a School

When it comes to spiritual growth and practical spirituality, many people naturally focus on having a healthy prayer life and devotional habits. Regardless of how it is defined, a basic element of success for many people is found in their relationship with God and the development of their spiritual practices. It would be a mistake to neglect this fundamental aspect of yourself in pursuit of anything else. The Gospel of Mark makes the point by asking this question, "For what will it profit them to gain the whole world and forfeit their life?"

While many people focus on their spiritual practices, many more overlook the opportunity to make the most of their situation. Meaning, many people have legitimate reasons as to why they are not able to commit to their spiritual walk in a significant way.

Spiritual practices take on multiple forms and are intended to help you transform. What is the benefit of praying like Mother Theresa, if you refuse to help someone in need? Why bother visiting the home of the soul through meditation, if your chanting does not support your changing? Why go worship every Sunday and still lack kindness, compassion, and a spirit of cooperation Monday through Saturday?

If your life is a school; your spiritual practices constitute the curriculum, lessons learned, and the extracurricular activities of your education. ▌

Today's Live Happy Practice

One of the best ways to increase your spirituality is to create a "rule of life" for yourself. That means developing some spiritual practices that you commit to on a regular basis. Once you create these rules, don't let anything deter you from following them.

DAY 173

Breaking the Strings That Are Holding You Back

You have been given the dignity of choice and the mental acuity to create and craft your life in a way that works optimally for you. Have you created and crafted that life yet? Though you are brilliant, vibrant, radiant, attractive, and talented, something may still be holding you back. Whatever that something is, know that it is not strong enough to stop you, once you know who you are and what you are capable of. When you recognize and value your unconditional worth, you will empower yourself to enjoy the benefits and blessings that are waiting for you.

In order to train a baby elephant to stay in its place, a small rope is used to tether the elephant's leg to a post. The baby elephant soon learns that it does not have the capacity to break free of the rope and eventually stops trying. But then as the elephant continues on its natural trajectory, it grows to such a powerful point that no rope is a match for its strength. Yet because of how the elephant was conditioned, and because of the number of times it has felt the sting, it will refuse to use its resourcefulness to display the power and capacity now at its disposal.

Life is full of opportunities. You must know how to identify, seize, and maximize each and every one of them. Your sense of deservedness is one of the most important factors in whether you will be able to have it. Napoleon Hill observed that most people could identify the faults of others easier than they can identify their opportunities. Is this you? If so, stop gazing at others, believe you deserve what you desire, plan a way to accomplish it, and take radically massive action. ■

> ### Today's Live Happy Practice
> Your only limitations are the ones you set up or accept in your mind. It is high time that you embrace your spiritual and personal power. Think about the limiting b beliefs you may have and develop a plan to overcome them.

DAY 174

Learn From Successful People

Have you ever been in a conversation with someone who talks with their hands and before you knew it, you were talking with your hands and being more expressive than usual? You carry mirror neurons and these neurons give you the ability to sense, and then mimic the feelings, actions, and physical sensations of another person. If you are going to model someone, you may as well make sure you are intentional and modeling the right kind of people.

That is why it is important to spend time with people who have traits, skills, character, and competence you want to develop. Link up with the people who have done what you desire to do and learn from them. You will slowly assimilate their characteristics. Note that this rarely occurs when you are the smartest person in the room. Study people you admire. Read their books and articles. Listen to their interviews. But do not just settle for the entertainment value. Study these pieces and tease out the valuable insights.

Today's Live Happy Practice

If you want to learn from people who are successful, you must be able to bring something to the table. Find your zone of genius. That means taking an evaluation of your own talents and knowing what you have to offer. Be a resource for them and sooner or later they will return the favor.

DAY 175

The Power to Choose

You have one of the greatest powers at your disposal. This power will enable you to create your life in so many wonderful ways. This power is the power to choose. You get to choose what you think, what you feel, and what you say. Other people may be able to influence you, but the choice is yours. You can literally do anything you want to do.

But, while you are free to choose, you are not free from the consequences of your choices. Thought settles in the form of choices, and the thoughts you hold in your mind will produce similar thoughts. That is the law of mind in action. Thinking causes your brain operate at different frequencies. When you make a choice, you flip your brain onto a different mode. You are the controller of your consciousness. The moment you choose to live a bigger life, your consciousness will devise, generate, and attract the ways and means of you having it.

Many people use the law of mind in action in reverse. Rather than using their choices to stretch, they use their choices to shrink. They consistently think in smaller terms. They unintentionally blur what they see as possible and remain confused about why they are unhappy. But the law of choice cannot fail you if you do not fail it. Recognize that you have complete control over your choices, you— and only you. Exercise that control. ▌

Today's Live Happy Practice

One of the best things you can do to improve your decision making ability is to follow your instincts. When you follow your instincts, you will be happier with your choices and won't end up second-guessing yourself.

Relationships Add Value

We are naturally hardwired for relationships. In fact, the more we reinforce, enhance, undergird the self-esteem of the other people in our world, the better we feel about ourselves. Relationships are an important part of your everyday life. Relationships are a means by which you add value to the lives of those who are important to you and receive the same in return.

But you are different from everyone else and those differences can sometimes manifest themselves through issues and disagreements. When your issues are not addressed and go unresolved, these same issues can have a harmful impact and become a breeding ground for conflict and resentment. While knowing how to successfully manage these conflicts may be difficult, it helps to simply determine if your relationship is worth it. As one writer said, "Your best relationships will help you meet your needs, fulfill your desires, gain clarity, and feel more connected."

Today's Live Happy Practice

You can improve the quality of your relationships when you pay attention to the whole person. Whenever you interact with someone, pay attention to their body language. Don't just listen to their words, but also take the time to read their facial expression and their demeanor. This will help you develop a stronger bond and a more meaningful connection.

DAY 177

Be Certain About Your Self-Worth

When Jesus advised asking for what you want, the instruction was not to simply remind you to be persistent in your demands. Embedded within the message is also a reminder about your self-worth. You are deserving of your good. Do you believe it?

When you are unclear about who you are and whose you are, it becomes easy to undervalue your worth. When your appraisal is off, the mind becomes filled with doubt, worry, or fear. However, when you get clear, you know that you have a right to ask, the motivation to seek, and the ability to knock. Guess what happens when you do these three things? When you ask...you receive. When you seek...you find. When we knock...the door is opened to you. Approach this practice with the same certainty as the mathematician, who has firm conviction that the numbers will add up.

How good can you stand it before you begin to feel like you do not deserve it? You can have it as good as you can stand it. Put another way, you can have as far as you can see but you will get no more and no less than what you believe you deserve. To the degree that you accept and believe in your worthiness, your subconscious nature will work to bring it to you. ■

Today's Live Happy Practice
Don't beat yourself up because things didn't go just like you had planned. Remember that everyone makes mistakes. When you learn and grow from your mistakes, you will eliminate any self-doubt and feelings of insecurity.

DAY 178

Put Some Feet to Your Prayers

Although affirmative prayer helps to broaden your perspective of principle, it is not enough simply to affirm things. Your power to use affirmative prayer is made more effective when you put some feet to your prayers. Not only does your affirmative prayer connect you with divine intelligence, it also pushes you to take action. As James 1:22 instructs, "Be doers of the word, not only hearers." While the context of the scripture is not related to prayer, the relevance of the message remains the same. Affirmative prayer is not a hopeful endeavor; nor is it an excuse for spiritual bypass or sticking your head in the sand.

Affirmative prayer and massive action helps you manifest everything necessary for the fulfillment of the good desires of your heart. Know that all things are working together for your good as you align your life, world, and affairs over to divine intelligence.

Affirmative prayer is not a passive activity. Instead, affirmative prayers are marching orders that help you align your actions with the will of God for your good. You should know that all things are working together for your good as you align your life, world, and affairs over to divine intelligence, and affirmative prayers help you get there.

Today's Live Happy Practice

When there is something you need to do, embrace the actions you need to take and open yourself to receive the guidance and direction that will lead you into right action. Then relax in the complete assurance that good will be your final outcome.

DAY 179

No Thought Lives in Your Head Rent Free

T. Harv Ecker observed that no thought lives in your head rent free. Put another way, each thought you have entertained has shaped who you are. I know what you may be thinking; what about the fleeting thoughts you have spent almost no time with? What about the thoughts that flew in and blew out? It may be improper to ask a question with a question, but to that I ask, have you ever tried to sleep with a tiny mosquito in the room or ever tried to drive with a gnat in the car? If you have, you know that size had no impact on how annoying it could be.

Likewise, there are lots of things impacting, influencing, or otherwise affecting you in ways that you may not be directing. The music you listen to, the people you hang around, and the conversations you engage in have affected you. Like a sponge, you are constantly absorbing things from you various environments. Whether your realize it or not, the things you absorb effect the weight and texture of your thoughts like water does the sponge. In order to make room for who you desire to be and what you desire to have, you will need to squeeze yourself and release the baggage you have absorbed.

The most important thing in this moment is that you be highly intentional about what thoughts you think. It was the Scottish Theologian Carl Bard who said, "Although no one can go back and make a brand new start, anyone can start now and make a new ending." Your future opportunities are unlimited and filled with possibility. Think positive thoughts and let today's absorptions serve a future that is more exciting and profitable. ∎

Today's Live Happy Practice

Being intentional is about being forward-thinking. One of the things you can do to live an intentional life is to be mindful of the media you consume. Chose those things that add value and meaning to your life.

DAY 180

The Price of Progress

Progress has a price. It invariably costs you something in order to have, do, and be all you aspire to. In order to do what you have never done, you have to become someone you have never been. That is why no less than 80% of your success is based upon what happens on the inside. Once you are resolved and determined internally, the next step is to take action. Therefore; the difference between thought and manifestation is the activity you initiate. Putting yourself into action is the price you pay to avoid staying in the same place.

There is an insightful story about a gentleman and his dog sitting on the porch. While the man enjoyed a glass of lemonade, the dog was lying next to him howling. A neighbor noticed, became curious, and went over to inquire about why the dog was irritated. Driven by his curiosity, the neighbor asked why the dog was howling in pain. The owner of the dog said, rather nonchalantly, "He's actually sitting on a nail." Now even more perplexed, the neighbor asked, "Why doesn't he just get up and move?" The gentleman took another sip of his lemonade, smiled wryly, and replied, "Well, it just doesn't hurt him enough."

Unfortunately, it is all too common to experience the consistent challenges of confronting the sources of your pain, focusing on practical solutions, and tapping into the courage to move, so that the source no longer pains you. Remember, the price of progress is action. ∎

Today's Live Happy Practice

Mustering up the courage to move past your pain may not be easy, but it is necessary. When you meet challenges in your life, be open to accept the support you get from those who care about you and want to see you succeed. Accepting help is not a sign of weakness. On the contrary, it is a sign of strength.

DAY 181

Breaking Out Of Limitations

Have you ever found yourself fighting for your limitations? If so, you have likely already learned that when you fight for your limitations, you get to keep them. Arguing for your limitations allows you to feel justified with your shortcomings, but know that your ascent was never meant to reach a comfortable plane or plateau. A better approach might be to find and develop new practices that will help you accomplish your desired end.

The obstacle to your progress is your limited thinking. Nothing derails the progress of your momentum like settling for the thinking that got you to where you are right now.

Thinking is vitally important because it is one of the ways by which you build your life. Therefore, new ways of thinking, resulting in new ways of learning, gives you an opportunity to grow into the greatness from which you were created. Noted psychologist Rollo Reese-May wrote that "all growth consists of the anxiety-created surrender of past values as one transforms them into broader ones." As a thinker, it is important to fight for new ways of doing things instead of clamoring to your limitations.

Drive is important. Momentum is important. Tenacity, determination, and commitment are all important elements in breaking out of your limiting behaviors and beliefs. A key element of having momentum is the ability to get over and beyond limitations that might otherwise be in your way. When you have momentum, you have the power to roll on. When you have life, you have the gift of creation and vision. When you have momentum for life, you can do, see, and be whatever you want. ■

Today's Live Happy Practice

A good way to break out of your limitations is to quit using the word "they". When you say "they" don't like me, or "they" are trying to hold me back, you are limiting yourself. Just go for it and quit making assumptions about what "they" are thinking.

DAY 182

An Attitude of Thankfulness for Yourself

Feelings of jealousy, emotional insecurity, or inadequacy can severely interfere with your ability to experience happiness. Choosing to eliminate these negative feelings can lead to you experiencing more joy. It begins with recognizing the futility found in comparing yourself to others. The fact is, comparing yourself to others cannot improve your sense of self-worth. Instead, self-worth comes from doing what is worthy. You will not find true worth for yourself, outside yourself.

The answer is not to compete with other people, but rather, to be the very best version of you. The key is to cultivate an attitude of thankfulness and appreciation for your own value. As the Talmudic scholar Abraham Heschel once said, "Self-respect is the fruit of discipline." When you embrace your own gifts, it can eliminate any feelings of hostility and intimidation you may feel toward someone who you perceive to be smarter, better, or more advanced.

After you make a conscious effort to be grateful for your own value, you should set about the task of self-improvement because there is always room for growth in all aspects of your life. You should strive to be the best version of yourself as possible. If you want to improve, it is incumbent on you to learn more in order to increase your skill level. ∎

Today's Live Happy Practice

Write down the good things you have done and are thankful for. Put them in a jar and pick one out whenever you need a pickup and encourage yourself.

DAY 183

What Is Better For You?

The gospel of Luke shares a wonderful story about the power of choice. Mary and Martha were hosting Jesus and, like most people serving as host, they had some last minute things that needed their attention before they would be completely ready. As Martha went about handling the customary responsibilities, Mary did something unexpected.

Mary chose to take a seat at the feet of the master teacher and she began listening to what Jesus had to say. This behavior upset Martha a little bit so she pointed out to Jesus that there was work to do and how Mary had left the work for her to do it. Jesus replied to Martha, "Mary has chosen what is better (for her) and it will not be taken away.

How often do you neglect to choose what is better for you? It may be time to challenge yourself to stop trying to fit in when you were made to stand out! Like Mary, it takes courage, conviction, and faith to come to yourself and choose what is better for you, especially if it means you might disappoint someone else's expectations of what you should be doing.

There may be an avalanche of evidence, all suggesting that you should stay in your place. But here is the truth, you have been set apart for a dynamic purpose. Stop trying to fit in when you were made to stand out. ■

> ## Today's Live Happy Practice
> It is better for you to be yourself and stop trying to fit into someone else's idea of who you should be. Don't try to be accepted by others. Instead, work to reach your own potential and follow the dreams of your heart because no one else has the authority to direct your life and your power to choose.

DAY 184

You Are the Real Deal

It is very difficult to rise above the level of your vision of yourself. Not impossible, but difficult. That may be why research shows that 70 percent of folks feel as though they are impostors at one time or another. Maya Angelou admitted, "I have written eleven books, but each time I think, 'uh oh, they're going to find out now. I've run a game on everybody, and they're going to find me out'."

As with the amazing Maya Angelou, it does not matter how accomplished you are, how much proof of competence you have, nor what kind of results you have produced, people with impostor syndrome are convinced that they don't deserve the success they have achieved. They somehow see themselves as unworthy. Though you may not see yourself as the Real McCoy, there is undoubtedly something within you that is far superior to the challenges you may be facing. The problem is likely that you have somehow mentally disconnected yourself from your internal support.

Like a hibiscus planted in a small pot, your growth can become stunted and you will only perform at a level of your limited vision when you refuse to see yourself as bigger than your current situation and circumstance. Oftentimes the best path forward is the one that allows you to step outside of your limited sense of self and move past your routine, stagnated ways of living and being. You deserve your accomplishments. Look more truthfully and see for yourself that you are not a fraud. You are not an imposter. You are good enough to enjoy success in every area of your life. ∎

Today's Live Happy Practice

Being authentic means that you make decisions to live according to your own dictates. Your day to day actions must line up with your ideals. Be sure to live in your own truth and not according to other people's priorities.

DAY 185

The Whole Is Greater Than the Parts

How much synergy do you have working in your life? If you realize that the whole is greater than the sum of the parts, you probably enjoy plenty of it. If you have a need to control everything, you probably have very little working for you. Synergy helps give you the motivation to forego working in counter-productive ways and with adversarial aims. Having synergy can help you alleviate the energy leaks that occur when cooperation is low.

Synergy opens the way to more trust, deeper commitment, respect, understanding, creativity, divergent thinking, evolution, and problem solving. When synergy is allowed, it tends to generate a multiplied effect of successful behavior and communication. The effective execution of this habit allows you to deepen your commitment and potentially earn more credit with your followers by building in deeper networks of trust.

Having synergy can help you more consistently share the risks and rewards related to getting things done. This systemic sharing will serve to communicate the message of lateral trust in your relationships. When you consistently find ways to work together and collaborate with others, you will reap the benefits and quickly recognize that the whole is greater than the sum of the parts.

Today's Live Happy Practice

When working with others, it is important to establish some ground rules up front. Think about what each individual will bring to the table and work out all the details in advance. Be sure that expectations and roles are clearly delineated.

DAY 186

You Have the Right to Be Happy

Happiness can be yours at any time, but it must come from within you. One of the best ways to condition yourself to consistently experience happiness is to determine whether you actually believe you have a right to be happy? If you do believe you have a right to be happy, then it's time to make sure your effort, creativity, and activity support your belief. Also, if you believe you deserve to be happy, why settle for less than what you deserve?

Happiness is a process of making progress, and progress is based on action. One of the actions you can take to add more happiness to your life is doing something for other people. In a study on happiness, researchers gave a small amount of money to two groups of participants. They gave the participants the choice to spend the money on themselves or on someone else either through charity or as a gift. Researchers found that the participants who spent the money on other people experienced a greater boost in happiness than those who spent the money on themselves. In fact, just recalling a time when you bought something for someone else can make you feel happier.

What I'm saying is that you deserve to be happy; and the more you give to others, the happier you become. ■

Today's Live Happy Practice

It is important to experience all of your senses and emotions in life. In order to be happy, you must acknowledge when things are not going according to plan. If you feel unhappy, let yourself experience the moment. After that, quickly let the moment pass, take a deep breath, and move on.

DAY 187

The Voice of Your Intuition

Each of us has multiple voices vying for our attention. The first voice you may want to give your attention to is the voice referred to as intuition. Intuition is your natural ability or power to know something. It is also a feeling that guides you to act a certain way or do a certain thing, perhaps even without your fully understanding why. This voice is one of your interior forces.

You might know the voice of intuition as your sixth sense, your hunches, or your ability to perceive your good guidance. Intuition opens you to a perception of truth that is independent of your reliable reasoning processes. It gives you the ability to understand and know through the power of your feeling nature rather than relying upon the facts. Your intuition will enable you to be in the flow of divine guidance. This voice will not make your choices for you, but it will prompt you in ways that can lead to your success and energize you in ways that help activate your awareness.

Today's Live Happy Practice

You can improve your intuition by paying attention to the physical cues. If you feel uneasy about a decision, it is probably a good idea to think again before engaging. Don't be afraid to listen to your body because it is designed to provide information for your best good.

DAY 188

Find Your Compelling Reason

Whenever you need to get yourself out of a situation that does not seem to work for you, it is important that you identify whatever it is that is keeping you there.

People do what they do because they don't have something more compelling to do. People stay where they stay because they have not found what makes their undesirable state so compelling. But if you can analyze the situation and identify the roadblocks in your path, you can learn how to release them so that you can live in a new possibility.

Whenever you decide to improve things in your life, remember it is not enough to simply change the outer effects; you also need to do some hard work. There are no short cuts to success. But if you find the compelling reason to make a change, and have the desire and determination, you will exponentially increase your chances of success. ■

Today's Live Happy Practice

In order to give yourself the best possible chance of success, it is important to understand why your goal matters. You may be able to clarify your reason why by completing the following sentence:

I want to _____ because _____.

Dig deep. Think about what really matters in your life and give yourself the best chance of success by understanding why things matter to you.

DAY 189

Sharpening Your Proverbial Saw

We can all benefit from the continual improvement within the structure of the soul; so the physical, mental, social, emotional, and spiritual aspects of being can be viable. It is important that these aspects of the soul receive the proper amount of attention in order for you to be your most effective.

Although people often put their best face on to glamourize and sensationalize their persona, life behind the mask is often a taxing experience. Frankly speaking, there are some unappealing, valley level experiences that can begin to weigh heavily on the best of us. Life sometimes comes with a great deal of pressure. You must have the ability to renew, balance, and continue improving your whole soul as a means by which to negotiate and move forward.

You need outlets that allow you to sharpen your proverbial saw. Give yourself the benefit of a consistent prayer and devotion life; a challenging, fruitful, and rewarding mental life; an exciting and enjoyable social-emotional life; and a healthy and fun physical life. Knowing and exercising these areas are important and should be considered as a "coming apart." Being in touch with, and consciously connected within, is vital and truly helps to be your best self. ∎

Today's Live Happy Practice

When you want to continuously improve yourself, don't make excuses. Excuses can slow you down and change your focus from moving forward to looking backward. So if you want to create the life you want, spend more time moving forward and less time making excuses.

DAY 190

Appreciate Yourself

How do you appreciate yourself and value the good you bring to life's experiences? You have to occasionally remind yourself that no one, aside from you, can give you the true appreciation of how valuable a commodity you are. You must reclaim your will and direct it so that you are supported in bringing forth a fulfilling life. One of the ways you appreciate yourself is by trusting the resourcefulness of your intuition and to allow it to guide you accordingly.

You can appreciate yourself by honoring the emotional state you find yourself in at any given moment. You can value yourself by facing your fears rather than burying your head in the sand of undesirable experiences, even when you are afraid. You can demonstrate your worth and live from your purpose by simply giving yourself to others through your service.

It can sometimes be difficult to adequately honor when you do not understand the various layers of your soul. Honoring yourself provides you with a chance to peel back the layers and get a better feel for the self. As you pray and meditate, you open yourself to two of the wonderful ways in which you nurture and appreciate the value you bring to your life's experience. ∎

Today's Live Happy Practice

It may be tempting to tear yourself down when things don't go according to your plans, but undermining your own worth and self-esteem is not productive. Learn to appreciate yourself by acknowledging your unique set of skills and abilities. Stop judging yourself harshly and recognize that you are an amazing individual who has been wonderfully made to do great things.

DAY 191

Take Responsibility for Your Life Now

One of the ways people give away their power is by overlooking their immense ability to take responsibility for their life. If you find that you sometimes behave in this way, it may time to seal up this leak and no longer give away your power. It is disempowering to transfer your responsibility.

While it may be easy to shift blame to someone else, intuitively you know the truth. It may be tough to stomach, but the more you take responsibility for your actions, the easier it will be to determine how to remake your reality by taking responsibility. George Washington Carver suggested that, "Ninety-nine percent of all failures come from people who have a habit of making excuses;" and habitually making excuses is like practicing to not take responsibility.

The only way to have the life you desire is to take responsibility for creating it and to do what must be done in order to make it happen. Reclaim the power you poured into feeling ashamed. Reclaim the power you used to prop up your old story. Reclaim the power that is occasionally deployed to recharge feeling victimized and powerless. Reclaim your power by accepting that the person who is responsible for the life you want is you. Taking responsibility is not about living in the past or the future; it's about what's happening in the present. Now is the appointed time to reclaim your power and take total responsibility. ∎

Today's Live Happy Practice

Stop blaming other people for your misfortune. Don't blame your environment and don't blame your past. Blaming only shifts the responsibility away from you and onto someone else. But when you fully accept responsibility, you shift away from being a victim to being a victor.

DAY 192

Make Room for New Fruit

One of the most enlightened choices you can make is the choice to release that which has fulfilled its purpose in your life. How can you tell if something has fulfilled its purpose? It is no longer fruitful. When the thing no longer delivers on what it was intended to provide, it is no longer fruitful. Most people underestimate just how important this choice is and so they do not make the choice often enough. We see this happen in nature as well. Some flowers will only share their beauty for an appointed time. When that time expires, the bud is no longer able to share the fruit of its beauty and dies. The plant will however continue providing energy to the spent bloom even though it can no longer fulfill its purpose. This energy can be used to produce new blooms and longer life and productivity for the plant.

Like plants, it is amazing that people can continue giving energy to spent experiences. This is unfortunate because that energy could be used to enhance life in so many beautiful and fulfilling ways. Your choice about what to release is no less important than your choices about what to create. Choose to identify and address the situations, conditions, and circumstances that are no longer producing fruit in your life. The consequence of neglecting this important choice is that you run the risk of never having your new fruit. ∎

Today's Live Happy Practice

Make a list of the things that are standing in your way and preventing your forward motion. Once you have your list of impediments, begin to systematically faze them out.
Releasing that which is no longer fulfilling will make room for that which is.

DAY 193

A View from the Top

Eagles and ants don't share the same worldview because eagles get a view from the top. Getting a view from the top means that before you react in negativity to people, conditions, or things, you take a moment to lift up your eyes unto the hills from which comes your help.

It means you contemplate all the changing, challenging experiences from the highest possible point of view. Regardless of the appearances, conflicts, or limitations, you can see things from the awareness of the perfection of God, the all-ness of life, and the ever-present substance of good. A view from the top gives you the opportunity to see things creatively, with an attitude that is constructive and optimistic.

Your grateful heart will always attract to itself in one way or another, through human hands or through wonder-working ways, the great things needed to solve the particular situation. It is a perfect outworking that you can invest your belief in. Remember that the source is truth and decide to only see good and express only truth. That's how you experience a view from the top. ∎

Today's Live Happy Practice

A great way to stay optimistic is to use the word "for" instead of "to". Life happens for you; not to you. So instead of complaining by saying, "Why is this happening to me?" try recognizing your blessing and say, "Why is this happening for me?"

DAY 194

Inhaling and Exhaling the Flow of Life

Breathing is one of the most urgent practices you will engage in all day. It is the kind of practice you do not notice until perhaps you have some difficulty doing it. Being connected to your breath is an amazingly valuable thing. As inhaling fills you with life, exhaling gives you an opportunity to release toxins, blocks, and negative build up. Your breath and your feeling nature are intimately connected. One of the best ways to stimulate your emotions is to consciously pay attention to your breathing.

When you breathe, you organically introduce the integration of the spirit, soul, and body. Breathing consciously and intentionally allows you to activate your mind and your heart. When you breathe, you unconsciously put yourself into the flow of life, where you are giving and receiving. You get to participate in each cycle of giving and receiving, as the intelligence within you works its perfect work. When you consciously and intentionally work with the life-force intelligence, it enriches your overall wellbeing. When you connect your entire being through your breath and into your whole body, you activate every level of your physical being, from the crown of your head to the soles of your feet; as well as activating the dynamic aspects of your soul and the subtle energies of your spirit. ■

Today's Live Happy Practice

Try this exercise to relax yourself and breathe in the flow of life:

- Inhale for a count of 5.
- Exhale for a count of 5.
- Continue this breathing pattern for at least a few minutes.

DAY 195

The Importance of Rest

We live a fast paced society where multi-tasking is at a premium. The busy-ness of life has nearly everyone believing that multi-tasking is the most effective way to do things and it should be done as often as possible. There are millions of webpages sharing information about how to become a better multi-tasker. This approach leads many people to believe that they cannot benefit from rest. They believe it is unproductive and that it prevents them from reaching their goals, when the fact of the matter is that taking breaks from your routine can rejuvenate you and help you become more productive.

Whether you are an ardent multi-tasker or not, you should not overlook the benefits and balance that comes from getting proper rest and relaxation. Rest and relaxation are particularly important because of the mental and physical health benefits they provide. Relaxation reduces your blood pressure and gives your heart the important rest it needs by slowing down your heart rate. As a result of being relaxed, you might experience more energy and better sleep. You may also experience enhanced creativity, increased concentration, and better problem-solving abilities.

Rest and relaxation helps you recharge your batteries as you take a break from work or other activities in order to refresh yourself and gain peace of mind and spirit. One of the best ways to relax is by listening to relaxing music. You can take a few deep breaths. You can read a good book. You can just lie down and do nothing. Relaxation can also be achieved by taking a few minutes to sit quietly and close out the noise in your environment. How you decide to do it is less important than that you decide to do it. ■

Today's Live Happy Practice

In order to get a good sleep at night, create a restful environment by ensuring that your room is cool, dark, and quiet. You might also try calming activities like taking a warm bath or reading just before bedtime.

DAY 196

Happiness Comes From Within

You would be amazed at the number of people who say they are not happy. Recent studies show the number of people in this category continues to rise. Many of these same people overlook the fact that happiness is generated from within. While your happiness may not always be constant, the fact that the happiness comes from within you is. In order to live happy, you have to embrace and fulfill your desire to be a person of contact as well as a person of impact. It is happiness by way of flourishing.

Unhappiness, on the other hand, is the result of life not happening the way you think it should. Just by choosing to be grateful, you will become happier. As one writer put it, "Have gratitude for all you have and you can be happy exactly as you are." In order to be happy, stop allowing your disturbed emotions to color how you see yourself. Happiness is not about deceiving yourself or ignoring the negativity. It is about adjusting your mind so that you can adjust your life and enjoy your reality. A change in happiness happens to a changed individual. This is a mental and spiritual law.

Today's Live Happy Practice

Staying in touch with your family and friends is one of the best things you can do to increase your happiness from within. Take the time today to contact someone you haven't spoken with in a while and catch up on old times.

DAY 197

Overcoming Setbacks

Being knocked down, rejected, or denied in life can impact your perceived worth. During a research experiment, a marine biologist placed a shark into a large holding tank and then released several small bait fish into the tank. As you would expect, the shark quickly swam around the tank, attacked and ate the smaller fish. The marine biologist then inserted a strong piece of clear fiberglass into the tank, creating two separate partitions. She then put the shark on one side of the fiberglass and a new set of bait fish on the other. Again, the shark quickly attacked. This time, however, the shark slammed into the fiberglass divider and bounced off. Undeterred, the shark kept repeating this behavior every few minutes to no avail. Meanwhile, the bait fish swam around unharmed in the second partition. Eventually the shark gave up.

This experiment was repeated dozens of times with the shark getting less aggressive each time. Eventually the shark got tired of hitting the fiberglass divider and simply stopped attacking altogether. The marine biologist then removed the fiberglass divider, but the shark didn't attack because it had been trained to believe a barrier existed between it and the bait fish.

Like the shark, experiencing setbacks and failures can cause you to give up and stop trying. Being unsuccessful in the past does not mean that you do not deserve what you are going after. Refuse to be like the shark; don't allow the real or imagined barriers keep you from achieving what you desire. ∎

Today's Live Happy Practice

The more you can answer "yes" to these questions, the more you can persevere and overcome setbacks in your life:

- I have clear career goals.
- I address my limitations.
- I bounce back from disappointments.
- I can adapt to change.

DAY 198

Reposition Yourself

You have the ability to become more than what you presently are. You have the capacity to produce more than you have. You can reposition yourself and create greater benefit for yourself and others. You also have the ability to see others in this same light and to live in a manner that celebrates the faith, potential, and motivation of all humankind. Do not overlook this amazing opportunity.

Enlightenment comes through education and exposure. These can serve as the foundation for love and sharing. There is a structure to unity and peace residing in your soul and this structure involves service, spiritual integration, the restoration of dignity of all mankind, and the realization that mankind has more resources than they have been given credit for.

Sometimes when you are feeling stuck in life, you may need to reposition yourself so that you can experience greater success by moving from one place to another. If you are spinning your wheels, try getting unstuck by changing your routine. You can do this by taking small steps. For example, get up five minutes early or read one page of a book. As you work to reposition yourself, you will find that your life will change for the better and you will realize your capacity to produce more than you ever have. ■

Today's Live Happy Practice

Clear your emotional clutter by paying more attention to your actions and being in tune with how you are feeling throughout the day. Is there anything you can do better? If so, adjust your actions by making small changes until you get yourself unstuck and into a better position to consistently hit your targets.

DAY 199

The Quality of Service You Give To Others

The space you occupy in this world is in exact ratio to the quantity and quality of the service you give to others. As Albert Schweitzer offered, "I don't know what your destiny will be, but one thing I do know; the one among you who will be really happy are those that have sought and found how to serve."

Serving others does not have to mean a significant contribution of money. Many churches and nonprofit organizations can benefit from your talent just as much as your money. So, if you want to improve your own quality of life, give back. Giving yourself in service to others helps you grow because when you are wrapped up in yourself alone, you make yourself a small package. ■

Today's Live Happy Practice

One of the things you can do to give of yourself is to mentor others. Mentoring is a great way to give back and make a huge impact without making a financial donation. Your advice and experience can have a major impact in the lives of the people you mentor.

DAY 200

How to Experience the Life You Desire

Some behaviors do not lend themselves to experiencing the life you desire. Here are some behaviors you may want to analyze and overcome:

- Indecision. Being unwilling to make a decision is, in fact, a decision. Inactivity is a decision to avoid paying the price for your progress and to remain stuck.

- Comparing yourself to others. I have heard it said that comparison is the thief of joy. It robs you of the awareness that your only competition is you.

- Worrying. When you worry, your faith remains smaller than your fears. In addition, taking a pessimistic approach to life steals away your joy and creativity. Worriers are like those people who miss the sunset because their attention is focused on the dark clouds.

- Complaining. Complaining does not accomplish anything; just stop it.

- Being unwilling to say "No." "No" can be a confrontational and uncomfortable word but it is a complete sentence. It is important that you be able to say, "No." Saying "No" is a means by which to establish your essential boundaries. ∎

Today's Live Happy Practice

Take a closer look at the behaviors above. Select one and commit to working on it until it becomes part of who you are.

DAY 201

Your Best Opportunity for Growth

Each of us is exceptionally gifted by God and we naturally do some things better than others. While it is sensible to consider what it is you do well, you may also want to give some thought to where you might fall short a little. What is it you need to work on to give you the best chance for promotion and increase? Don't make the mistake of thinking that the things you are good at will be sufficient. It is always worth improving your skills because you never know how important that might be for your future.

As you develop your strengths, be sure to do so within the context of why you are engaged in the activity, what you intend to accomplish, and who you desire to become. It is more difficult to gain clarity if you are not candid about your shortcomings, so be honest with yourself and be open to engaging in those activities that give you the best opportunity for growth. ▉

> ### Today's Live Happy Practice
> Think about where you want to be five years from now. Write your future self a letter expressing your appreciation and admiration for what you've become. Seal the letter and plan to open it five years from now. Immediately begin work on becoming the person you want to be when you open that letter.

DAY 202

Shaping the World of Your Dreams

Your mental models influence the way you live your life and those models play a major role in how your life is shaped, developed, and transformed. Your metal models are not only limited to your urges to overgeneralize, but they also serve as the powerful core of your thinking. And it is those patterns of thinking which begin to shape and mold your world.

If Henry David Thoreau observed correctly that "The mass of men lead lives of quiet desperation," then despair can be traced back to what you think and feel about your individual world as well as the world around you.

Eventually, your mental models begin to serve as identifiers of how you see yourself. As such, these mental models add context and continuity to your life. Consequently, your assumptions can seem more congruent with who you are and where you find yourself, regardless of the legitimacy of those assumptions.

Generally, people will fight for their limitations and attempt to justify them according to their mental models. At times it could be easy to slip into this trap since you are comfortable with the models that have shaped and permeated your life. But if you feel the urge to defend certain assumptions that you intuitively know are no longer serving you, release them and free yourself to begin shaping the world of your dreams. ■

Today's Live Happy Practice

You can shape your dreams and break out of your old routines by doing things different than you have been. Try working on a different project at work or start a different hobby at home. This will enable you to think differently, gain inspiration, and help you explore new possiblities for your life..

DAY 203

Look For Common Ground

When you consider the benefits of ensuring the integration of your soul, remember these few words, "As within, so without." This simply means that the activity taking place within the space of your thoughts and emotions will express itself through the experiences of your life.

The dignity of total self-integration is a radical paradigm shift. The motivation toward a compartmentalized distinction of self has always existed. Many people seem to take pride in identifying or creating differences, but working together and creating partnerships can yield great dividends.

To grab hold of the notion of oneness of humanity may require a quantum leap. But much like the results of a quantum leap within the scientific realm it is an incredibly grand possibility that requires little more than the right conditions for the leap to occur. The amelioration of common ground can be found when we are committed to it. ■

Today's Live Happy Practice

When you work with others, it is important to demonstrate respect. One way to do this is to show appreciation for your teammenbers. Tell them how valuable they are give them tokens of your appreciation. It could be as simple as a thank you email or text.

DAY 204

Look Beyond Your Limitations

When is the last time you took a good look at your life? What you see is usually in alignment with what you expect, and what you expect is directly related to what you believe you deserve. Your outlook is shaped by your perceived limitations. That is why you are most likely beset by the belief that you are not good enough to have what you want. The other hang-up is the belief that there is not enough of what you desire for you to have it.

Do an assessment of how you see the world. Determine if your perspective supports your ability to live happy and feel good on a consistent and regular basis? Do you see yourself as magnetic and attractive? Are you willing to grow yourself and give yourself permission to feel good? Can you do whatever is required to ensure that your life goes well? What do you need to change in order to have your life work the way you desire? Do you see abundance instead of lack? You can attract plenty of every good thing, including health, happiness, prosperity, and peace of mind. However, it will require you to adjust your viewpoints and see beyond your limitations. In order to sail to new horizons, you have to leave the shore. ∎

Today's Live Happy Practice

Transform you life by breaking out of your limiting behavior. In order to get ahead, try contacting at least 5 potential clients everyday for the next week.

DAY 205

You Are Love in Expression

Love means different things to different people but how do you know it when you see it? What are the ways and means by which you make love active and practical in your life, world, and affairs? One thing you can do is allow love to be the lens through which you see yourself. Regardless of your mistakes, missteps, and mishaps, you are love in expression. None of your shortcomings can measure up to the presence of love that shines forth through you. Love is your true identity. Make it your practice to cooperate with yourself.

You would be surprised at the number of people who attempt to motivate themselves and change their behavior through some form of internal guilt, shame, blame, or self-criticism. Loving yourself is a much more compelling and effective way to recondition your behavior.

If you cannot feel compassion for yourself because you feel undeserving, you have to find a way to challenge this interpretation. Explore compassionate ways to view the situation because you are love, you are loving, and you are loved. ■

Today's Live Happy Practice

If you acted in an unloving, unhealthy, or irresponsible way, ask yourself what might have influenced your behavior. Perhaps it was the intensity of the moment or some unresolved issue. We are often more lenient with others than we are on ourselves, so you might approach your love practice by considering how you would respond if you were dealing with a friend, instead of yourself.

DAY 206

Give Yourself Permission to Honor Yourself

Sacred scripture contains some amazing and insightful focus-recalibrating instruction. There is a particular instruction that is credited to the Apostle Paul which reads, "Finally, beloved, whatever is true, whatever is honorable, whatever is just, whatever is pure, whatever is pleasing, whatever is commendable, if there is any excellence and if there is anything worthy of praise, think about these things. Keep on doing the things that you have learned and received and heard and seen in me, and the God of peace will be with you."

This is a great reminder for how you can recalibrate how you see yourself and others. As you go through the ebb and flow of your day, you have many occasions to see yourself and others anew. What would happen if you began to see your interactions, exchanges, and transactions through the piece of excellence and glimmer of praiseworthiness that existed in them? How would your life evolve? How much easier would it be to see the God of peace in your everyday life, world, and affairs? There would be no more idle waiting for the big miracle because there would be showers of blessings, falling like raindrops, and drenching you in tiny miracles…all because you looked for the true, honorable, just, pure, pleasing, and commendable in your daily life.

Give yourself permission to honor yourself. Learn to be gentle and compassionate with yourself. You deserve your love. Instead of being judgmental about yourself, look for that which is true, honorable, just, pure, pleasing, and commendable and the God of peace will be with you. ■

Today's Live Happy Practice
Honor yourself by creating a feel-good list. That is a list of anything you enjoy doing. Then pick one thing to do from your list each day.

DAY 207

Make Your Decisions On Purpose

Life is decision driven and knowing how to address and improve your decisions can dramatically improve your life. What is a decision? A decision is the creative control and intentional plan you establish for what will happen in your everyday life. The problem is that most people do not make decisions by design. They make decisions by chance. Your ability to decide is the equivalent of your ability to consistently select what works and reject what does not. That is why you must prioritize what you pay attention to.

Decide to pay attention to your results. It was James Allen who wrote, "In all human affairs there are efforts, and there are results, and the strength of the effort is the measure of the result." Your results you give you very clear insight into whether your decisions, focus, and actions are working out as you want them to. Your results simply show you that what you achieve or fail to achieve, is the result of how you choose to use the power of your decision. Your decision-making gives you a power that you can use or misuse, all day every day. ■

Today's Live Happy Practice

Decide what your priorities are. What is it that is important to you? How do you avoid having your daily agenda be disrupted by someone else's request, emergency, call, boredom, or poor planning? Prioritize what you choose because you cannot choose it all and you cannot do it all. Use your time to accomplish your priority.

DAY 208

Pay Attention to Your Results

Are you paying close enough attention to your results? Are you really getting the messages that accompany each and every situation, condition, and circumstance showing up in your life? Every result is telling you something that holds immeasurable value, but are you getting it? Paying attention and getting it is advantageous because doing so allows you to either change what is not working so you can get different results or keep doing what you have been doing so that you can continue getting results that work for you.

So again, are you paying attention to your results? Which of the environments of your life is causing you the greatest challenges? What are your challenges trying to teach you? Why some of your relationships working very well and some others are not? Is it time to divorce yourself from certain thoughts, feelings, words, actions, or reactions? Your results are always telling you something. ∎

Today's Live Happy Practice

As a part of your commitment to pay closer attention and in order to better examine the thoughts, behaviors, motivations, and actions that led to your results, ask yourself the following questions to bolster your ability to add to better future: What did I do? What was my motivation? How do I feel about my results? How did I produce what I produced? What was I trying to accomplish? What lessons did I learn? How can I use this information to design a better future?

DAY 209

You Are the Solution

I have some great news for you and it is this…you are here to be the solution, not to complain about the problem. However, in order to accomplish this, it will require a few things from you. It will require you to hold positive, constructive, uplifting thoughts about yourself and others. It will require you to speak life when conversations turn negative. It will require you to avoid complaining and communicate with those who can help you fix what you might otherwise merely complain about. It will require you to hold yourself and others accountable in ways that prioritize intentional action. It will require you to corral your emotions so that your feelings are not easily high-jacked when things do not necessarily go your way. It will require you to reject rejection, doubt, shame, worry, and criticism.

Throughout this entire day, remember that you are the solution. Extend grace. The easiest thing to do, whenever you are going through a difficult season, is to overlook what has been given to you. The easiest thing to forget when others fall short is that you have been there before. Encourage yourself and others. It will not cost you anything and it can immediately help you feel better. Be grateful. You cannot be afraid, angry, worried, and grateful at the same time. Share a compliment. There are plenty of wins to go around. Pray. If you do not know how; no worries; just try, "Thank you so much for so much."

As the solution, you are T.B.T.F. Too big to fail, so do not be afraid to make a big impact. ■

> ## Today's Live Happy Practice
> Smile because you have unspeakable joy. Laugh at yourself, instead of someone else. It will give you an opportunity to not take yourself so seriously.

DAY 210

Align Your Thoughts

In order to create a life you love, you have to align your thoughts with your aspirations; then ensure that the entirety of your being works in concert with your desires. You have one of the most powerful tools ever invented. It is your mind. This creative tool will help you coordinate your outcomes, direct your performance, exercise of your will, and produce the results you are seeking.

However, accomplishing this will require getting over the negativity that seems to be streaming on demand or dancing around in your head. Although you were born with a clean slate, by now you have not only been programmed, but also hindered by the many negative and limiting beliefs you have accepted. That is why it is not enough to only think about your desired state.

When you think about it, you will find that you have many options to help you overcome every negative situation. You will likely need to be creative and contemplate solutions that would typically lead you to believe that you can do it. You have more options than settling for negativity. All you have to do is align your thoughts with your aspirations. ▮

> ### Today's Live Happy Practice
> Engaging your entire being means thinking the right thoughts, while feeling as though you deserve your desires, while speaking in favor of your good regardless of the appearances, while working in accord with the fulfillment of your desires, while responding in ways that let you release what does not work and embrace all that does.

DAY 211

What Do You Want?

What do you want to experience? Most people view this question through the lens of their perceived limitations rather than through the panorama of their possibilities. The question is a version of the question Jesus asked the man by the pool in Bethesda. Jesus asked the man if he wanted to be made well. Frankly, it seems like the answer would be obvious, especially since the man had been waiting for that very opportunity for 38 years. But rather than answer in the affirmative, the man defaulted to the limitations of what he had become accustomed to experiencing; not being well.

Unfortunately, his response was more common than you might imagine. In fact, you may have a firsthand experience with something similar. Particularly since many factors shape your experiences, including your beliefs, your environments, your support systems, your motivation, your relationships, and your sense of self-worth.

It has been said that doing the same things and expecting a different result is the definition of insanity. So, consistently neglecting to even consider what you want to experience will not work. The man by the pool got distracted but you get to be crystal clear about what you want. It does however require that you own it.

∎

> ### Today's Live Happy Practice
> Be mindful and avoid overlapping the question of what you want with the question of why things are not working out the way you want them to.

DAY 212

Progress Leads To Momentum

You have what it takes to transform your life. Not convinced? You should be! If you know how to change your mind, you have the foundation to change your life. If you know how to accept a new belief and you believe you can change, you can change. You absolutely have what it takes. The question is; are you committed to doing what it takes in order to bring about your change.

Once you change your mind and adopt a new belief, it is time to take action. Put one foot in front of the other and remember; progress leads to momentum. You do not have to begin fast, you just have to begin and remember; slow motion beats no motion. You will probably have to renew your commitment; remember to hold the image of what your better life looks and feels like. You have what it takes. They see it, even if they do not say it. Be your own advocate. You have what it takes to experience the benefits of change. You can live a prosperous life now. Abundance is within your reach. Do not stand in your own way. ∎

Today's Live Happy Practice

Do not listen to the doubters, haters, or naysayers. Remember, people who do not chase their dreams can come to resent you for chasing yours.

DAY 213

You Have Greatness in You

You have greatness in you. Are you experiencing the success that should accompany your greatness? If not, it may be a result of your negative thinking. Social behaviorists have predicted that for the majority of people, over three-quarters of their thoughts are negative. That means that three out of four of your thoughts are counterproductive and work against you. That is what you might call self-sabotage.

Studies have shown that by the time the average teenager turns eighteen, they have heard the word "no" or has been told what she could not do approximately 148,000 times. This unfortunately has the effect of conditioning us toward negativity.

Repetition is a convincing argument, so, how can you break the repetition of your negative conditioning? First, you embrace a new belief. This is a critical first step as your beliefs dictate you effort, energy, and enterprise. Embracing a new belief that is aligned with your realization about your greatness will not only help you eliminate negative thoughts and feelings, it will also help you stop yourself from overreacting negatively. Examine your beliefs about yourself and be willing to release those things that are in conflict with your awareness about who you are and what you are capable of. ∎

> ### Today's Live Happy Practice
> Eliminate any negative thinking by taking some time each morning to focus on the good qualities you desire. Take ten minutes to think about the person you want to be and the qualities you want to have.

DAY 214

The Resources Are Already Within You

Your money is an energy that can flow to you in abundance or in pinches. The good news is that you can have lots of money just as easily as you can have a little of it. Those who amass wealth have recognized the existence of an invisible source. This source, responding to your thoughts and beliefs, flows in quantities equal to the capacity of your mental equivalent and settles as your awareness of wealth.

Like the story of the Prophet Elisha and the widow, there are some secrets that help you harnesses your power to attract and produce wealth in abundance. The widow went to Elisha to inform him that a creditor had come to take her two children in exchange for what was owed. Elisha said to her, 'Tell me, what do you have in the house?' She answered, 'I have nothing in the house, except a jar of oil.' He said, 'Go outside and borrow vessels from all your neighbors. Then go in and start pouring into all these vessels. When the vessels were full, she said to her son, 'Bring me another vessel.' But he said to her, 'There are no more.' Then the oil stopped flowing.

The story helps us see that lack and abundance are not separated by much. Unfortunately, it is sometimes easy to lose sight of the resources you have available to you and within you. The widow thought she had nothing. However, what she did have was exceptional and it was right within her own house. Likewise, there is something exceptional in you that is far superior to any apparent sense of lack or need you may be facing. Used properly, what you have can cause an abundance of wealth, good, provision, or whatever is required. █

Today's Live Happy Practice

How do you make other people's lives better? Take stock of your talents by thinking about the things that you are good at and celebrate that awareness.

DAY 215

Releasing That Which Does Not Work

It is not always easy or convenient to change the performance that you have been practicing, especially if you have been behaving that way for a long time. Change necessitates that you leave your past behavior without the certainty, comfort, or clarity of knowing what will happen next. Repetition is a convincing argument and the repetition of that which is not working for you cannot produce progress.

Deciding to release that which has completed its course in your life is even more important than the decision to welcome new. Like a fully saturated sponge, without releasing, there is no room to take on more. You may be clear about where you intend to go. The challenge is that you must be equally clear about what you are going to leave behind. You cannot effectively walk forward and look behind you at the same time. The old wine skins of past experiences will not be adequate to hold the new wines being poured into your life. Trust your intuition as it reveals the patterns you have outgrown. You may have convinced yourself that you do not like change but that is not really true. You change every day in so many amazing ways. Do not delay on what you should release today. ∎

Today's Live Happy Practice

What habits, attitudes, dispositions, thinking, behaviors, or persons must you be courageous enough to cut ties with? Now, don't just think about it; do it!

DAY 216

The Vibration of Wholeness

In the science of prayer, nothing is thought to be incurable or beyond help and all things are possible. This means you can experience wholeness through virtually any expression you desire; be it emotional, psychological, physical, financial, relational, or otherwise. It is important to match your desire for wholeness with the reality of health. The reality is...health simply is. The reality is...wholeness simply is. Alignment is awareness in action. We say there is nothing to be healed, only God to be revealed.

When thinking about your health, vitality, strength, animation, energy, and zeal for life, consider this; a thought about not having access to perfect health is a vibrational mismatch to health and wholeness. On the other hand, it is a vibrational match to God is withholding His healing power from me. Know that you are an extension of the source of life, and that source is nothing but well-being. In order to access this well-being, you must vibrate at the same frequency!

Every time you have a thought or are in a conversation with others about what is missing, what is lacking, who is against you, your bad luck, etc., remember to shift your thinking and reconnect to the vibration of wholeness. ▮

Today's Live Happy Practice

Do not look for love and approval from other people. Your wholeness is already inside you. Use your resources and energy to express the love and compassion that you already have inside of you.

DAY 217

Your Mind Is a Powerful Resource

Your life is not unfolding by chance and luck plays a much smaller role than you might imagine. That is why living your life without personal purpose increases the likelihood that you will not be as fulfilled as you could be. Personal purpose is the intention you use to design, influence, create, and express your life. Personal purpose also helps ensure that your life is not unfolding by accident. Rather, that which happens in your life, world, and affairs does so because you have caused it to, as a result of your purposeful thinking, feeling, speaking, and acting. You are always your own experience. Knowing that what happens to you, happens because of you, is incredibly empowering.

Your personal purpose is most directly influenced by your thinking. Whether you are making decisions, choosing between options, analyzing your experiences, selecting what works, or rejecting what does not, your thinking is causative. It is suggested that thought travels 930,000 times faster than the sound of your voice. Some even suggest that the speed of thought is faster than the speed of light. Your mind is a powerful resource and an element of force. It is unlimited and inexhaustible, flexible and forceful. Unfortunately, very few people are truly aware of the possibilities inherent within their thought power.

If you hold thoughts of success and steady your focus, you will attract more success and fulfillment. Your thought force is like rich soil and the seeds of thought flower and attract opportunities for pollination. Using your thinking capacity with personal purpose is a part of the cornerstone upon which you help success come to you, as your successful living is founded. █

Today's Live Happy Practice

Use the power of your mind to focus on the good things in your life. Allow your mind to associate all the things around you with good memories. Let your coffee mug remind you of your favorite book; or let your bracelet remind you of your favorite friend.

DAY 218

Self-talk

When it comes to living your truth, you do so as a part of your self-image and level of personal regard. Your level of self-esteem is the result of the positive and negative thoughts and feelings you hold about yourself. For most people, nearly 80% of their thoughts are negative. Those thoughts are frequently expressed through your internal dialogue. Whether you are conscious of it or not, whether it is in the background of the foreground, your internal dialogue is always playing. This is more commonly known as self-talk.

That is also why you have to be able to stand up to yourself, for yourself, inside yourself whenever you notice that the messages you are sharing with yourself are negative. Not only that, you have to be able to stand up to those who would stand in your way by dumping their negative garbage out on you. If someone communicated a negative message to you in a language you did not understand, it would have no impact upon you. The meaning you give is what makes the message powerful.

We all know how to spend too much time ruminating on a failure episode or focus too much attention on a negative comment or being excessively offended. It is time for some new behavior so instead, invest more thought, feeling, energy, and effort in the things you feel good about. When you do a good job, give yourself permission to feel good about it! Do not just hurry on to the next thing that needs to be done. Make honoring your work a priority. ■

Today's Live Happy Practice

The thing you must remember is that whether a negative message is generated internally or externally, the power is not in the kind of message you receive, the power is in what you decide to do with the message.

DAY 219

Taking the Right Actions

Do you have a spiritual plan? If not, hopefully you will design one before you decide to make your spiritual growth a priority. If you do have a plan, does it include taking massive action along with your prayer, meditation, fasting, devotion, study, and service? There is a passage in the book of James which says, "The body without the spirit is dead, so is faith without works dead." It gives us a clear indication that, not only must you work in the spiritual realm, but you must also work in the natural realm.

The step that must accompany your spiritual plan in order to make it successful is action. The right actions will naturally feed into how you get to where it is you desire to be. The right actions in the right sequence will always produce better results than random, unplanned, undisciplined behavior. You do not have to be special in order to know how to do the right things. However, you do have to be motivated and committed to the result those actions produce.

Consider for a moment, the Apostle's Cycle of Sabotage. In writing to the church in Rome, the Apostle Paul admitted to not knowing something important about how he moved in manifesting his plans. He shared, "I do not understand my own actions. For I do not do what I want, but I do the very thing I hate." Being unable to dictate and determine your actions does not occur by mistake. Rather, it occurs when you are not in alignment. ■

> ### Today's Live Happy Practice
> What is the motivation behind your spiritual plan? What is your "why"? Knowing these answers will give you the insight you need to know why you do what you do.

DAY 220

Going From Information to Action

One of life's most consistent challenges is getting the most from the things you learn. That is why transforming what you know into what you do, will be one of your greatest levers to change yourself and improve your life. It is not enough to know what to do. You must apply your knowledge in order to make it work for you. Knowing enough to get a gym membership will never be enough to help you improve your health or fitness. Going from information to action is the key.

Neither talent, nor skill, nor giftedness, nor resourcefulness will work for you, if you will not work. Most things are easier said than done. Yet a thought not coupled with action will leave the thought undone and the potential of your destiny unfulfilled.

The difference between information and transformation is motivation, integration, and execution. Do you truly have the desire and motivation? Will you integrate what you know as a means by which to transform yourself? Can you consistently execute and stay in action toward your best life? You can do it if you will do it. That may sound like shorthand or motivational speak but taking action is not difficult. Sometimes it will be easy and sometimes it will not. There is a price to be paid for gaining knowledge and that price is application. ■

Today's Live Happy Practice

Getting yourself to take action is the issue. So put your information to work. Do not read another book or take another class until you have integrated and acted on something from the last book or class. Get moving now!

DAY 221

The Legitimate Use of Your Will

This may seem like an obvious statement but you were born to be you. You are equipped to fully express all that God designed you to be. You get to be you but you must be willing to realize and accept that you can be you. Otherwise, you unwillingly become a summation of other people's decisions. Your will is what moves all your other capacities to action. A strong will with nothing to do is like idling the engines of a G5 jet but never flying it anywhere. You need more than willpower—you need a direction to point it in.

Will is your capacity to say yes or no to your options and opportunities. The higher expression of human will is willingness, while the lower expression is willfulness. Nature enables you to see that least effort is expended in your willingness: grass does not try to grow, it just grows; birds do not try to fly, they just fly; fish do not try to swim, they just swim; flowers do not try to bloom, they bloom. Each aspect of nature simply releases what is intrinsic to its nature, as it functions with effortless ease.

When you know what to think and do, then you must use your will to compel yourself to think and do the right things. Willingness helps you do it with harmony, understanding, and love. The challenge for many people is that they hold the power of will incorrectly. You do not have to apply willfulness to compel good things to come to you, any more than you have to use your will power to make the sun shine. Remember, the sun doesn't try to shine, it just shines. ∎

Today's Live Happy Practice

Use your will to keep yourself thinking and acting in the ways that are consistent with your purpose and goals. That is the legitimate use of your will.

DAY 222

The Pull of Prayer

Like the beads of a rosary, there are so many reasons to pray. Regardless of one's station in life, something always seems to be pulling humans toward prayer. Whether it is the medical diagnosis of a family member, the opportunity of a new business proposal, or a shooting at a school, there are many things calling us up to the action of prayer.

Yet while many of us feel compelled in the way of prayer, prayer means different things to different people. The English word prayer finds its roots in the Latin word precari, and it means to have intentionality or earnestness in ones asking. It also refers to a form of entreating that easily lends itself to the notion of begging or beseeching God when one finds them self in a difficult spot. Interestingly enough, the word also carries the same root as the English word precarious and indeed, many of us are most content to pray when life seems to be unwinding at the seams.

Even with our varied interpretations of what to pray for and perhaps even how to pray, there still seems to be an innate magnetic pull, lifting us to some higher way of being, if only temporarily. Prayer in the purer sense is purposed to move us from the divine state of being the place of divinely-guided doing, as our time of prayer brings us back into the well-grounded being-ness that only comes through our communion with God. ■

Today's Live Happy Practice

Dr. Shoma Morita suggested that, "When running up a hill, it is all right to give up as many times as you wish, as long as your feet keep moving." When it comes to prayer, remain intentional and earnest, regardless of the appearances.

DAY 223

You Are the Result of Your Thinking

There is a relationship between what you think, what you feel, and what you do. Not only that; your thoughts produce conditions in your physical body. That is why when you change what you think, you can change your life. You are the offspring of infinite intelligence and as a creation of infinite intelligence, you are also intelligent. The Greek philosopher Plato said that thinking is the soul talking to itself. Thought is power. It is the driving force behind the things that happen in your life.

Certain laws exist that are related to your mind, and they are absolute and eternal. One of these laws dictates that you are the result of your thinking. Based on the law of suggestion, your subconscious mind is responsive to the thoughts it receives from your conscious mind. Your conscious mind sends impressions to your subconscious mind, and your subconscious mind faithfully reproduces and carries out the suggestions it receives.

The subconscious mind is the storehouse for beliefs, and beliefs are powerful because they influence what you think, say, and do. Since the subconscious mind has control over your body, it acts as a mental and spiritual storehouse for your body. Your subconscious mind, then, accepts inputs from your conscious mind and then produces according to those inputs. Whatever your subconscious mind receives will be manifested in your life. It is the life principle of reaping and sowing. ∎

Today's Live Happy Practice

In order to use your brain to think in a more positive manner, think of ways to make boring things into a game. You can increase your engagement if you can think of ways to make things more compelling and more challenging for yourself.

DAY 224

Erroneous Thoughts Have No Intention of Moving Out

What you are today is a result of what you have been thinking up to this point in time. If you sow ideas of disease, then you will reap a harvest of disease; but if you sow ideas of health, prosperity, and happiness, then you will reap a harvest of health, prosperity, and happiness. Since you are what you think you are, you can change your life by changing your thinking.

You have authority and dominion. In order to manifest dominion in, and over your life, you must persistently think in alignment with God. Doing that helps you stay aligned with your good. Stay determined. It takes tenacity and sagacity to condition your mind toward the consistent and conscious contemplation of the good you desire, especially if you expect to consistently demonstrate the good desires of your heart in your life.

Be mindful about dwelling on what is missing. I was counseling a parent who had recently sent their child off to college and I asked them how long it had been since their child had been gone and the parent said, "In three weeks, it will be a month." In other words, the child had only been gone for one week.

Just like that parent, sometimes your thoughts are subtly centered in what you do not have, with the subconscious fear that you do not have enough. Much like an unwanted houseguest who has been in your home for too long, erroneous thoughts have no intention or motivation for moving out easily. ∎

Today's Live Happy Practice

Take time to pay attention to the good things around you. Focus on the sunshine and the flowers. By doing so, you can train yourself to look for the joy that exists everywhere.

DAY 225

Take Your Thinking Off the Peanuts

As a thinker, you determine your experiences. Once you realize this, there is nothing that can oppose you except your own mental and emotional patterns. Trainers learned the hard way that elephants are more interested in eating the peanuts found scattered on the ground than in walking in a disciplined line for the amusement of humans. These skilled trainers have to recondition these majestic creatures to take hold of the tail of the elephant directly in front. In so doing, the elephants became far less consumed with the peanuts lying on the ground. If you can take your thinking off the peanuts of erroneous thought, you can more consistently experience the happiness you desire.

In order to persistently hold on to what you want to have, do, and be, you have to be stubborn, tireless and steadfast with it. If you want to experience transformation, then you must be persistent in thinking thoughts of power and strength in alignment with the principle of truth. If you are presented with anything that is inconsistent with what you want, you have to remember to let the guidance and direction within you, inform you about whether you should entertain that.

Your thoughts have profound implications for your life. You have been given authority and dominion over all ideas, and the dominion you have been given is over your own stuff. You have not been given authority or dominion over any soul but your own because you are the only person you are responsible for changing. ∎

Today's Live Happy Practice

If you want to create your ideal situation, take note of the excuses and alibis you use to play small and stay stuck. Pay attention and persistently think thoughts of power, strength, and dominion that are in alignment with truth.

DAY 226

Your Attitude Matters

The term "attitude" is one of those words that carry with it many different connotations. Attitude is often used as a synonym for someone's mental and emotional perspective, behavior, and disposition. In some settings, attitude is considered to be a precursor of character. In many homes in many countries, attitude is something children possess and parents correct. Your attitudes are the lens through which you view and go through life.

Your attitude is a function of the way you feel and is a part of what you use to determine what a thing is worth to you, based upon what you think about it. Your attitude helps bring clarity to the things you accept and reject.

This is why you can think you deserve something; for example a raise or a harmonious relationship, but your attitude rejects it. If this happens, you will find yourself frustrated because you have not learned how to align your attitude with the activity of your thought.

A good attitude allows you to see and seize the opportunities ahead of you and without a good attitude; you will miss what is right in front of you. Both the hummingbird and the vulture fly over the desert. Vultures only see rotting meat, because rotting meat is all they look for. It is their preferred diet. But hummingbirds ignore the rotting flesh. Instead, they seek out the colorful blossoms of desert plants. The vultures live on what was. The hummingbirds live on what is. Each bird finds what it is looking for. Attitudes make it so that we all do. ∎

Today's Live Happy Practice

Try smiling every half hour throughout the day. Smiling boosts your attitude and makes you feel happier. Smiling helps you adopt a positive attitude even if you don't have a reason to smile.

DAY 227

The Power of Beliefs

The beliefs you hold are powerful. So powerful in fact, that they can make something, not only seem true, but look and feel true. That is why it is necessary to put your beliefs through this litmus test: Does the belief inspire you or does the belief expire you? Does the belief give you life or does it make you feel less good about yourself? Does the belief stimulate your creativity or does it rob you of your energy? Like most people, you have thousands of beliefs about yourself and what you are capable of. What you believe about yourself and you capabilities will ultimately impact and dictate what you do.

Your beliefs do not all hold the same level of intensity for you. You have held some beliefs for a long time and you have only recently accepted certain others. Some of the beliefs you hold are factual and some are not. But what are your beliefs designed for? Beliefs are the guiding force to tell you what will lead to inspiration and what will lead to expiration. These generalizations guide all of your actions and therefore the direction and quality of your life.

It will help you to remember that just because you believe something, your belief does not make it true. In fact, most of your beliefs are generalizations about past experience and the story you told yourself about the experience. The way you interpret your experiences has real consequence. Begin by being more intentional and conscious about what you believe. ▮

Today's Live Happy Practice

It is time to stop accepting things that do not work for you. Challenge your beliefs, especially those which are based upon your misinterpretation of your past experiences. When you do accept a new belief, remember that the meaning you give it is based only upon your interpretation and nothing more.

DAY 228

Prayer Is an Invitation to Transformation

Prayer is your invitation into spiritual life and soul growth. Prayer is your invitation to transformation and change. The more consistently you accept the invitation, the more thoroughly you will find your life being transformed. Prayer is the kind of invitation that you receive but may not necessarily show up for. In fact, our hyperactive culture has convinced us that we should be content with the notion of being so busy that we are too busy to stop and pray. Yet anyone who is serious about transformation and personal growth will take up the spiritual practice of prayer.

Jesus shared this parable of the spiritual invitation to pray and how we sometimes handle it when he said, "Someone gave a great dinner and invited many. At the time for the dinner he sent his servants to say to those who had been invited, 'Come; for everything is ready now.' But they all alike began to make excuses." In life, there will always be an alternative to preoccupy your time but life, being what it is, is best handled with prayer. Still, prayer is more invitation than obligation. ■

Today's Live Happy Practice

You can improve your spiritual life by looking for the deeper meanings in your habits and behavior. This will help you have a greater control of your spiritual growth, as well as your personal destiny.

DAY 229

The Law of Good

The gospel according to Matthew offers some very practical and valuable direction about life action when you are in a relationship with someone who is in disagreement with you. The life action direction is, "So when you are offering your gift at the altar, if you remember that your brother or sister has something against you, leave your gift there before the altar and go; first be reconciled to your brother or sister, and then come and offer your gift."

While the direction may be inconvenient and the responsibility unwarranted, especially if all you want to do is honor and release your gift, it is important to free yourself of the energetic ties you likely do not even know exist. It is difficult to remain in the light while the shadow of a past exchange looms over you. Reconciling does not necessarily involve apologizing or making amends. Reconciliation rather, is your chance for forgiveness and healing. Reconciliation is your opportunity to demonstrate that the *Law of Good* does not only work for you but is extended from you.

Bless the good you will do. Bless the peace you will share. Also, bless the good that others will do and the peace others will share. In doing so, you make it so much easier to share the good gift you want to share. ∎

> ### Today's Live Happy Practice
> Bless yourself and bless those who have something against you. It may be tempting to give an eye for an eye, but it is much more powerful to give an abundance of good.

DAY 230

Success Is Something You Create

What do you want to have? What do you want to accomplish? Is it better health? Deeper spirituality? More wealth? Enduring love? Peace of mind? Sense of purpose? Whatever it is, in order to have it, you have to be committed to creating it. Success is not something you just accomplish. It is something you create. It begins with creating a new you. If you are not willing to become a new person, it will be more difficult to create your new reality.

Commitment to your aspirations requires that you become a creator. Having what you want is something you create and attract based on the person you want to become. Whatever your dreams, in order to make them a reality, you will have to think, feel, speak, and act in terms of the fulfillment of your aspirations. ■

Today's Live Happy Practice

Practice affirming that your cup is overflowing. Practice living in the expectation that not only is your good flowing abundantly, it is also being multiplied. Practice being in the midst of an ever-present good. Practice being highly intentional with the law of mind action, as the law is bringing everything of its nature into your life.

DAY 231

Dedication Helps You Grow

In life, there are things that we must work for and there are things that we must wait for. Either way, you can still give yourself a greater degree of personalized service if you begin each day with dedication. When you begin the day with dedication, you are better positioned to end the day with satisfaction.

Dedication to the daily improvement of self, precedes a future filled with greater possibilities. When you are dedicated to learning and being better in the simple things like having a better walk in faith or being a better parent, your dedication facilitates and supports your growth.

Dedication helps you grow and when you grow, you expand your vision, you attract more options, you open more opportunities, and you optimize your potential. You must remember that the law of increase is subjective; the soil will willingly accept the seed and do its part of help the seed transform into a plant; it does not however determine if it is making a tomato or potato. No matter where you find yourself planted, it is your dedication to remain true to the potential of what you can become that determines what you will produce.

New things are usually difficult before they become easy and too often the difficulties become a deterrent that prevents people from becoming better. Every worthwhile experience of growth and achievement requires dedication and determination. ■

Today's Live Happy Practice

The people who grow the most are the ones who consistently practice and prepare to grow day after day. Find one thing that you can do today to be better.

DAY 232

Working Well With Others

Lifting up others and wanting to see the team be successful above and beyond your personal needs is not always easy but it may sometimes be necessary in order for you to be your most successful. Knowing how to lead and be led so that you are able to reach a mutually agreed upon destination sometimes requires tough decisions and nuanced actions. The way you determine your course is a crucial factor for how you construct your identity. That is why, where you intend to go should not be overshadowed by how it is you intend to get there.

When you make the mature decide to be accountable and responsible for ensuring that your decisions and actions will be in alignment with the overall objective, you position yourself to lead powerfully. Likewise, your ability to navigate the process impacts the expectations for what kind of behaviors will be acceptable for the future. While these factors may not eliminate the tensions that sometimes exist between competing objectives, they do provide you with a position that frames and guides your decisions and makes things just a little bit easier.

When you understand and appreciate the various nuances by which you can engage the people you are aligned with, the framework for how you best work with them becomes clearer. This is important since clarity is 80% of the process between growing in your personal and professional life. █

DAY 233

Seek First To Understand

Do you possess the emotional and interpersonal intelligence you need in order to add to your relationships? It is not an exaggeration to suggest that your ability to work with other people is among the most important ingredients for your success. Some time ago, the Carnegie Technological Institute suggested that 90% of all people who fail in their life's work fail because they cannot get along with people. That is why you must understand the individual and collective dynamics of your relationships and also have the ability lead, live, and grow as a participant.

Emotional and interpersonal intelligence not only helps you create a home-court advantage in your relationships, they also help you grow. What kind of person are you becoming because of this relationship? As a framework of engagement, seeking to understand and be understood is a segue to influence in your relationships. Seeking first to understand and then to be understood opens the way for you to pay attention to the individual needs of the people you are in relationship with. ■

Today's Live Happy Practice

Be aware of who is with and around you because your relationships can either enhance or drown you. What is the nature of the relationship? Is it spiritual? Is it intellectual? Is it professional? Is it social? Pay attention because it makes a difference.

DAY 234

What's Holding You Back?

The starting point to making better decisions is to stop making poor decisions. What are you trying to do? How are you trying to do it? Is there a better way? Whenever you are frustrated about what you trying to accomplish ask these three questions.

Be willing and prepared to say "No" to those situations, conditions, circumstances, and people that are not in alignment with your purpose and desire to be better.

The quality of your choices equals the sum of the quality of your life. Always look into yourself first for the limiting factors that may be holding you back. ■

Today's Live Happy Practice

Use these steps to make good decisions:

- Gather as many facts as you can.
- Brainstorm possible choices.
- Weigh the pros and cons of each choice.
- Solicit feedback from those you trust.
- Make your decision and monitor the results.

DAY 235

Releasing the Repetitive and Unproductive

Do you agree with the assessment that insanity is doing the same thing over and over and expecting a different result? If you agree and you also take the appropriate corrective action, you may be one of those high-functioning people who strategically and intentionally releases the repetitive and unproductive in favor of your new opportunities for a new you. If this is you, know that you fall into a small percentage of folk. You may stop reading now and continue doing what you have been doing in order to grow and become better.

There comes a time when things belonging to you, though incredibly familiar, no longer really fit the current version of you. Have you ever owned a pair of shoes that fit comfortably in one season of your life, but when attempting to wear these same shoes while in another season, they were just too tight? What was once comfortable had become uncomfortable, if not unbearable. So it is with the things you have outgrown. You will outgrow many things such as environments, attitudes, habits, mindsets, emotional instabilities, addictions, toxic people, and the like. If there is something in your life that no longer has the ability to serve and support you, it may be time to let go of what may well be a repetitive-unproductive. ■

> ### Today's Live Happy Practice
> One of the best ways to release unproductive habits is to replace them with productive ones. As soon as you recognize that you are engaging in a negative habit, find a way to replace it with a more productive one.

DAY 236

Tomorrow's Adventure Are Being Written Today

How many times have you told that story? You know the one; your go-to story. The one that gets you artificial sympathy, insincere attention, or a temporary feel good but no healing. Yes, that one. You may have even embellished it some. By now the story is somewhat fictional, maybe even fantastical. People often do that to make themselves look better. What is your best guess at how many times you have told that story?

You probably use the account to describe, or maybe even justify, some experience or behavior or choice from your past. If you are like most people, you star prominently in your story and others make up your supporting cast. There may be an antagonist but there is most certainly a payoff; for you anyway. Have you come up with an answer yet for how many times you have told that story? Once you know what the quantity is, you may see the value in retiring it or giving it a rest, at the very least.

Here is why it is worth rethinking. Regardless of whether you are the hero or the heel in your story, most people you tell simply do not care. They do not want to insult you but they would rather not listen to that story again. At least not until you tell the story in a way that empowers you to own your responsibility for the actions you did or did not take in your life. It is time for the turning point in your story; a new version with a new story to tell. So be exciting, courageous, vulnerable, genuine, or whatever else aligns with your narrative but also be current because tomorrow's adventure are being written today. ∎

Today's Live Happy Practice

When your story is getting you nowhere, try these two things to get yourself back on track. First, ask yourself what's getting in your way. Second, seek out the people and resources you need to get yourself back on track.

DAY 237

Wait For It or Work For It

Your ship may not be able to pull in so you will have to be prepared to swim out to it. For everything there is a season. You do not want to get caught waiting in the season of working. That is why some say you can wait for it or you can work for it.

Expand your understanding so that you can be the solution. There is an enlightening story about a minister who was preparing for service. While preparing, she was preoccupied with thoughts of how she would ask the congregation to come up with more money than they were expecting for repairs to the church building. She also became annoyed to learn that the regular organist was sick and a substitute had been brought in at the last minute. The substitute wanted to know what to play. "Here's a copy of the service," she said impatiently. "But, you'll have to think of something to play after I make the announcement about the finances." During the service, the minister paused and said, "Family, we are in a difficult spot; the roof repairs cost twice as much as we expected and we need $4,000 more. Any of you who can pledge $100 or more, please stand up." At that moment, the substitute organist played "The Star Spangled Banner." And that is how the substitute became the regular organist!

If you can take action and do something about it, laser focus your energy and efforts and get busy doing something about it. ■

> ### Today's Live Happy Practice
> If you are going to give birth to your greatness, you must take initiative. Taking initiative means that you not only recognize that you have agency in determining the course of where your life is going, you also accept your responsibility to adjust so that the things that need to change do change, and the things that need to get done, get done.

DAY 238

Stop Complaining and Start Creating

One of the greatest habits that keep many people stuck is the habit of being content with complaining. Stop complaining and start creating. Challenge yourself to abstain from complaining and negative conversations. These activities condition your mind to be satisfied with negativity. Complaining is talking about things you do not want rather than focusing on how to get what you do want.

Remember your power to create by speaking the word. Isaiah 55:11 reads, "So shall my word be that goes out from my mouth; it shall not return to me empty, but it shall accomplish that which I purpose, and succeed in the thing for which I sent it. Proverbs 18:21 reads, "Life and death are in the power of the tongue."

People sometimes complain because they want to belong. We all have an innate need to be acknowledged and accepted by others. Sometimes they complain to get attention from others or to relieve themselves of responsibility. Complaining helps to distract us, which makes it a little easier to justify inaction. It may also be used to inspire envy in order to get someone to appreciate you.

People may also complain in order to excuse bad performance. But while it may not be ideal, an excellent mechanic can still get excellent results with lousy tools! ■

Today's Live Happy Practice

If you are a complainer, you can change your behavior by finding a way to articulate your feelings in a healthy way. Instead of complaining, find a place to vent in private so that you release the emotions. Venting lets you articulate your frustrations without knee-jerk emotions of the moment.

DAY 239

Adding To Others

Some people add to your relationship and life. Enjoy them. And while you're at it, why not become one of those people yourself. Anyone who desires to, can become better at adding. The only requirement for becoming an adder is an intention to uplift people and a commitment to follow through on the actions you agree to. One research article on adding through volunteerism showed that people who volunteer enjoy longer lives, have stronger immune systems, experience fewer heart attacks, recover from heart attacks faster when they do experience them, have higher self-esteem, and their lives have a deeper sense of meaning and purpose than those who do not volunteer.

People who add to those with which they are in relationships recognize the value of assisting others in experiencing their wholeness. They recognize that they do not lose themselves simply because they add to others. In fact, adders often come to realize that they have plenty to share; plenty of love, peace, happiness, joy, understanding, etc. Adders realize the importance of supporting others. They are there when you need them, not just when they need you. Sometimes being there for your relationship is as simple as listening. Listening is the most important part of the communication process. Developing this skill helps you to do as Steven Coven suggested, "Seek first to understand, then to be understood."

Ralph Waldo Emerson wrote that it is one of the beautiful compensations of this life that no man can sincerely try to help another without helping himself. Put another way, great levels of happiness, fulfillment, and self-satisfaction are experienced by those who have found a way to add to others. ∎

Today's Live Happy Practice

One way you can add value to others is by making them aware of opportunities. If you see an opportunity, think about who in your circles can benefit from it, then pass it along.

DAY 240

The Power of Prayer

Praying together is not just a spiritual practice, it is also a tool that has undergirded families for centuries. We are hardwired for relationships and we all deserve to be in healthy relationships. Through your healthy familial engagement, you learn to shine ever brighter. That is why your soul longs for such interaction. It also helps to know how to facilitate prayer-filled relationships and invite family in to function within the framework of what you are facilitating.

One of the greatest resources a family has available to it is the dynamic power of prayer. Prayer gives you the ability to persevere through the storm and be grateful for the good. Prayer gives you the strength you need to overcome the hardships and improve your family life. Prayer has an additional benefit of enabling you to grow in the primary relationship you have in your connection with God. But you must know how to access and use the science and faith of prayer in order to benefit from it in your family unit because interesting things can happen within the context of family when you pray. █

Today's Live Happy Practice

When you pray, remember God's love and grace. Be sure to pray for your family and be thankful for the prosperity that you have experienced in your life, world, and affairs.

DAY 241

Naysayers Have Nothing to Do With You

It is amazing how people who have quit on their dreams are constantly trying to convince you that you cannot achieve your dreams. That is why it is critical that you learn to be independent of the good opinion of others because if you can stand free in the face of good opinions, you can certainly be liberated from your naysayers. So know that if you are truly committed to living from your own unique form of greatness, there will be people who will try to keep you down or hold you back.

Theodore Roosevelt put it beautifully, "It is not the critic who counts; not the [one] who points out how the strong [one] stumbles, or where the doer of deeds could have done them better. The credit belongs to the [one] who is actually in the arena, whose face is marred by dust and sweat and blood; who strives valiantly; who errs, who comes short again and again, because there is no effort without error and shortcoming."

Your naysayer's issues really do not have anything to do with you. You are simply the mirror, reflecting back expressed possibilities to a stale and stagnant pessimist. Hating your progress is just their way of saying, "Please slow down. I do not want it to look like I have actually stopped trying. Plus I find it more convenient to distract myself by focusing on you but I do not know how to say, 'I admire what you are doing.'" Cut your attachment to their opinions and continue to soar. ∎

Today's Live Happy Practice

Do not waste another moment worrying about what your critics think. Redirect that energy to clearing and cleaning up your relationship environment. Consider limiting your exposure to anyone who does not know how to provide what you need from them.

DAY 242

Are You Willing To Pay The Price?

Your seeds have potential but the yield of that potential is produced in conjunction with your strategies for sowing. That is why you will want to have strategies for successfully sowing your seeds. Success does not come cheap. You must be willing to consistently pay the price for its confirmations. So one of the most difficult decisions you will consistently make is whether to quit or try harder. The gospel of Matthew shares a parable that that demonstrates this fact. It is called the Parable of the Sower.

The first approach the parable shows is that your seeds are valuable. You may not have realized this before now but your seeds can become your harvest. Do not doubt your ability to be successful in your sowing. Your seeds are your thoughts, your seeds are ideas, your seeds are beliefs, your seeds are words, your seed actions, and these seeds are valuable. You can reshape what you believe is possible by listening intently and carefully to God not others, and not even yourself, if you are not giving yourself proper feedback. The second strategy is to recognize that hard experiences are sometimes a part of life. Difficulty usually affects people in one of two ways: It serves to challenge you to greater effort or it subdues and discourages you from trying again. ■

Today's Live Happy Practice

Do not put any additional, unnecessary pressure on yourself. Whether you had a tough day at the office, a difficult class, an uneasy relationship, an unwanted diagnosis from the doctor, or a lack of understanding regarding a particular topic, do not doubt your ability to be successful. If it were intended to be easy, everyone would do it.

DAY 243

Chose Relationships That Multiply You

Relationships are an important part of life and truly enrich our experiences in living. Each of us is wired to enjoy healthy, productive, reaffirming relationships. We all benefit from human contact, personal touch, and emotional connection. Yet all relationships are not created equally and unfortunately, in the absence of healthy relationships, we are too often willing to settle for the unhealthy ones.

It has been suggested that you have four different types of people in your life; those who add to you, those who subtract from you, those who divide you, and those who multiply you. Simply put, those who add to you help you do more than the sum of what you could do alone. Those who subtract from you leave you with less than you had before the interaction. Those who divide you leave you fragmented, with a sense of separation. Those who multiply you help you expand exponentially.

Where healthy relationships help you feel fulfilled, unhealthy relationships have the potential to rob you of the joy, peace, and unity that comes from walking with another. In order to get the most of your relationships, it really helps to be self-aware and self-reflective. Both tools are critical when it comes to evaluating your relationships. Self-awareness and self-reflection enables you to examine the nature of your relationships and potentially better understand who you are involved with. When you are truly self-aware, you will chose relationships that multiply you. ∎

> ### Today's Live Happy Practice
> While you may be able to build meaningful relationships with those who subtract and divide, just remember, changing them is not your responsibility. It's best to develop relationships with those who multiply you.

DAY 244

Healthy Relationships Require Commitment

Psychiatrist and expert on the subject of self-esteem, Nathaniel Branden wrote, "No factor is more important in people's psychological development and motivation than the value judgments they make about themselves. Every aspect of their lives is impacted by the way they see themselves." Considered through another lens, you build and expand your relationships by deciding to connect with other people and allowing them to connect with you.

A fringe benefit of sharing in relationship is to increase your alignment with love, truth, and power, and thereby enjoy more wholeness. Any connection that clogs your filter or pulls you further out of alignment should be addressed. Just know that you get to unhook yourself from any relationship that does support you.

Refusing to change is choosing to stay the same, and choice is the voluntary act of selecting that that is preferred. A conscious relationship requires effort and commitment on both sides. One person should not and cannot carry the whole relationship alone. ∎

Today's Live Happy Practice

What combination of love, truth, and power do you share and look for in order to connect with others? In order to have a healthy relationship, you must insist that your relationships serve to increase your power rather than diminish it.

DAY 245

You Are Not Your Role

It is very easy to confuse what you do with who you are. In fact, in order to be exceptional at anything, not only must you be committed but you must also pour yourself into it. This reality is a major factor in why the roles you decide to take on often take on a life of their own. But no role can truly encompass all that you are or contain all the facets that make you. In order to effectively navigate and mitigate this dynamic, you can distinguish yourself from the roles you fill. Because you see, clouding yourself with the roles you fill is a setup.

Your role is not the real you and mistaking you for your roles only serves to reinforce the error in how people treat you. In order to preserve your peace of mind and solidify your true sense of self, it is critical that you understand this, so that you can perceive, use, manage, and decipher your interactions without losing yourself, as you retain control over whether your self-worth is being risked with your interactions.

So ground yourself in your true identity. No one else can do this for you and it is not anyone else's responsibility. Ground yourself in the truth of who you are and whose you are. Doing so will prove to go a long way in enhancing your sense of self-love, focus, and meaning. ■

> ### Today's Live Happy Practice
> Pay attention to the people in your life. You may find that your environments are filled with people who maneuver in the role misperception by reinforcing the persona that suits their expectations of you, rather than dealing with the whole you.

DAY 246

Your Body Is a Gift

Your body is one of the best gifts that you have ever received. When you were younger you likely learned that one of the behaviors that demonstrates good manners is saying, "Thank you" when receiving a gift. However, you may not have been preoccupied with giving thanks for your body as it was being formed. After you and mommy were done pushing so that you could become somewhat independent, celebrating your body was likely secondary to taking in your new environment.

Nevertheless, the gift remains, even until this day. Many people and things have come and gone but the gift of your body keeps on giving. Perhaps now is as good a time as any to fall gloriously in love with your age-old gift. Maybe it is time to accept it for what it is; custom designed for you and you alone. Worthy of honor, acceptance, peace, harmony, respect and so much more. Your administration will energize it, regardless of the state it is in right now. Your body is committed to reflecting what you affirm about it. It is listening intently to every word, regardless of whether it is verbalized or not. It has agreed to be with you for your whole lifetime so it will not be deceived from believing whatever your mind believes.

It also comes with a connection to the all-knowing intelligence so that if you start to trip a circuit, it has a backup system to keep you going and in the game. No matter where you are or what you go through, the journey of a million miles begins with the first step you take in your body. ∎

> ### Today's Live Happy Practice
> Take care of your body by doing something you enjoy every day. You might try dancing, yoga, gardening, painting, walking, biking, or any other activity you like.

DAY 247

The Benefits of Exercise

If you want to keep your body energized, exercise is an excellent way to do it. Exercise helps to renew your body while enhancing your brain's ability to learn. You exercise whenever you activate your field of gravity. Whether you walk to the kitchen or walk up the stairs; run around the block or on the treadmill, sit, stand, carry supplies, or clean your garage. As long as you are using your limbs, working your muscles (including your heart), and breathing deeply, you are exercising. What counts is not only what you do for an hour at the gym, but how much you have moved by the end of each day. The following are additional benefits of regular exercise.

- It strengthens your bones and the muscles that support them.
- It improves joint function and helps diminish the effect of arthritis.
- It improves circulation and strengthens heart muscles.
- It improves blood flow and lowers cholesterol.
- It improves thinking and memory and helps to decrease the effects of dementia.
- It relieves stress.
- It improves your digestive system and relieves constipation.
- It helps you sleep better.

Today's Live Happy Practice

It's the little things that matter. You can develop an energizing lifestyle by taking the stairs instead of the escalator, or by parking your car a little farther from the store.

DAY 248

Forgiveness Is Freedom

Forgiveness is a wonderful way to journey back to wholeness and like most other things; this journey begins with you. Many people overlook and undervalue the amazing restorative decision that is made when someone decides to forgive themselves. You, as much as anyone, deserve your own forgiveness. Your forgiveness unlocks a blessing that opens the flow of cleansing and healing energies with your body, mind, and emotions. Forgiveness is based on mental cleansing and that mental cleansing occurs when you relieve your soul of past experiences.

Forgiveness is a form of freedom. Forgiveness is your personally gift wrapped grace. The fact that it is coming from you, is all the more reason to give it to you. ▮

Today's Live Happy Practice

Choose to forgive and free yourself for each and every time you judged yourself but you did not judge rightly. Choose to forgive and free yourself for each and every time you spoke harshly or negatively to yourself. Choose to forgive and free yourself for each and every time you neglected your happiness. Choose to forgive and free yourself for each and every time you deemphasized prioritizing what you thought was important. Choose to forgive and free yourself for each and every time you acted in a way that was inconsistent with your highest ideal of your beloved self. Choose to forgive and free yourself for each and every time you held an unproductive belief about yourself and what you were capable of. Choose to forgive and free yourself for each and every time you did not trust your intuition.

DAY 249

Forgiveness Makes You Stronger

The unwillingness to forgive establishes barriers in the soul, and these barriers prevent you from working with the life force. As Brian Tracy shared, "The *Law of Forgiveness* states that you are mentally healthy to the exact degree to which you can freely forgive and forget offenses against you." Holding on to stuff is a uniquely human feature. Though it may be attributed to the fact that we are actively conscious, it seems that all other creatures feel and still have the ability to move on. But most people do not. People accumulate experiences, give them meaning, and store the interpretation in their bodies.

Holding on to pain, anger, hurt, and hatred is not healthy; and doing things that are not healthy takes a toll on you. There is an enlightening anecdote about a woman who had just come through a tough surgery. She was doing well and was starting to recover when one of her daughters came to the hospital to visit her. The mother thought the daughter was too busy with her own life to visit more often and the mother became irate. The mother had just come through a very difficult experience but she thought her daughter was being selfish. The mother refused to let go of her hostilities toward the daughter. In fact, she became so angry that the emotional trauma caused her to relapse and slip into a coma.

She was a perfect example of how the unwillingness to forgive can create a barrier in the soul and prevent the life force from working in someone's life. █

> ### Today's Live Happy Practice
> It's in order to enjoy your full potential and maximize your deep and rich capabilities, you have to forgive yourself and anyone else you have something against...and...wait for it...anyone who has anything against you. Forgiving does not make you weak, it makes you stronger.

DAY 250

Your Gifts Are Wrapped In Problems

There is so much great stuff within you. There are so many treasures, dreams, gifts, and blessings. The problem is that getting all of them out is not easy. Nothing in life worth achieving is easy. Can you pull it off? Absolutely you can, but you will never pull it off unless you put your faith to work and set yourself on fire with making it happen.

You are one of the most powerful forces on the planet when you believe in yourself and your ability. You are formidable when you dare to aim high and go confidently after the things you want from life, despite the issues and obstacles that get in the way. Disappointments, frustrations, and failures are a natural part of life, let alone anything you want to accomplish with your life. As Norman Vincent Peale said, "When God wants to give you a gift, He wraps it in a problem." Problems do not stop you when you understand that they point out where you can improve. Give yourself an energy charge by finding solutions and overcoming obstacles. ∎

Today's Live Happy Practice

Whenever you experience disappointment, don't try to deny it. Instead, feel it and let it go. You can accomplish this by discussing your emotions with a family member or friend. You could also try writing in a journal or talking it out with a therapist.

DAY 251

Take Small Steps to Overcome Fear

It is impossible to achieve greatness if you are held back by fear. Fear is a choice, and if you succumb to it, it will prevent you from achieving a state of total happiness. Fear is a decision based on your perceptions and if you are not mindful, your fear can triumph over your faith. Danger may be real, but fear is an illusion.

You may be faced with something that antagonizes you, or a rival that always seems to get the best of you or generally causes you problems. You may have a fear of failure or a fear of success; or you may have a fear of losing a great relationship or of being alone. Whatever obstacle that may be in the way of total happiness, you must overcome it if you truly intend to be happy.

When people feel afraid to move forward by a "thing", they are generally not afraid of the thing; instead, they are afraid of the feeling of fear that they are experiencing. Consequently, it is easier to tackle the fear than to ignore it. By taking action and facing the fear head-on, it helps you to dis-empower the thing that is causing the fear in the first place. ∎

Today's Live Happy Practice

The more you tackle the fear, the less power it has. For example, if you are afraid of speaking in public, the best way to push past the fear is to speak in public. Speak up in small, private, and comfortable settings. Tell a story or joke during the family meal. Share your perspective at the weekly staff meeting. The more comfortable and familiar you become with your public speaking voice, the more consistently you will be taking small steps to overcome a big fear.

DAY 252

Focus On Your Target

Having a target to aim for is a very important part of your transformation and success. Targets are critical because you cannot hit what you cannot see. In order to achieve amazing things in your life, you must absolutely have an idea, image, and target of your goal. This target will not only serve as an organizing focus to help guide your decisions, but it will also be a yardstick by which to measure, compare, and contrast your thoughts during the process of turning them into your reality. Know that your limitations and obstacles should not influence setting your target. Once you have a target, you can laser focus in on it and begin to unleash a reservoir of valuable resources.

Your target becomes the central focus of your attraction, attention, and activity. Thought is magnetic so your attraction is the force that draws charged bodies together. Your attention helps narrow the concentration with which you direct your mind. Remember, where your focus goes, your power flows. Your activity is the energetic animation, liveliness, and movement. Accomplishing the many great things seeking to be birthed through you requires that you decide your target and commit yourself to hitting it.

Once you have a target, it will become much easier to determine how well you do at hitting it and what adjustments, if any, you must make in order to successfully improve your life. Your priority is to design your blueprint so that you will have very clear picture of where you are going and what it will look like when you get there. █

Today's Live Happy Practice

Ponder these questions for clearer focus: Where is my attention? Is it on the events from my past? Is my attention on the problems that exist in the present? Or is my focus on what I want to create?

DAY 253

Life Is Biased On The Side Of Abundance

Most of nature lives with the purpose of advancement and unfolding of life. But when we pay closer attention to the DNA of the divine, you see the plan and pattern by which God seeks to express. The simplest way to put it is to say, the thing that makes you want to experience more good, that makes you want to have more, do more, be more, and give more is the same thing that makes an oak tree produce acorns, and some of those acorn seedlings become the beginning of a new oak tree. That cycle just continues to repeat itself for it is life seeking fuller expression.

Life is the divine inclination toward activity and life is biased on the side of your abundance. That is why you are designed to achieve the good desires of my heart.

Likewise, it is natural for you to want to experience success in your life, world, and affairs. It is one thing to want it. It is another to remain committed to working for it in a way that allows you to experience the good you desire. The question is, are you working it the right way?

You were made to live a bigger, fuller life; a life wherein you are gaining those favorable, helpful things. This desire aligns with the intentions of God, and the intentions of God are thorough and unfailing. The thing to remember is that you must open yourself to it and expect to receive it. It is like flipping a light switch. The source is already available and waiting. It is up to you to determine which areas will receive the light. ∎

Today's Live Happy Practice

Develop an abundance mindset by setting up win-win situations. One person doesn't have to lose in order for the other to win. Try brainstorming until you develop a solution whereby both parties are satisfied.

DAY 254

Step Outside Your Comfort Zone

As Joshua was preparing to lead the children of Israel into the Promised Land, he received a much needed word of reassurance. The message was that he should not betray his divine assignment, for just as God had been with Moses, God would also be with him. The word was that he should be strong and courageous and that he should not be afraid or dismayed.

Have you ever had that moment when doubt was leaning on you and needed clarity or encouragement? Something to let you know you were on the right path or reading from the right page? Whether at the hands of another or if you victimize yourself, betrayal can be painful. You betray your possibilities when you do not believe in the potential or promise, especially when you have difficulty seeing the possibilities that God put in you.

Like Joshua, we tell ourselves stories and become convinced that God has made a mistake in calling us up to bat. We betray the talents and abilities we have been given because we are not sure we are the one who is called to make a significant contribution. But sometimes it's in the place of our greatest uncertainty that God will speak and helps us to see our potential, which often times leads to our greatest improvement. Step outside of your comfort zone and trust God to do exactly what He said he would do! ■

Today's Live Happy Practice

Try getting out of your comfort zone by reframing your fear into excitement. Sometimes fear and excitement can feel the same, so let you mind substitute excitement for fear and just go for it!

DAY 255

Develop a Winning Attitude

To be clear, attitude is a nuanced idea. The term attitude is one of those terms that carry with it many different connotations. Attitude is often used as a synonym for our mental and emotional perspective. It is used as a synonym for how we behave and for our disposition. In some circles, attitude is even considered to be a precursor for character. In many homes around the country, an attitude is something to be repaired. Maybe this also happened to you when you were younger and began acting as if you were dissatisfied. And for whatever reason, you let that dissatisfaction be known to your mother or father. Mom or Dad would then say, "I don't know what's wrong with you, but you better fix that attitude before I do." So, attitude can also be a thing to be repaired.

An attitude is many different things to many different people. But when we look at an attitude from the standpoint of how it is impacting our life, it is important to know that our attitude is a function and part of our subjective nature. Attitude is a part of the memory mind. It is a part of the soul that is taken from a memory and then crystallized into form or function. Attitude is said to impact our altitude. If you want to fly higher, make a greater contribution, and accomplish more, you must develop a winning attitude. Are you truly ready to fly? ■

> **Today's Live Happy Practice**
> Your actions are dictated by your own vibrations so never make excuses. Be accountable to yourself. Own both your successes and failures and always look to the bright side of things.

DAY 256

Thoughts and Emotions

You have two forces that work together to help bring about the good you desire. Those two forces are your thoughts and your emotions. The better you are at directing these two elements, the more consistently you will be able to design the life you deserve. Commit to putting more structure, intensity, and intention behind these twin forces and watch the circumstances of your life begin to change.

When you understand the power of your emotions, you will come to realize that this force is a part of the genesis of everything you produce. This is why you must be able to perceive, understand, use, and manage your emotions in ways that allow you to easily apply the right or best emotion, when you are faced with a particular decision, situation, or opportunity.

Whether you are embracing the desires of your heart or avoiding the thing you fear, you will most consistently attract that which ignites your emotional force. The more you desire or fear something, the more likely you are to see it show up in your life, world, and affairs. Your thoughts and emotions can either facilitate the expression of your desires or bring about your worst fears. The psychic marriage of these two forces cannot be overstated. Thoughts stimulate emotions and emotions feed thoughts. It is uncommon to have one without the other. A thought, disconnected from emotion, lacks the power to manifest the seed potential. An emotion, not stimulated by thought, causes the leak and misdirection of energy. However, when your thoughts and emotions are consistently aligned, you have an undeniable force for manifesting what you desire. ∎

Today's Live Happy Practice

Use your thoughts and emotions to visualize what you want. Close your eyes and imagine all of the details of your accomplishment. After you visualize the goal, get to work on performing the tasks needed to bring it to fruition.

DAY 257

Releasing Negativity

Do you have a program or process for eliminating stuff from your life? How do you determine when the time is right to let go? Most people have no problem deciding what they want, but very few have the same level of clarity about what they need to release. As the saying goes, "There are few of life's problems that can't be conquered with a little strategy and commitment." So how do systematically release those things from your life that produce unhappiness, mediocrity, negativity, and any other undesirable state?

One-way to get more from your life is the release the negativity. Regardless of whether it is gossip laden conversations, unproductive thoughts, or energy draining people, you can give yourself permission to release that which does not work for you. That is why deciding to release requires honesty, humility, and courage to face what is not working because you cannot fix what you will not face. Your happiness and peace of mind are absolutely worth it.

If you are like most people, there will not be a lack of reasons for why you might stay stuck in the negative. The negative side of life has likely conditioned you. So much so, that you may have come to see it as normal. So instead of producing answers, you may be coming up with excuses. It is time to break those patterns and release what no longer works. ■

Today's Live Happy Practice

The three things you must examine in order to release negativity are: 1) Your level of attachment to the negative conversations, thoughts, and people you continue to hold on to; 2) Your payoff for holding on to them; and 3) Whether or not it is working and worth it to you.

DAY 258

Changing Unproductive Habits

Behavioral consistency refers to the tendency you have to behave in a manner that matches your past decisions and behaviors. As you have amassed experiences, you have also accumulated behavioral patterns. Your behavioral patterns form the essence of your habits and your habits largely dictate your life. The challenge lies in the fact that if your habits are not productive, they will become one of the obstacles to your becoming the best version of yourself. The better version of you has better thinking habits, better emotional habits, and better communication habits. All of which lead to you having a better road to the better version of you.

While habits can be developed, they can also be weakened and disabled. Your habits either support a better you or your habits stand in your way. If your habits do not enhance your life, they are most likely obstacles. Habits that do not work for you can be changed. That is great news if you have a lot of unproductive habits. Habits are best when they enrich your life and serve you and your goals. Remember, adversity reveals bad habits and releasing your energies for a fresh start with better habits.

J.K. Rowling went from living as a single mother on state benefits to being a multi-millionaire today. Rowling attributed her considerable achievement to her ability to prepare her focus and develop her habits toward the things that mattered to her the most. The success of *Harry Potter* is not only a tribute to her ability to bring forth abundantly, but it is also in indication of the hidden power of habit within each of us. When you choose to develop your mental and emotional habits, you unlock and tap into an amazing ability to immediately change yourself. ▋

Today's Live Happy Practice

Joining forces with somebody is a great way to change unproductive habits. You can hold each other accountable, motivate each other, and celebrate victories together.

DAY 259

Success Means Doing a Little Bit More

What percentage of your potential are you using? When you consider your spiritual, mental, emotional, and physical resources, what would you be able to do if you were to use just 5% more of your ability? Being able to get more from your ability is key if you desire to experience more happiness and success. Regardless of the situation, condition, or circumstances you find yourself in right now, you have the immense ability to have more, do more, be more, and give more. You have never been limited by your past, as much as you have been limited by what you get from yourself. By accessing your potential, you can achieve more than you have before and push beyond your self-imposed ceilings. You simply have to assess the current level of what you are giving, determine what you could do if you gave just a little bit more, commit to getting more from yourself, and taking action.

The only thing you have to control is what you think and feel. Social behaviorists have predicted that for the majority of humans, over three-quarters of our thoughts are negative. That means that three out of four of your thoughts are counterproductive and work against you. It is what you call self-sabotage. To be your best, it helps to know who you are and why you think and feel the way you do. You have to understand the impulses and influences that formed you. When you understand that, you can do a little bit more, and that's when your success will skyrocket.

> ### Today's Live Happy Practice
> Being self-aware goes hand in hand with inner happiness and achieving your aspirations. You cannot grow unless you change and you cannot change unless you understand why and how you respond to your environment. Pay very close attention to your environments because your environments are full of clues.

DAY 260

Your Mind Is the Starting Point of Every Thought

To be successful, you have to think above your current situation. What you are and what you will become is up to you. You are where you are at this very moment because your choices have brought you there. You get to choose your thoughts, words, and actions. Choosing to take no action is a choice to remain in the position you are in right now. You have to think beyond situations, conditions, and circumstances currently appearing in your life. The experiences you have and everything you become because of those experiences is based upon how you think. When you change your mind, you change your life.

You cannot let your thinking get trapped by what is showing up in this moment, because this moment was created at a moment before this one. This moment was created by the past; it is not an indication of where you can go or what you must settle for. Greatness is in your bones. Greatness is in your soul. Greatness is in your mind, and your thinking has to catch up with your greatness. You catch up with you innate greatness by the way you use your mind.

Your mind is the starting point of every thought, feeling, and spoken word. Reclaim focus and control so that your mind can be established and you can stop it from accepting so many random impulses. ∎

Today's Live Happy Practice

In order to unleash the vast potential within you, you must begin to live more consciously. You can do this by allowing yourself to be more alert, more awake, and more enthusiastic.

DAY 261

Our Gratitude Is Always In Order

The grace and mercy of God is always sufficient in every need. This, of course, is not a new concept. Yet, considering how we sometimes encounter difficulties that seem to be too much to bear, it does help to be reminded of this truth from time to time. As you think this out a bit further, if the grace and mercy of God is always sufficient, then our gratitude is always in order.

When God begins to move, it's wise to either get out of way or get in the flow. As Gary Simmons says, "You're either the way of God or in the way of God." I want to be the way of God.

Reflecting on the idea of God being merciful and filled with grace, and that grace being provided to each of us, I submit to you that when you think about the law, you think about the law as this hard and unrelenting aspect of God. But I submit to you that since the law was established for your benefit, the law is therefore, a product of grace and mercy. Since the law was established for your benefit by the beneficent, then the law is intended to be a product of grace and mercy. And that's worthy of our gratitude. ∎

Today's Live Happy Practice

Try these things to practice more gratitude:

- Smile more.
- Create a gratitude list.
- Watch inspiring videos.
- Say "thank you" often.
- Focus on your strengths.

Finishing What You Start

Are you committed to changing the course of where your life is going? If so, it is critical to finish what you start.

Your commitment must be coupled with your persistence; which requires keeping your commitment to your commitment. There was an excellent example of this in the Mexico Olympic Games in 1968. The marathon was the final event on the program. The Olympic stadium was packed and there was excitement as the first athlete, an Ethiopian runner, entered the stadium. The crowd erupted as he crossed the finish line.

Way back in the field was another runner, John Stephen Akwhari of Tanzania. He had been eclipsed by the other runners. After 18 miles his head started throbbing, his muscles were aching and he fell to the ground. He had a serious leg injury and officials wanted him to retire from the race, but he refused. With his knee bandaged Akwhari picked himself up and hobbled the remaining 7 miles to the finish line. An hour after the winner had finished, Akwhari entered the stadium. All but a few thousand people in the crowd had left. Akwhari moved around the track at a snail's pace, until finally he collapses over the finish line.

It was regarded as one of the most heroic efforts of Olympic history. Afterward, asked by a reporter why he had not dropped out, Akwhari said, "My country did not send me to start the race. They sent me to finish." ▌

Today's Live Happy Practice

What does being committed look like? How will you know if you are committed? When you change your mind and behavior, you will know that you have tapped into commitment. When you do not feel like doing something that is in alignment with your aspirations, do it anyway. That's how you tap into commitment.

DAY 263

Inherent Intelligence Aligns With the Life Force

Since thinking creates reality, happiness and health are the direct result of our beliefs and thoughts. The good news is that you have the power to impact your health because you have the power to change your beliefs and your behaviors. Health, vitality, and energy are your natural physical state. Your body has a natural, regenerative capacity to support the predisposition toward health. Your body will produce an abundance of energy if you will cooperate with the flow and activity of health seeking to express through you.

Inasmuch as sickness is due to improper or imbalanced approaches to living, you can maintain good health with the right knowledge and improved action. In other words, your body is designed to recover and renew the properties of wholeness when you no longer deploy mental or physical interference and stop doing what does not work. The inherent intelligence realigns the energy of the body and aligns it with the life force.

In order to do all you are capable of doing, you will want to have a radiant, healthy body. Your health is vital to your success and being without disease and pain means you will be able to do more. ■

Today's Live Happy Practice

Eating breakfast every morning is a great way to boost your energy level and help increase your overall health and wellness. Eating breakfast will help you get going in the morning and will prevent you from being hungry and feeling drained of energy.

DAY 264

The Law Is Designed To Support You

Approaching your life with mindfulness and intentionality gives you an opportunity to design the type of experiences you want to have. Designing experiences you do not want can cause you to believe that you are being punished for something. But the truth of the matter is that the law is not designed to punish you, the law is designed to support you. The law is designed to be the faculty that holds every thought and act strictly to the truth. Therefore, it is not God's responsibility to make you think in ways that are consistent with what you want. It is God's responsibility to provide a system and the intelligence that would incline you to use it intelligently.

God is so merciful that He set up a system for your good, put omniscience within you, and then naturally presumed that you will use what you have to create what you want. You are always using what you have, you just may not always be using it intelligently.

What you have to remember is that the law is a mathematical faculty. It is not biased on anybody's side. You must understand the specificity with which law works. When you understand the law, you recognize that water will boil at 212° on your stove and on your neighbor's stove. It is specific. All things being equal, it works the same every time. It is the law. The law will freeze the water at 32° regardless of whether you are incredibly spiritual or not. ∎

> ### Today's Live Happy Practice
> Think about what you want out of life and then design your plan to get it. When you identify the things you want, it helps you focus your energy and intelligence in a way that allows you to use what you have to get what you want.

DAY 265

Sometimes You Will Have To Quit

There are so many connotations around quitting, even though quitting is far more common than anyone would like to admit. In order to be happy and successful, sometimes you will have to quit. Oprah Winfrey quit working as a TV news anchor before she became a media mogul. Michael Jordan quit his first love baseball to focus on basketball then he quit an illustrious career in basketball to play minor league baseball, he then quit minor league baseball to go back to winning championships in basketball. Dwayne Johnson, who was one of my son's favorite wrestlers, not only walked away from the ring but he also quit The Rock persona, in order to become a major movie star. Arnold Schwarzenegger quit being a movie star in order to become the governor of California. Successful people quit all the time.

Knowing when to quit is not always easy. So how long should you go before you throw in the towel? In the words of the legend B.B. King, "You never want to make your move too soon." When you think about the possibilities attached to achieving your objectives, the human mind is programed to keep going. This is a vital thing because like most people, your objectives may not be accomplished easily.

Perhaps the greatest difference between quitting too soon and quitting successfully is found in your ability to redirect your energy and effort toward something new. ∎

Today's Live Happy Practice

Whether you are quitting a goal, a job, or a relationship that is no longer working, you will need to redirect your energy to the things that give an opportunity to be happy as you move on to the next.

DAY 266

Let It Go

Whether it was super-successful or not, your past was never intended to be a permanent holding place for you. Your past is simply a point of reference, not a prison. The thing to remember is that you cannot drive forward with your attention focused in the rearview mirror. Unfortunately, far too many people live life that way. There is an interesting story about a man who got stuck waist deep in mud. As it turned out, he was too embarrassed to call for help. Here is the rub: after trying, on his own, to get out of this mud for more than four hours, he still would not use his cell phone to call for help. Fortunately, some fishermen were passing by and he finally asked for help. Still it took an emergency services team another seven hours to get the man free because he refused to undo his pants so that they could extract him more quickly.

While you might be unable to comprehend the man's actions, you would be amazed at the number of people who say they want to be free and yet they are stuck holding on to their issues. Just like the man in the story, they are unwilling to undo, release, resolve, liberate, change, relinquish forgive, let go, or say good-bye.

The good you desire has already been prepared, are you ready to possess it? In order to create the capacity to possess all that has been prepared for you, you have to do one of two things; you must either get a larger bucket or empty the bucket you already have. ∎

Today's Live Happy Practice
Before you can possess something new, you have to release that which no longer serves you.

DAY 267

The Law Is Consistent

The law is specific, intentional, and consistent. The law of gravity says that what goes up must come down. You can count on it. That is why it is important that you be careful about the people you misuse on your way up because you will likely encounter those same people on the way down. You can count on it. The law is consistent and mathematical and always on point. And so, the law of thermodynamics says that the only thing that you can get out of a thing is what you put in that thing. When you look at your life, you do not have to look at it with judgment, guilt, and shame. All you have to do is look at it through the lens of the law and say, "What I am getting out is the byproduct of what I am putting in."

The law is established for your benefit. The Book of Jeremiah says, "Before I formed you in the womb, I knew you. Before you were born, I consecrated you." Meaning the omniscient God established a system, then equipped you to move intelligently and successfully in that system. So, if you are the type of person that majors in minors, it is time to do something different. If you fall into that category, remember that you were not made that way. And, if you were not made that way, you have somehow gotten that way. Take a look and make the adjustments so that you can begin to get different results. ■

Today's Live Happy Practice

Get the most out of your life by getting rid of the distractions. Take a look around and evaluate the things that get in your way but don't add value. Focus on what's important and don't waste time on the things that don't matter.

DAY 268

Making Your Mental Life a Priority

One of the most efficient ways to improve yourself is to improve your mental life. Your mental life is the predominant cause behind what you experience. You may be familiar with the saying, "You reap what you sow," or "what goes around comes around." Another way to think of it is, in order to get what you want in your life; you must first have the mental version of it. When you have the mental version, the physical version naturally follows.

Whenever you see a shadow, you can rest assured that the shadow has not been caused by the sun. The shadow is the result of something obstructing the sun. Likewise, the random results in your life are not because you do not deserve better; on the contrary, the obstacles in your thinking limit the flow of your better life. But you can correct that. The more effective you become at making changes on the inside, the more effective you will be at creating success on the outside.

When you decide to change your mental patterns, you do not only have to overcome your existing programming, you also have to contend with the whirlwind of your daily life. Unfortunately, your commitment to be better competes with your routines, habits, needs, and demands. Commitment shows up in what you do. Therefore improving your mental life has to become a priority. It is like being too busy driving to stop for gas. Eventually, the decision catches up with you and you are forced to reprioritize and make sure that your commitment is expressed through what you do. ∎

Today's Live Happy Practice

Improve your mental health by setting up a getaway. It can be a simple evening in the back yard listening to music or as elaborate as a vacation away from everything.

DAY 269

Your Vision Was Given To You for a Reason

No one else has to get your vision. Though you may want to share it, it is no one else's responsibility to get it, accept it, or bring your vision into fruition. You have to know that it was given to you for a reason. It is your vision. It is your revelation. It is your insight and it is your responsibility to bring forth. You are the one who will need to breathe life into it. You will need to set yourself on fire with it and when you do, people will likely come to watch you burn hot with your vision. But whether they do or not, you have to commit yourself to bringing the vision you have been given into manifestation, in spite of the many difficulties you will likely face along the way.

You will face doubters. You will face critics. People you thought you could count on will not come through. You may even question why the vision came to you. But you were given the vision because you can grow and thrive through the adversity. You are not just made for the easy road. You are hard wired for tenacity and perseverance. Trust that God knows exactly why you were given the vision. So whenever you have a "why me" moment, remember, God uses who He chooses and since nature does not waste anything, you can be trusted with the vision. That is why it was given to you. ∎

> ### Today's Live Happy Practice
> Execute your vision by going the extra mile. Anticipate objections and develop valid answers to the questions that may arise.

DAY 270

Don't Take on Other People's Baggage

As a general rule, your behavior follows your attitudes. That is why it is really difficult to talk yourself out of something you behave yourself into. In order to develop a winning attitude, you have to use the power of persuasion to your advantage. You have to make sure that if you are the message source for your own soul, the things that you are saying to yourself are in alignment with your desire to develop a winning attitude.

One of the greatest barriers for developing a winning attitude is the tendency to complain, criticize, and gossip about stuff. People often forget that it is not necessarily what happens to them, rather, it is what is happening within them that makes the difference. Do not get lulled into believing that you cannot control what is happening within you. You are infinitely equipped to handle what is happening in you.

The responsibility is not to shield yourself from what might happen, but rather, to position yourself to walk in power when what happens to you is not happening through you. Just because it happens to you, does not mean that it has to dictate what's happening in you. Someone in your circle of relationships may have a problem with. But it is not your problem. It is only your problem if you make it your problem. It only becomes your problem when you adopt the essence and energy of the problem that they had. Instead, adopt the attitude and tell yourself, "I did not pack a bag to take this trip with you." ∎

Today's Live Happy Practice

Avoid taking own other people's baggage by establishing boundaries. Get proficient at saying, "No". In addition, you may need to reduce your social interactions for a while.

DAY 271

You Are Bigger Than Your Past Pains

In order to allow yourself to heal emotionally, it is important that you take the step to forgive yourself and others. For many people however, forgiving themselves or others is a neglected, radical, and little understood practice. Forgiveness is radical because it involves making a rare practice a regular practice. Forgiveness is radical because it involves doing what is important before it becomes urgent. Forgiveness is radical because it involves a transformation in thought and a healing of the heart. Without forgiveness, you may find yourself sliding down old hurts rather than climbing new mountains.

In order to free yourself from the toxins, blocks, and negative emotional build-up, decide to no longer harbor anger, hatred, hostility, bitterness, and animosity. It is much harder to lay down the burden if you will not first reconcile the emotional baggage related to a past experience. Stop struggling against your feelings. It is important to refrain from inflicting emotional violence on yourself by reliving the past painful events and situations. Let your desire to be better be fueled by your commitment to forgiveness and healing.

Today's Live Happy Practice

Embrace and then improve upon any sense that you are in any way inadequate. Give yourself the benefit of your own confidence by proving to yourself that you are bigger than your past pains.

DAY 272

Develop Your Plan

One of the most consistent ways to get what you desire from life is to grow yourself, but personal growth and development is not easy. In order to make success easier, develop and plan for how to grow yourself. Just as a building follows from a blueprint, so does the desire to become all you can be. If you do not design a conscious, highly intentional plan to assist you with your personal growth, you will find yourself at the mercy of those who have a plan for you.

If you design your blueprint and develop a plan for your new goals, it will go a long way toward helping your enjoy better results. Your new plans will help you better work within the creative field of energy and intention, as you connect to manifesting your own destiny. You have an inexhaustible ability to grow and make something good happen in your life. ■

Today's Live Happy Practice

Follow these steps to develop your plan:

- Write down your goal.
- Divide it into small chunks.
- Enlist the people and resources you need.
- Review you plan regularly.
- Make adjustments as necessary.

DAY 273

Be Prepared

If you are the type of person that major in minors, you have forgotten who you are and whose you are. If you are a person who major in the minors, you may fall in the category that H. Emilie Cady referred to when she said that most people believe themselves to be in bondage to the flesh and the things of the flesh. If you fall into that category, remember that you were not made that way.

Focusing on minor things in life can cause problems to your mental health and prevent you from moving forward to get the things you want out of life. You might think it's the big things that cause the most problems, but the small things can add up and take over your thought consciousness.

One of the things you can do to refocus your energy and stop majoring in the minors is to be prepared. When you are prepared, you can minimize the impact of the small things, but you will also know that you have done all that you can in that situation. The more prepared you are, the happier you will be. So, invest the time and resources into getting yourself prepared and stop worrying about the small things. ∎

Today's Live Happy Practice

Be prepared for anything by staying in the moment. Don't focus on what happened in the past or what you think will happen in the future. When you stay in the moment, you can remain calm and be grateful for where you are at any given time.

DAY 274

The Power of Clothes

The global pandemic had a profound effect in many areas of our lives, especially when it comes to the clothes we wear. It seems that everyone simultaneous decided to dress down; mostly, just throwing on a t-shirt and a pair of jeans. It almost feels that we collectively adopted the mindset that the world doesn't deserve our best. But I recently discovered something fascinating when I made a conscious decision to start dressing up again. One day I wore a pair of green pants and was particularly intrigued by the impact my clothes had on individuals around me. Most people responded in a predictable manner, making judgements about my financial success or coming to conclusions about my trustworthiness or intelligence.

While we have always known that our clothes strongly influences other people's perception of us, new research has shown a powerful link between your emotional state and the clothing you wear. In the "lab coat" study at the Kellogg School of Management, researchers gave a white lab coat to two groups of participants. One group was told that it was a doctor's coat and the other group was told that it was a painter's coat. The group that believed it to be a doctor's lab coat performed better than the group that believed it to be a painter's coat. The researchers confirmed a definite connection between how people dress and how they feel. Wearing ill-fitting clothing can impact your confidence and make you feel self-conscious throughout the day. On the other hand, natty clothing can actually make you smarter and affect your ability to perform a task. Even the colors you wear can impact your mood. The old adage is true, when you look good, you feel good. So, do yourself a favor and put on some good clothes because you're worth it, and the world is too! ■

Today's Live Happy Practice

Take a moment to think about the clothes you've been wearing over the last year. Make a conscious decision to take out your good stuff and wear them every day.

DAY 275

A Smooth Sea Never Made a Skilled Sailor

Life as a sailor was one of the most exciting and unpredictable experiences that I have ever had. For months at a time, we literally lived on the margins of society far beyond the reach of land. Our living quarters were cramped and noisy, and the sea conditions dangerous. We always faced the possibility of having to abandon ship on short notice and constantly lived with the risk of falling overboard and the hazards of working with dangerous machinery.

But don't get me wrong. I don't mean to imply that life as a sailor was as bleak as that; in fact, a life unencumbered with the restraints of life ashore is appealing and intriguing in many regards. And because of the adversity inherent in life on the seas, it also presents a wonderful opportunity for growth and development.

Some people view adversity as hardship or misfortune. However, adversity can be a catalyst for growth if you reframe how you think of it. When you are able to reframe adversity as a challenge instead of as stress, then you will be better able to process it. Challenges give you additional energy and increased adrenaline. That's why past adversity makes you more resilient. It also explains why people who experienced adversity have better mental health and well-being than those who don't. Sailors know this all too well because the best sailors are the ones who have experienced adversity on the high seas. So whenever you face a challenge in your life, remember that a smooth sea never made a skilled sailor. ∎

Today's Live Happy Practice

Use these tips if you're dealing with any adversity in your life:

- Find a sense of humor. Laughter is always the best medicine.
- Take stock of the adversity you have already faced and reflect on how you overcame it.
- Reframe the adversity as opportunity and look for possibilities for growth.

DAY 276

The Power of Saying Nice Things

We've all heard the saying, "If you can't think of anything good to say, don't say anything at all." I disagree with that. I believe that if you can't think of anything good to say, you're not thinking hard enough. Saying nice things to others can give you a warm glow inside. It increases your sense of well-being. Sometimes, just thinking about saying something nice can improve your mood and increase your happiness. But why do saying nice things make you happy?

Did you ever notice that when people around you are in a negative mood, it can bring you down? Did you notice that, when people in your circles experience a loss and feel sad, you empathize with them and often you feel sad too? Scientists refer to this as a "mirroring" affect.

In an experiment with monkeys, they noticed that when researchers picked up food, the same neurons fired in the monkey's brains as those in the person they were watching. In other words, when watching the person pick up food, the monkey's brain reacted as if the monkey itself was picking up the food. The mirroring affect explains why, when you see someone yawn, you also get an overwhelming urge to yawn.

The same thing happens when you say something good. When you say something that makes someone else feel good, it makes you feel good as well. So if you want to lift your mood and increase your own sense of well-being, say something nice. ■

Today's Live Happy Practice

One of the nicest gifts you can give to someone is a few positive words, like; you look great today; you have the best smile; or, that color looks perfect on you. Use the power of saying nice things and practice saying something good to everyone you meet today.

DAY 277

The Color of Birds

Birds are, hands down, the most colorful living creatures on the planet! Take for example, the dramatic red feet of the red-footed booby; the chorus of colors on the puffin's bill; the brilliant blue feathers of the mountain bluebird; or the dazzling crisp yellow bill of the mallard duck. While serious birdwatchers thrill at the amazing variety of colors of these wonderful creatures, most of us completely miss their beauty.

This is unfortunate because it's the little things in life that matter the most. Too often, our focus is on relishing the big moments, achieving the big goals, or giving the big gifts. By doing so, we underestimate the little things in life that mean so much. A small gesture of kindness to someone who's having a bad day could do wonders. A smile to a stranger could have a ripple effect. You may never know how much a small act of generosity can completely change the course of someone's life.

It's the small things that can have a great impact on your life as well. The little things help us put things in perspective. When you take the time to enjoy the small things, you will have a greater appreciation for life's beauty.

Do you ever feel that there isn't enough time in a day? Do you sometimes feel that life is moving too fast? Why not slow down and enjoy the time that you do have? Instead of rushing through your life and missing the small things; stop and take the time to savor the delicious smell in your kitchen when you bake a cake. Throw a blanket over yourself and snuggle up to take a nap in a comfortable chair while reading a book. Look up at the sky and bask in the warmth of the sun on your face. Take a little time every day to enjoy the small things in life and savor the experiences as often as possible. ■

Today's Live Happy Practice

Get a book or search the internet for pictures of birds and marvel at their vibrant colors.

DAY 278

Sing Like Nobody's Listening

Did you know that there is a whole community of people out there who want to learn from you? You have a lot to offer the world but it's up to you to birth your ideas and to live your dreams. One of the things that keep us from living the life we want is the feeling of being self-conscious. This often happens because we are too aware of ourselves and it causes us to hold back on some of the things we want to do. We often ask ourselves, "What if something happens?" or "What if this doesn't work out the way I want it to?"

While we hold back on doing things because of fear of the consequences, the real consequence is missing out on doing the things we want to do in life. The best cure for this is to learn how to live your life uninhibited. It's like signing in the shower when no one is listening; or dancing when no one is watching. Have you ever noticed how great you sound? Or well you dance? That happens because you are not holding back.

What would happen if you lived your life that way? The possibilities would be endless! You would begin to recognize that other people are not nearly as concerned about you as you might think. When you live your life uninhibited, you will begin to love yourself. You will begin to free yourself from the shackles of other people. You will become completely comfortable with who you are.

Don't worry about what other people are thinking and don't change your behavior based on someone else's disapproval. Go ahead and live life without inhibitions, and remember to sing like nobody's listening. ■

Today's Live Happy Practice

Instead of saying, "I can't do something," ask yourself, "How can I do it?" There is always a way. There is nothing you cannot do, but you have to affirm the possibilities rather than declaring the negative.

DAY 279

Return on Full

Recently, one of my family members decided to move out of her apartment. These days that doesn't present much of a problem because you just pull up TaskRabbit or some other App and hire movers to get the job done. All you have to do is rent a U-Haul truck and show up. The movers do the rest. They meet you at your apartment and load the truck. Then they drive to the second location and unload. They even place the boxes in the appropriate rooms and set up your bed. And after it's all over, you simply return the truck.

But here's something I noticed during the move. One of the instructions for the truck was to "returned on full", which meant that you have to fill up the gas tank before returning the truck.

Success in life is kinda' like that U-Haul. Just like the truck, you must refuel your body after every use. How do you refuel? You do it by eating the proper foods during the day and getting the proper amount of rest at night. There is an additional cost if you don't return the truck on full. And just like you have to pay for not refueling the truck, the same goes for your body. Without sufficient food and rest, you will pay a price in the form of sluggishness and increased chance of illness.

Another very important point with the U-Haul is that you must give yourself enough time to get the gas. If it is not back by the deadline, you will have to pay an additional charge. So in order to avoid extra charges, you have to give yourself enough time to stop for gas, refuel the truck, and still get it back on time. The same is true with your life. Be sure to give yourself enough time to get where you need to go and do what you need to do. When you give yourself the time you need, you will experience less stress and your anxiety levels will decrease. So be sure to refuel your body and don't forget to give yourself enough time to do so. ∎

Today's Live Happy Practice

Wherever you go today, leave 20 minutes earlier than you have to. You will be the better for it.

DAY 280

If It's Out Of Your Hands, It Deserves Freedom From Your Mind Too

If you've ever seen a rip current you know that it is a very powerful, fast-moving channel of water that can flow faster than an Olympic swimmer. Rip currents are dangerous and many swimmers won't survive if they get caught in one. The best chance of surviving one is to remain calm, go with the flow, and ride out the surge. But many people feel a lack of control and their first instinct is to fight the current. This is generally a bad idea because trying to swim against a rip current is impossible and only uses up your energy. It's best to just let go and conserve your energy so that when you're out of the current, you can swim safely back to shore.

In life, one of the things that stand in the way of some people's happiness is the fact that they can't let go of control. It could also be the result of being too attached to a specific outcome. But if you want to achieve true inner peace, you must let go. Letting go means more peace, joy, and freedom. Just like the swimmer caught in the rip current, things will go more smoothly in your life when you allow them to happen instead of fighting against your circumstances.

You will be happier when you trust that things will be okay regardless of your current situation. Don't limit your options. Open yourself up to the possibilities. Recognize that some things are out of your hands. And if it's out of your hands, it deserves to be out of your mind too. ∎

Today's Live Happy Practice

Try employing some of these strategies if you're struggling to let go of control:

- Accept that some things are out of your control.
- Set realistic goals for yourself.
- Welcome feedback.
- Distance yourself from past events.

DAY 281

Believe Life is Rigged in Your Favor

The beliefs that you hold are an important part of your identity. They affect the quality of your life because what you believe is what you are. The stronger your beliefs become, the more unshakable they are. But you should keep in mind that the beliefs you held yesterday may not be the beliefs you hold tomorrow; and the beliefs that got you where you are now won't necessarily get you where you want to be in the future.

You may have religious, cultural, or moral beliefs and they may be rational or irrational. There is some basis in your experiences for your rational beliefs; however, your irrational beliefs are simply a function of mistaken convictions.

Since your beliefs are assumptions that you hold to be true, and since they stem from your life experiences, there is a very rational reason to hold the belief that life is rigged in your favor; especially given the fact that you have always lived a blessed and highly favored life.

So if your beliefs are not serving you well, how can you change them? One way to change what you believe is to change the language that you use. The language you use will determine the way you interpret things, and it will also influence what you believe about the world around you. Your words have power. They drive your behavior, dictate what you believe, and ultimately, create the world you live in. So it is no wander that if you believe life is rigged in your favor, it is! ∎

Today's Live Happy Practice

Believing that life is rigged in your favor could be as simple as telling yourself good things over and over. Repetition is the most powerful tool to imprint something into your mind. Whatever you say or hear regularly will be more valid than something you are exposed to only occasionally. So go ahead and tell yourself repeatedly that life is rigged in your favor and see what happens.

DAY 282

Done Is Better Than Perfect

While it is important to do things in excellence, you should not sacrifice done for perfection. In order to complete my studies and receive my doctorate degree, I was required to write and produce a dissertation. A dissertation is a very long document that summarizes the research in a Ph.D. program. The dissertation is perhaps the most difficult part of any doctoral program. It can take anywhere from 12 to 18 months to complete. It is in the dissertation phase where most doctoral candidates fail.

As you might imagine, there is a lot of anxiety around completing the dissertation because you cannot graduate without it. Given that reality, it is no wonder that many students are concerned about their dissertation; so much so, that the dissertation mantra is "a good dissertation is a done dissertation." That statement is repeated frequently to suggest that the dissertation doesn't have to be perfect, it just has to be done.

While perfection is a noble endeavor, completion is equally important. Are you a perfectionist? Do you refuse to accept anything short of perfection? Do you set excessively high standards for yourself that can never be met? If that's you, take a look at your motivations. If your perfectionism gives you the motivation and determination to overcome adversity, then it's a good thing. On the other hand, if it paralyzes you and gets in the way of finishing, then it is an unhealthy fast track to frustration. When trying to reach your goals in life, remember that perfection is good, but done is better than perfect. ■

Today's Live Happy Practice

Think about the last project or goal that you did not finish. If it is incomplete because of perfectionism, tell yourself that mistakes are a great way to learn and give yourself permission to submit it regardless of the criticism.

DAY 283

Assume Whoever You're Listening To Knows Something You Don't

Know-it-alls can ruin a perfectly good day and they can be exhausting to be around. They tend to be very judgmental and overbearing, and often congratulate themselves for their perceived intelligence. They may even try to make you feel bad about yourself because you don't know some minor piece of trivia.

Know-it-alls are convinced that they are right and demand that even the most ridiculous assertions be taken serious. But if you know everything, you can't learn anything. However, the good news is, if you are a know-it-all, you can change your behavior. Here's how:

- Listen. Listening means keeping quiet and silencing your inner voice. Don't mentally rush the person you're listening to so that you can spew the comeback you've already planned in your head.
- Assume that whoever you're listening to knows something that you don't. There's a great chance that they do.
- Ask. Asking is one of the most important aspects of communication. People who are curious, ask; and when you turn up the volume on your curiosity, you will win every time.

Being an active listener shows people that you care about them and their wellbeing. When you do that, they will enjoy chatting with you and they will be grateful for the encounter. And what's not to like about that? ∎

Today's Live Happy Practice

Try these tips if you're in a conversation with someone else who is a know-it-all:

- Avoid getting into an argument with them.
- Always respond with kindness.
- Let their comments or criticisms go in one ear and out the other.

DAY 284

If You Change the Way You Look At Things, the Things You Look At Change

If you want to live your dreams and be truly happy, you must have mind discipline. Mind discipline refers to the discipline it takes to engage in the mental practices you need to make your vision a reality. It basically means taking ownership of your thoughts. Your self is simply a reflection of what you believe it to be; therefore, if you change the way you look at things, the things you look at will change.

Elite athletes know a little something about mind discipline. In order for them to become elite and perform at such a consistently high level, it is critical that they exhibit mental discipline. This is most important just before a performance. Just before they go on, elite athletes settle down and focus their attention on their actions, thoughts, and emotions. If they discover that they are distracted from the big moment, they make the appropriate adjustments by changing what they're focusing on or how they feel. For example, they might change their breathing patterns to gain control of their heart rate, or they may go through their pre-game to-do list.

Just like elite athletes, you can discipline your mind by focusing on what you want to see in your world. Make this a focus every morning by taking five minutes to visualize success. This is a great way to prepare your mind for the opportunities you might encounter during the day. After all, the self-aware person will draw circumstances into his or her life consistent with their highest self. ■

Today's Live Happy Practice

The best way to gain mind discipline is to understand the reason why you are doing what you are doing. Try writing down your "why" on a sticky note and put it on your refrigerator or on your computer. The constant reminder of "why" will help you gain greater discipline and make it more likely that you stick to your plan.

DAY 285

Yellow Lines in the Middle of the Road

One day I was driving my car contemplating the meaning of life when something jumped out at me. It was the yellow lines in the middle of the road. I thought about it for a moment and realized that they were telling me something. I could pass other cars when the yellow lines were broken, but no passing was allowed when there were two solid yellow lines. In essence, the yellow lines in the middle of the road were there to establish boundaries for me.

Just like we have boundaries in our roads, we also have them in our life, world, and affairs. Our personal boundaries are guidelines that communicate to other people how to behave towards us. Our boundaries define our likes and dislikes and are essential to healthy relationships. Without them, we could be taken advantage of or disregarded, and poor boundaries could lead to resentment, hurt, or anger.

Empower yourself to set personal boundaries and take responsibility for your own well-being. Boundaries help you take care of yourself by giving you permission to say "No". Clear boundaries help others know what is okay and what is not, and they help build healthy, and respectable relationships. Being assertive and honest about what you need is not the same as being unkind or rude. Learning to be confident is the first step to setting personal boundaries and managing your self-care. Taking the time to set and communicate your boundaries will go a long way in improving your relationships and help you live a happy and healthy life. ■

Today's Live Happy Practice

- Think about a situation where your personal boundaries have been crossed.
- Next, decide what action you can take. For example, letting the individual know how they made you feel.
- Finally, communicate your boundaries clearly and directly to the individual.

DAY 286

Don't Let Yesterday Take Up Too Much of Today

Disappointment is inevitable. It is a fact of life. Everyone will experience some disappointments because things don't always work out the way you want them to. Whether you wish you had better prepared for an opportunity; or you wish you could take back some insensitive thing you said; you can't undo the past. There is nothing wrong with reflecting on your mistakes and learning from them, but if you find yourself endlessly replaying what happened yesterday, you're giving it too much attention.

The best way to deal with disappointment is to learn from the experience and move on. Learning from your disappointments mean that you process what happened and determine how to deal with it in a constructive manner. Continuing to focus on things that did not go your way will only cause you unnecessary stress.

Disappointments that manifest themselves in your experience are not meant to destroy you; on the contrary, if you learn to make them rewarding and beneficial, they can strengthen you and make you a better person. That means greater insights and wisdom. So although you may not be able to prevent disappointment from coming, you can choose how you deal with it. The key to dealing with the frustration of being let down is to keep a positive mental attitude, and not let what happened yesterday take up too much of your time today. ■

Today's Live Happy Practice

Learning to let go of disappointment is crucial to maintaining mental well-being. Try the following tips to change your disappointments into something positive:

- Don't take it personally
- Review your expectations
- Try again

If It Doesn't Open, It's Not a Door

Superheroes can do amazing things! Take Luke Cage, for example. Luke is known as Power Man, the first Black superhero to star in his own comic-book. He has superhuman strength and unbreakable skin that can stop bullets. When he wants to get the bad guys, he simply kicks the door in or tears it off the hinges; and if there is no door, he goes through the wall. But if you're not a superhero, you probably won't be going through the wall. So if you're beating your head against a wall trying to do something that is not doable, or reach something that is not reachable, then it might be time to change directions. Bottom line; if it doesn't open, it's not a door.

If you don't like the direction you're going, change it. Unfortunately, change can be a challenge for some people but it can be done with the use of micro habits. A micro habit is an action that requires minimal effort to complete. These small steps can build over time into something big. Think of it like compound interest in an investment. The question is: "would you prefer to receive $1,000,000 thirty days from now, or receive a single penny that doubled every day for thirty days? Most people would take the $1,000,000. However, if you took a single penny and doubled it every day, you would have $5,368,709 at the end of thirty days.

That's how micro habits work. Assume that you don't read but you want to get in the habit of doing so. You might begin the micro habit of reading just one page every night before going to bed. This is a small goal that anyone could do. Before long, you'll discover that you have created a habit with very little effort. So a tiny devotion to micro habits may require minimal effort but they can make a huge impact in transforming your life. ■

DAY 288

Love People for Who They Are, Not For Who You Want Them to Be

According to research, good social relationships are the most consistent predictor of a happy life. However, satisfying relationships not only make you happy, they also improve your health and wellbeing. But what happens when the people who are closest to you do not behave the way you want them to? That's when it is important to love people for who they are and not for who you want them to be.

But remember, it's actually not the love that is disappointing, it's the expectations. Sometimes we have trouble with loving people for who they are because their behavior does not live up to our expectations of them.

An important step in loving people for who they are is to accept your differences. Try to appreciate the other person's uniqueness, no matter how unusual it is. Recognize that everyone is a distinct individual and avoid being judgmental. It may help to affirm to yourself that you accept the person for who they are.

There is no question that you can't depend on someone else to make you happy, but it is clear that satisfying relationships lead to better health, greater happiness, and in some instances, longer life. So if you want to have a happier life, be sure to love and appreciate the people in your life for who they are and not for who you want them to be. ■

Today's Live Happy Practice

Think about a person in your life who has disappointed you. Write down the expectations you have of that person. Do an honest assessment to determine if you expectations are realistic. Now let go of your expectations and start to accept them for who they are and what they mean to you.

DAY 289

If It's Not Going to Matter 5 Yrs. from Now, Don't Spend 5 Minutes Upset By It

Being concerned is a natural way of thinking about life's challenges. Being worried, on the other hand, is destructive and can lead to stress and anxiety. While concern is natural, constant worrying and negative thinking can take a toll on your mental and physical health. Worrying can also interfere with your emotional wellbeing and leave you feeling jumpy and unbalanced. But if it is not going to matter 5 years from now, you should not spend 5 minutes worrying about it today.

Instead of worrying; think positive. Positive thinking is an attitude that focuses on the good things that can happen and it puts you in the frame of mind to expect results that will benefit you. When you think positive, you anticipate happiness. You anticipate good health and success, and you train your brain to adopt an abundance mindset. After you have firmly adopted an abundance mindset, the next thing you can do to eliminate worrying is to create an action plan. This will help you evaluate the situation and come up with some concrete steps for dealing with whatever challenges you may face. If you follow this practice, you will be well on your way to living a life without worries and spending less time on things that do not matter. ∎

Today's Live Happy Practice

Steps to create an action plan:

- Brainstorm and make a list of possible solutions.
- Select the best option to deal with the challenge.
- Identify the steps needed to execute your solution.
- Attach a deadline to each step.
- Identify the resources needed.
- Determine how you will measure your progress.
- Start today.

DAY 290

It's Okay to Take a Break

Do you feel that taking a break from your routine is some sort of guilty pleasure? Or, are you reluctant to take a break because you feel that you are shirking your responsibilities? Your daily routines can cause stress to creep into your life so it's important to take a break every once in a while. The human body is designed to endure short bursts of stress, but when your daily routines turn into prolonged tension, real health challenges could set in. At some point, even positive activities can drain your energy, so taking a break is a way to take care of yourself and ensure that you have the stamina to perform at your best level.

If you pay attention to your body, it will let you know that it's time to take a break. You may need a break if you are experiencing low energy, have trouble sleeping, or can't concentrate during the day. If this happens, you should start planning some downtime right away. Taking a break will help you restore your physical and mental health. If you feel sluggish, a break can restore your creativity and increase your productivity. A break can also be beneficial to your personal and business relationships.

While vacations away from everything can be very beneficial during these times, it may not be necessary to leave town. Just chilling around the house doing nothing; or relaxing with a glass of lemonade may be enough to do the trick. All you need to do is break from your normal activities long enough to disrupt the stress response cycle. You can do this by taking a bike ride or enjoying a movie. Regardless of how you get your downtime; do it; because everyone needs a break sometime since taking a break can leave you refreshed and restored. ∎

Today's Live Happy Practice

Listen to your body and determine if it's time to take a break. Plan your time off and anticipate the pleasure you will feel from the experience.

DAY 291

The Way You Speak to Yourself Matters

Take a minute to think about what is going on inside your head and reflect on what you said to yourself today. Was your self-talk negative or was it positive? Was it critical or was it helpful? Was it meaningless or was it insightful? Self-talk is something that we naturally do throughout the day. Your internal dialogue is influenced by your subconscious mind and it is clouded, either positive or negative, by your outlook on life.

In order to get an idea of how self-talk might influence your behavior, a study was done where researchers asked patients with anorexia to walk through a narrow doorway. In general, when an individual walks through an opening that is smaller than their frontal body dimensions, they will automatically rotate their body to the side to safety pass through the opening. In the study, the anorexic patients rotated their bodies in order to fit through the doorway even though the opening was large enough and they were perfectly capable of fitting through it just walking straight. Through self-talk, the anorexic patients told themselves, "I am fat and therefore; I will not fit through this opening." The researchers determined that negative self-talk influenced the anorexic participants in a way that made them unconsciously believe that they're bodies were larger than they actually were.

We can see from this study that the way you speak to yourself matters. One of the best things you can do to increase your positive self-talk is to surround yourself with positive people. Since you will naturally absorb the outlook of the people you associate with, be sure to surround yourself with people who are positive whenever you can. ■

Today's Live Happy Practice

The best way to improve your self-talk is to practice it daily. Pay attention to what you are saying to yourself and challenge any negative thoughts. Make a list of the positive things about yourself and practice thinking those good thoughts.

DAY 292

The "Be" Attitudes

In the bible, the beatitudes are sayings that were attributed to Jesus in his Sermon on the Mount as recounted in the Gospel of Matthew. They are sayings that begin with the phrase, "Blessed are…" and each saying speaks of a divine favor toward those who are less fortunate. For example, blessed are those who mourn, for they will be comforted; or blessed are the meek, for they will inherit the Earth.

Each of the beatitudes begin with the word beati, which means happy or blessed in Latin. The phrase itself, "Blessed are…" implies that the individual who possess the qualities espoused in the scripture will receive a divine blessing and perfect happiness. Therefore, Jesus is literally calling out a group of people who are normally thought to be unfortunate, and proclaiming that they are blessed. In practical terms, it means that Jesus is telling those who are underprivileged that they, in fact, can have their best life; the one that they were intended to have.

Although there is some debate as to exactly how many beatitudes there are, the prevailing thought is that they consist of eight proverb-like sayings. But they are not just cute sayings to be rattled off by bible toters; they are actually affirmations that should be used as markers for your life. So, over the next eight days you will embark on a journey of "Be" attitudes that are in the same vein as the beatitudes in the Sermon on the Mount. But these "Be" attitudes are not those sayings that Jesus espoused; instead, they are behaviors and mental attitudes that you should adopt in order to improve your life and gain greater happiness. In other words, if you can adopt the eight live happy practices espoused in these pages, you will be that much closer to enjoying extreme happiness and living the life that you were intended to live. ∎

Today's Live Happy Practice
Read the beatitudes in the Gospel of Matthew and affirm that you are blessed.

DAY 293

Be Awesome

The 1st "Be" attitude is a live happy practice encouraging you to be awesome! Robby Novak is awesome! But who is Robby Novak and why is he awesome? Robby is a young Black boy from Tennessee who loves to dance and give pep talks to the world.

He is known as Kid President and here is his first pep talk," People of the internet! Get off the internet! Get off your Facebook and listen to me! If it doesn't make the world better, don't do it!" He was eleven years old when he said that.

Here is his second pep talk, "This is life people. You got air coming through your nose; you got a heartbeat. That means it's time to do something."

These are profound insights from a young boy, but it's not the corndogs or the dancing that makes Kid President awesome; it's the fact that he was born with a bone condition sometimes referred to as "brittle bone disease," which makes his bones break easily. By the time he was eleven years old, he had endured more than 70 broken bones; yet, he goes around dancing and encouraging other people. He said that he does it because he really wants the world to be filled with awe. He never complains. He just keeps spreading joy and happiness to the world.

You can do it too. Why settle for good when you can be awesome? You can do what you want to do and be what you want to be. That means that you can live life without restrictions; refrain from complaining about its imperfections; and spread as much joy as possible. And that's awesome! ▪

Today's Live Happy Practice

Think of three things you can do to be awesome today by spreading more joy in the world.

DAY 294

Be Weird

The 2nd "Be" attitude is a live happy practice encouraging you to be weird! It's okay to be weird! Throughout history, some of the greatest people on Earth were weird. William Shakespeare and Albert Einstein were said to be weird. So was Michael Jackson and Prince. But what made these great people great was precisely their willingness to stand out in the crowd and be perceived as weird. Every great creative and scientific breakthrough was considered to be weird because the creator had to think like no one else thought in order to go beyond existing paradigms. The good news is that your weirdness might just be innovation. If you have a fresh perspective that challenges the status quo; it could be your super power. Therefore, if you are perceived to be a weird person, learn how to use the power of your uniqueness; it's what makes you special.

Kobe Bryant was one of the greatest players to ever play the game of basketball. His teammate, Shaquille O'Neal said that Kobe used to practice without a ball. Shaq said that Kobe would be cutting and grunting and dribbling and shooting with no ball. He said he thought that was weird, and then Kobe became one of the greatest players to ever suit up. There's a lesson in that. Live by your convictions and gain the freedom to be who you are and do what you want. Kobe wanted to be the greatest and didn't care how weird it looked getting there.

When you live your convictions and gain the freedom to do what you want, that's when your creative juices begin to flow. In actuality, it means believing in yourself, and that's one of the most powerful things you can do. ■

Today's Live Happy Practice

Being weird means that you are unusual in some way; which only means that you are unique. Take some time to think about the things that make you unique and reflect on the benefits of the things that make you different.

DAY 295

Be Curious

The 3rd "Be" attitude is a live happy practice encouraging you to be curious! There is an old African folktale about the benefits of being curious. In the story, the elephant never drinks water because he won't go to the river, and the hippo never eats grass because he won't go on land. One day a hare tied one end of a rope to the hippo and the other end to the elephant. He asked the elephant, "Do you think if I tied myself to you, you could pull me out of the river?" And he asked the hippo, "Do you think you can pull me in?" They both replied, "That would be easy. You're but a very small thing."

So the hare tied one end of the rope to the elephant and the other end to the hippo. When he was out of sight, the hare tugged both ends of the rope and hopped off. The hippo began to pull and so did the elephant. They each pulled for a long time and became curious. How could a tiny little hare be so strong? When their curiosity got the best of them, the hippo headed onto the land and the elephant headed to the river. When the hippo saw the elephant, he said, "Ah, it is you." They each had a good laugh and became lifelong friends. And that's how the hippo came on the land to eat grass and the elephant went to the river to drink water.

Just like the elephant and the hippo, curious people experience great benefits. Curious people are happier and they know more things because they ask questions. Here are four reasons curious people prosper better than those who are uninterested; first, curiosity makes your mind active instead of passive; second, it makes your mind observant of new ideas; third, it opens up new possibilities; and fourth, it brings excitement into your life, world, and affairs. So, if you want to increase the level of happiness in your life, be curious. ∎

Today's Live Happy Practice

Be open and look for new ways of doing things. Ask other people for their opinion and perspective on something you are trying to do.

DAY 296

Be Intentional

The 4th "Be" attitude is a live happy practice encouraging you to be intentional! Do you often feel stuck as if you're not making any forward motion toward your goals? Do you ever feel like you're going through life on a treadmill? Like you're constantly going in a forward motion but getting nowhere? If so, you may be stuck on autopilot and need to find ways to be intentional in your everyday life. Being intentional means that you take action and make decisions by choice. It means that you get clear upfront and determine what you want to achieve in advance. When you do this, you begin to live life on your own terms and create the life that you want to live; one with meaning and purpose.

After you figure out your goals and your dreams, then you can line up your actions in a way to accomplish those goals. Take a moment to decide what it is you want to do and how you want to do it. Write your goals down. Avoid getting trapped in social media and other things that might take you off the path to your objectives. That means you may have to learn to say "No" sometimes.

After you think about what you want to do, take the time to prioritize. Move the things that are most important to the top of your list and plan to do them at the beginning of the day. Prioritize the next important thing second, and so on. Nothing that you do is good or bad, per se. It's really all about your intentions. As long as you are prioritizing and doing the things that matter to you, you are well on your way to being intentional and living the life you want to live.

Today's Live Happy Practice

Spend 5 minutes being intentional about today. Decide upfront how you want to spend your time and think about the time traps you want to avoid. Develop a plan and make a commitment to only do those things that are most important to helping you reach your goals.

DAY 297

Be Excellent

The 5th "Be" attitude is a live happy practice encouraging you to be excellent! Comedian and filmmaker, Robert Townsend said, "If you don't do it with excellence, don't do it at all!" That makes sense because excellence just means doing your best at whatever you do. But how can you be excellent and what are the benefits of it?

Excellence is the quality of being outstanding or being extremely good at something. The benefits of doing excellent work are enormous. You get good feelings when you do something to the best of your abilities, and it increases your confidence and self-esteem. Success begins inside of you. It is a state of mind. When you adopt and attitude of excellence, you will begin to see yourself as the person you want to be.

One of the first things you should do if you want to be excellent is to do what you love. Think about what you are passionate about and pursue those things as your goal. Doing things you love will drive you to greatness. If you want to be excellent, you will need to develop a strategy to get from where you are to where to be. Be sure to spend the time developing your strategy. Part of your strategy should include working smarter, not harder. It means studying people who have already achieved success in the area you want to pursue. Study their success and learn from their mistakes. This can help you achieve your goals faster than you may have thought possible. And above all, if you want to be excellent, be willing to work hard and ask for feedback. It's always good to get another perspective on things, sort of like a second opinion. This can help you avoid the blind spots and get you where you want to be a lot faster. One of the hallmarks of excellence is recognizing that there is room for improvement; and being willing to go there. ∎

> ### Today's Live Happy Practice
> In order to be excellent at anything, follow these two tips:
>
> 1. Practice intensely.
> 2. Seek expert feedback.

DAY 298

Be an Iceberg

The 6th "Be" attitude is a live happy practice encouraging you to be an iceberg! Statistically speaking, about 90 percent of an iceberg is found under water, which means that the part that is visible is minor by comparison. Success is like that. What people see are the trophies and the star performances. What they don't see are the hours of loneliness and setbacks. They don't see the crises of confidence or the late nights and early mornings. A successful performance, no matter what field of endeavor, is usually a result of years of perseverance and commitment.

Take the life of a minister as an example. Many people only see the glory and success of the message preached from the platform, but they don't see all the costs that a successful minister has paid over time. What people see above the surface is the final result of the hard work and dedication; but they don't see what happens below the surface; the commitment and sacrifice, the sweat and the tears, or the failures and the disappointments that contribute to the final win they see on Sunday morning. In other words, they only see the tip of the iceberg.

All of these things happen below the surface where they are generally unseen. Many times it is easy for people to look at someone else and think that they have a good life. But the truth is that success is like that iceberg where spectators only see the top layer of final results. So if you really want to be successful and to make your dreams come true, be like an iceberg. Do the things that people don't see and success will naturally follow.

Today's Live Happy Practice

Think about your dreams and determine the "below the surface" costs of success. Are you willing to pay the cost? If your answer is "Yes," then get back to work. If your answer is "No," then get yourself a better dream.

DAY 299

Be an Encourager

The 7th "Be" attitude is a live happy practice encouraging you to be an encourager! The benefits of receiving encouragement have been well documented. It is true that encouragement will lift the other person's spirits by giving them confidence and hope, but the good news is that you also gain benefits from saying good things to people. Studies have shown that the very act of helping others boosts your happiness and sense of well-being. The bottom line is that doing good deeds like encouraging people actually make you feel good. There is some evidence that helping other people feel good triggers a physiological change in your brain that is linked with happiness. Researchers have found that helping others gives you a sense of purpose and satisfaction.

Everyone tends to be busy working on their own dreams and goals, but when you give someone else confidence and hope, it can do wonders for your outlook on life. Giving words of encouragement to others can make you feel rewarded and empowered. It can give you a sense of renewal. In addition, people who do good things for other people have been found to have greater self-esteem and overall wellbeing. So be an encourager because motivating someone else encourages you too. You will get an amazing feeling when you make a difference in someone else's life. Make a habit of saying good things to other people. The more you encourage others, the more confidence you will gain and the more happiness you will experience in your own life. ■

Today's Live Happy Practice

Seek to become a full-time encourager. You can do this by cultivating the habit of encouragement. As you move through your day today, look for things to encourage in everyone you meet.

DAY 300

Be a Good Listener

The 8th "Be" attitude is a live happy practice encouraging you to be a good listener! We've all heard the saying that humans have two ears and one mouth so that they can listen twice as much as they talk. We've all heard it but apparently some of us don't believe it. What I'm saying is that some people talk too much!

If that's you, don't worry, you're not alone. Science tells us that humans are programmed to talk; after all, it is how we communicate. Generally, talking is not a problem. The problem is that our favorite subject to talk about is ourselves so we tend to talk more than we should. This is unfortunate because, in a good conversation, each person should speak about half the time, which means that you are quiet the other half. People who know this understand that silence is a great source of power because when you are silent, you not only hear what is being said, but you hear what is not being said as well.

It doesn't mean that having the gift of gab is all bad, but it does mean that you should be careful not to cross the line from interesting conversationalist to compulsive talker. Compulsive talkers are rarely good listeners and generally tend to over-talk everyone else.

One of the things you can do to improve your conversation skills is to pay attention to non-verbal cues like facial expression or body language. Another thing you can do is to ask for the other person's perspective before you share your own. Being a good listener can pay dividends because people who listen are perceived positively and they are better liked. And as an added bonus, people who are good listeners are more likely to be promoted at work, and that's money in the bank! ∎

Today's Live Happy Practice

Try listening more than speaking in all of your conversations today.

DAY 301

Cleaning Up For the Cleaning Lady

The other day a cleaning lady come to clean my house and something occurred to me. I thought about the old cliché of someone cleaning up for the cleaning lady and considered how silly it sounded. Why should you clean up for the person who's coming to clean?

I thought about that for a while and after some careful consideration, realized that there is some merit to the notion of tidying up a bit before she arrives. For instance, before she arrives, you should put away any important documents and secure any valuables such as jewelry and small electronics. One thing you should keep in mind about a cleaning service though, is that they don't maintain your home forever; they just assist you in your efforts to get it into the shape you want.

Something similar happens when you get a coach. A coach is someone who helps you maximize your full potential and helps you reach your goals. They can help you with specific objectives and hold you accountable. They may also give you encouragement and help you grow by challenging limiting beliefs and helping you develop a plan of action that can enhance your chances of achieving the outcomes you want. But it would be a mistake to think that a coach is some sort of magic bullet for success. They can help and assist you on your journey, but you have to put in the work. Just like the cleaning lady, there's some things you must do to get the most out of a coach. First, do your homework up front and be prepared before every meeting with your coach; then, do the follow-up work afterward.

Today's Live Happy Practice

If you are thinking about getting a life coach, it's best to first have a good vision for your purpose in life. Think about what you do well and consider what skills and talents you possess. Then, brainstorm how you might turn your passion into something meaningful to you.

DAY 302

The Best Time to Plant a Tree Was 20 Yrs. Ago. The Second Best Time is Now.

An old Chinese proverb tells us that the best time to plant a tree was 20 years ago, but the second best time is now. In essence, it means that, when you want to do something, it is better to start early; however, it's never too late. If you have goals or dreams that you want to accomplish but you never acted on them, start now. Don't let time hold you back. Allowing age to hold you back is purely a limiting belief that has no place in your conscious. You should look at age for what it is; just a number. It is simply a measurement of time and should not be used as a barometer to restrict your life. Don't let it define you, and don't let it be a barrier to you going after your dreams.

Morgan Freeman received his first Oscar nomination when he was 50 years old; Ray Kroc started McDonald's when he was 52; Laura Ingalls Wilder published her first "Little House on the Prairie" book when she was 65; and Grandma Moses began painting when she was 78. These people represent good examples that it is never too late to start something new.

Let go of your limiting beliefs and outdated opinions about age. You are in control of your life so it's never too late to do what you want to do. You only live once so be sure to make the most of every opportunity because whatever you want to accomplish, it is always a good time to start now. ■

Today's Live Happy Practice

Think about the thing you wanted to do but now think it's too late. Decide why it's important to you and prioritize it in your life. If it is something you truly want, find a way to make it happen.

DAY 303

Create a Happy List

You might be surprised at the benefits of writing things down. Writing things down provides a psychological payoff to your brain and creates advantages for your health and wellbeing. Many people live a hectic life and can feel overwhelmed by the deluge of things they need to get done every day. When you write down the things you have to do, it allows you to clear your mind, which in turn, reduces a significant amount of stress. The psychological benefits of writing your goals and intentions can be significant because, when you write them down, they become real. They are no longer just ideas or thoughts in your head, but they become part of the physical world. Writing can also give you a sense of accomplishment and make you more efficient.

While writing things down can help you recall things when you need them; the purpose of writing is not simply to store facts to be retrieved later. Instead, the purpose is to document your thoughts so that they become concrete things that exist in the real world; that's why making a list of the things that make you happy is a great way to actually improve your happiness.

A happy list is not only a great resource to help you acknowledge that things that bring you joy; it can also be used as a reminder to help you find the good when things are not going your way. Make a list and display it somewhere you can see every day. Read it often and think about the things that you are grateful for that brings happiness to your life. ■

Today's Live Happy Practice

Write down the following things that make you happy:

- Things at home that make you happy
- Places to go that make you happy
- Food that makes you happy
- Music that makes you happy

DAY 304

Contact a Distant Relative

The family is one of the most important institutions in our society and is a critical component in shaping our social and mental wellbeing. Families are generally there to help each other grow and develop, and to assist in meeting the basic needs of other family members. Family connections can provide a sense of purpose and offer a safe environment in order to build and prosper into a functional and productive adult. The benefits of spending time with family cannot be overstated. Not only do close family connections reduce the occurrence of depression and mental illness, but it can create a strong emotional support system that can help get you through the challenges you may face in life.

But as families grow, they face many forces that can threaten to pull them apart. Family members grow and start their own families, and begin to lose touch with each other. One of the most common reasons families fall apart is distance. Another reason families grow apart is through disagreements that cannot be resolved, which could result in growing apart both physically and emotionally.

Disagreements are a normal part of any relationship but it does not have to mean an end to the family unit. The important thing is how you choose to handle the situation. Your actions can have a great impact on the healing process. Choosing to forgive your family member can have a powerful benefit on your family unit, both physically and emotionally. It can be helpful to ask yourself how important the disagreement is. Is it worth losing a family member? Think of ways to let go of the anger and negative feelings and move on because your family is worth it. ■

Today's Live Happy Practice

Contact a family member today that you haven't spoken with in a while. Enjoy the connection and catch up on old times.

DAY 305

Just Put on Some Active Wear and See What Happens

If you want to achieve great things in life, you need to motivate yourself to do the things you need to do to move toward your goals. But motivation is an elusive concept. Motivation is an important element to your success and just about every area of your life. Motivation is the process that guides your behavior. It is the thing that propels you to act and do the things that you do. When you get out of your chair to get a drink of water, you are motivated by thirst; and when you read a book you are motivated by the desire to gain knowledge or entertainment.

Motivation is the driving force behind all of your actions and it can be either extrinsic or intrinsic. Extrinsic motivation arises from outside and generally involves rewards such as money or social recognition. Intrinsic motivation is something that arises from within and is based on personal gratification or satisfaction.

So how do you get motivated to take action? Many people miss the mark because they are trying to figure out how to get motivated to do this or that. But the truth is that you can't get motivated to do something. On the contrary, motivation comes after you begin, not before. The motivational speaker Zig Ziglar used to say that "motivation follows doing," and he was right. Getting started on something is a form of inspiration that naturally produces momentum. Once an object is in motion, it tends to stay in motion; therefore, after you begin a task it is easier to continue moving forward. It means that the key to getting motivated is to start. So if you want to move forward, stop waiting for motivation to strike. If you want to start a class just register; if you want to read a book just turn to the first page; and if you want to start exercising just punt on some active wear and see what happens. ■

Today's Live Happy Practice

The best way to get motivated is to just start. So take the first step and put on your workout clothes; you'll be amazed at what happens next.

DAY 306

Doing Nothing Is a Great Way to Change Nothing

You remember Kid President. He's the young boy who has brittle bone disease and goes around spreading joy by dancing, eating corn dogs, and giving the world pep talks. One of his pep talks goes like this, "Doing nothing is a great way to change nothing." This kid is wise beyond his years.

Sometimes you may get overwhelmed and not know what to do to reach your goals, but one thing we know for sure, and that is that failure isn't fatal, but doing nothing is. You can't move forward if you do nothing. That's why it is critical to take action. This is true even if the action does not work out the way you would like. You will learn and grow when you try things. Even if the things you try don't go your way, you will be one step closer to achieving what you set out to do.

One of the best things you can do to reach your goals is to do something toward it every day; even if you spend just fifteen or twenty minutes. When you spend a few minutes every day, it can become a habit, and that's where your power lies. So just do something. Anything! Don't focus too much energy on what the results will be because that can create fear. Instead, focus on doing things and see where it takes you. It's okay if you're not particularly good at it, and it's okay if you do it badly. The key is to just do it. Free yourself to mess up and you will be liberated from your inaction. ∎

Today's Live Happy Practice

Spend fifteen minutes today working on your goal. Do something toward it now, no matter how small.

DAY 307

Opportunity Dances With Those Already on the Dance Floor

Have you ever been to a party and saw a fine woman or man that you wanted to dance with? You could sit on the sideline and try to figure out how to approach that person, but most of us will notice the people who are already on the dance floor have a far better chance of getting that coveted dance than those who are not.

That's how it is with opportunity. You are going to be in a much better position to take advantage of opportunities as they arise if you are already in the game. What does this mean? It means that you need to be prepared.

For years, the Boy Scout motto has been, "Be prepared." For the Scouts, it means that they should always be ready to perform when needed. One of the greatest benefits of being prepared is that you put yourself in a position to take advantage of opportunities when they arise. But there are other benefits too. For instance, being prepared instills confidence and it saves time.

There is nothing like a boost in confidence to help propel you forward in life. When you prepare for things in advance, your confidence goes through the roof. Your knowledge level also increases, which makes you more efficient in every situation. Being prepared also helps you save time by allowing you to be organized. Many people loose hours of productivity every day because they are unorganized and haven't planned in advance. Sometimes opportunity only knocks once; are you ready for it? ■

Today's Live Happy Practice
Take some time today to prepare for the thing that you want most in life.

DAY 308

The Joy of Winter

Some people seem to have developed an inability to tolerate winter. They complain about the icy winds, the snow on the sidewalks, or the frozen slush that impairs driving conditions. The fact of the matter is that winter makes up one quarter of every year, and thus, one quarter of your entire life. When you think about it that way, it makes sense to reclaim the joy of winter. After all, why should you be miserable and complain about a fourth of your life.

Wearing the proper clothing is essential, however; it is the mental space that may present a challenge for most people, but it doesn't have to be that way. Just take a look around you and take in the actual beauty of the season. Welcome it and embrace it. Notice the calm spirit of winter and contrast that with the frantic energy of summer. Appreciate the beauty of the fresh snowfall and the transformation of the picturesque landscape.

The joy of winter is about living in the moment. It's about relishing the small miracles that go unnoticed all year long. Take the time to slow down and use this opportunity to turn inward and reflect on how good life is. Even in the midst of the ice and snow, don't neglect to indulge in the warmth of the sun on your face on those bitter cold days. And don't forget to let the child in you come out through the many winter activities like making snowmen, roasting marshmallows, or skiing. Find new ways of experiencing the joy of winter and reclaim that quarter of your life that you may have long forgotten as you transitioned into adulthood. ∎

Today's Live Happy Practice

Try one of these live happy practices to get more enjoyment out of the cold winter days:

1. Cook up some warm, comforting recipes like soup, chili, or gumbo.
2. Treat yourself to a few little luxuries like a movie under a warm blanket and a cup of hot chocolate.

DAY 309

The Greatest Show on Earth

For years the circus has been known as the greatest show on Earth, and one of the greatest is the UniverSoul Circus. Whenever I visit the circus, I am amazed at the skill of the performers. They always seem to be super humans who are able to defy gravity and pay no attention to the laws of physics. One of the most thrilling things about the circus is the fun and enjoyment you get from the outing. But there are more benefits to be gained from the circus than just fun and games; it can actually make your life better. Here are three ways the circus makes life better:

- It can be an outlet to help you relieve stress. It is important to have an outlet for your emotions and worries. The pure joy of observing the physical activities and participating in the show allows us to escape and release emotions that have been pinned up inside.
- It is inspiring. Most people are inspired by others, and there's no place better to get inspired than the circus. Watching the magical moments can push you to be what you want to be and do what you want to do. When you watch a circus, you recognize that anything is possible.
- It helps us learn the value of teamwork. One of the most fantastic things we learn from the circus is the value of teamwork. Although each member has their own role to play and their own unique set of skills, the circus is ultimately a team effort. All of the talents work together to complement each other. ∎

> ### Today's Live Happy Practice
> Take some time to attend the circus and enjoy the many benefits of it. You will be happy you did.

DAY 310

Unfollow People Who Make You Feel Bad

When you follow someone on social media, you will be able to see their posts and keep up with them on a regular basis. But sometimes it makes sense to unfollow people, especially if they are someone who leaves you feeling worse after you've interacted with them. Unfollowing is an important concept and you should apply this same philosophy to your life outside of social media. It means that sometimes, you have to cut people loose from your life. The people you surround yourself with should inspire you to feel more engaged and leave you feeling positive about yourself and your goals; if not, then it may be time to let them go.

People who make you feel bad are often referred to as toxic. When you have someone like this in your life, it can be a futile effort to try the change them. Not only is trying to change someone a waste of time, it can also be a drain on your emotional energy. So the best thing that you can do is remove yourself from the situation and try to avoid the interaction in the first place. Sometimes toxic people can make you feel as if you did something wrong. If this is the case, remind yourself that their behavior has nothing to do with you.

If you are dealing with someone who makes you feel bad or tries to manipulate you, you should make yourself unavailable. If you scale back the amount of time you spend with toxic people, eventually they will move on. The bottom line is that you do not have to put up with abusive behavior in your life; and you shouldn't.

Today's Live Happy Practice

If you are dealing with a toxic person in your life, slowly fade them out by reducing your meetings, calls, and text with them.

DAY 311

Attack Your Goals Like a General

General George Patton had his flaws just like any other man. According to historians, Patton was arrogant, publicity-seeking, and personally flawed, but when it comes to developing a goal and going after it, he was one of the best. He created a colorful image of himself, and developed the philosophy of leading from the front to inspire his troops. In order to further cultivate his flashy and flamboyant image, he carried an ivory-gripped, silver-plated Colt Single Action Army .45 caliber revolver on his right hip, and an ivory-gripped Smith & Wesson .357 Magnum on his left. He was known for riding atop a brightly painted tank to oversee training maneuvers, and expressed a deep desire for glory on the battlefield. All of this translated to an offensive spirit along with an aggressive determination to attack and destroy the enemy in order to gain victory in battle.

Just like General Patton cultivated an aggressive determination on the battlefield, it is important for you to be aggressive in the area of goal setting for your life. Aggressive goals force you to make a plan and they make you think about what you might do to reach them. When you set aggressive goals and attack them, they propel you forward and fuel your drive to succeed. Aggressive goals should be slightly hard to reach, yet obtainable in order to motivate you to do your best. Be sure to make your goal aggressive enough that you have to stretch to reach it; at the same time, don't make it so hard that it becomes impossible. You should also create a multi-faceted approach to your goals; meaning that you set both short-term and long-term goals for yourself. That way, you can keep your forward momentum by reaching your short-term goals, which will give you the energy to keep pushing toward your long-term ones. ▋

Today's Live Happy Practice

Review your current goals and make sure they are aggressive enough to stretch you. Be sure to break them down into long and short-term.

DAY 312

When You Focus on the Good, the Good Gets Better

It is true that when you focus on good things, you attract more good things. The power of positive thinking has been used so much that it can sometimes feel like a cliché; however, the benefits of thinking positive cannot be overstated. There are many benefits for the positive thinker. Positive thinkers will enjoy a better mood and a happier life. They will also experience less physical challenges such as hypertension and depression. If you want to experience the benefits of positive thinking, you must focus on the good; and when you do that, the good gets better.

One of the things you must do in order to focus on the good is to transform your negative self-talk into positive self-talk. Sometimes it's hard to notice negative self-talk but you can do it if you pay attention. Whenever you catch yourself doing it, just stop and replace those negative thoughts with positive ones. When you focus on the positive side of things, your relationships will flourish. Your emotions will remain in check and you will be less prone to emotional ups and downs. Another benefit of focusing on the positive is that you will spark your creativity. When your creative juices begin to flow, you will suddenly discover powers that you never dreamed possible. That means that you can turn your failures into lessons.

When you focus on positive things, you attract positive things into your life. The universe dictates that whatever you imaging and hold in your mind's eye can be yours if you make a plan and take action on it; and that's good news. ■

Today's Live Happy Practice

Think about a goal that you have made for yourself. Focus on that goal and think about all of the positive aspects associated with it. Now think about all of the positive benefits that will come your way when that goal has been accomplished.

DAY 313

Back in the Day R&B

Have you ever noticed how listening to music takes you back to a time in your past? Do you sometimes hear a particular song and all of a sudden begin to reminisce about the good old days when you were in school; or got married; or went on a road trip somewhere?

The reason music takes you back to those special times is because the music encodes the experiences in your brain and turns them into lasting memories. When this happens, the song and the event get bound together in your brain so that when you hear the music later on, it triggers the good emotions and the sound helps to bring it to the front of your mind.

Not only do you get good feelings when you listen to music, but there are other benefits of listening to musical recordings as well. Research has found that people who listen to familiar music improves your mood and relieves feelings of depression. These benefits can be experienced by intently focusing on the music or just playing it in the background. Most of the time when you hear those good ole back-in-the-day songs; you can't help but sing along. But you might also dance or move to the music as well, which can provided added physical benefits as well. If you decide to listen to new music that you haven't heard before, you can benefit from that too. Even unfamiliar music can stimulate your brain. But if you really want to reminiscence, try listening to some music that was released when you were younger. It'll put a smile on your face! ■

Today's Live Happy Practice

Relax and listen to some music from your childhood or young adult years and enjoy the experience.

DAY 314

Live Your Dreams According to You

Never allow yourself to be defined by someone else's opinion of you. Be brave enough to live the life of your dreams according to your vision, not the expectations and opinions of others. Your dreams are precious, and above all, they are yours. You may only get one shot at your dreams so it is important to maximize your efforts and give it all you've got.

Think in terms of possibilities, not limitations. Although other people may believe that you have an impossible dream; that is their baggage, not yours. Life is limitless so don't put restraints on yourself.

If you want to make something happen, go for it. Don't make excuses for what is possible. There may be gaps that you need to fill, but don't think that you need to have all the answers up front. Be sure to leverage the skills and knowledge of those around you. Use your resources. The universe doesn't reward those who don't act; it rewards people who move on their instincts and chase their dreams in the face of uncertainty.

The best thing you can do is focus on the things you can control. Don't spend a moment worrying about the things you can do nothing about and don't waste your time and energy on goals that are unrealistic. Wishing things were different gets you nowhere, so stay focused on what matters and your diligence will pay off big! ■

Today's Live Happy Practice

Spend some time today thinking about your dreams. Are they realistic? Do you need to enlist the help of other people in your circles? If so, move on it!

DAY 315

Embrace Your Mistakes

Mistakes are an inevitable part of life. They happen and that's okay, but you cannot move forward in the pursuit of happiness unless you let go of your mistakes and forgive yourself. When you hold on to the past and don't forgive yourself, you keep relieving the thing that is preventing your happiness in the first place. Another problem with not letting go of mistakes is that it affects your decisions. You feel paralyzed by your past.

You must make a conscious decision that you want to let it go in order for you to move forward. Look at it objectively and acknowledge the mistake. Focus on what you've learned instead of the mistake. When you think of it as a learning experience, it helps you move forward.

Forgiveness means letting go but sometimes letting go can feel like you're giving up a part of yourself. The best way to forgive yourself is to recognize that you have done your best. Society might try to tell you that anything that is not perfect is bad and deserves to be punished. As a result, you may want to beat yourself up when something doesn't go the way you planned. You may even try to cover up your mistakes and hide them. However, it is best to admit that you made a mistake and take ownership of it. That is the best way to learn from your past experiences.

Think of it this way: if you never make a mistake, you're probably not doing enough. So try to view every experience as a learning opportunity and move forward as quickly as you can. ■

Today's Live Happy Practice

Think of a mistake that you made and can't seem to get past. Do you keep reliving it over and over in your mind? If so, write it on a piece of paper, find the lesson in it, and burn it. Then apply that lesson to your life and move on.

DAY 316

The "I'll Be Happy When" Syndrome

Have you ever uttered the statement, "I'll be happy when…?" Will you be happy when you find love, get a better car, live in a bigger house, or get that dream job? It turns out that thinking you'll be happy when something specific happens is a sure way to live an unfulfilled life.

One of the biggest myths surrounding happiness is that money and other material things will make you happy. But *things* will never make you happy because there is always more things to be had; therefore "when" will never come. Researchers conducted a study to measure the level of happiness in two groups of people. The first group were recent lottery winners and the second group were recently paralyzed from the waist down.

As you might expect, immediately after the life changing event, the lottery winners were ecstatic, whole the paraplegics were devastated. But when researchers followed up a year later, they found that the happiness level of both groups had returned to where it had been before the event. This is referred to as your happiness set-point. It's the point where your happiness lives. Temporary fluctuations may occur to move your happiness level up or down momentarily, but then you become accustomed to the life changes, your happiness level will adjust accordingly.

It means that the best way to improve your happiness level over the long-term is to be grateful for the things you have, not the things you want. █

Today's Live Happy Practice

It's okay to think about the things you want but don't let your happiness depend on them. Take some time today to reflect on the things you have now and be grateful for them.

DAY 317

Habit Stacking

If you've ever had a bad habit that you wanted to break, you know how difficult it can be to stop. But did you know that it can be just as hard to start a productive one? As it turns out, every habit starts with something called a habit loop. There are three parts to habit loops. First, there's the cue; which is the trigger that tells your brain to act. Second, there's the routine; which is the behavior itself. And third, there's the reward; which is something your brain likes that helps it remember the habit in the future.

One of the most powerful tools you can use to help your brain create good habits is something called habit stacking. Habit stacking works like a chain that links events together to associate a new habit with an old habit that already exists. It allows your brain to create new habits by taking advantage of old ones. For example, you already have strong habits associated with your morning routine. When you get up in the morning, you don't have to remember to brush your teeth, take a shower, comb your hair, and make a cup of coffee.

So if you want to create a habit of praying every morning, you can pair praying with your current habit of making coffee by telling yourself, "After I make my coffee, I'll pray for two minutes." This can work in almost any area of your life. If you want to develop a habit of working out every day, you might stack the habit of taking off your work clothes with putting on your workout clothes. This type of behavior creates a simple set of rules for your brain to follow. It's a way to create a habit loop because the existing behavior acts as a cue tells your brain what to do next. ∎

Today's Live Happy Practice

Think about a good habit that you want to create. Now think about other habits that you do automatically. Stack the habits together and practice it for the next couple of weeks and see what happens.

DAY 318

Stand for What You Believe In Even You Stand Alone

Standing up for what you believe in doesn't always come easy. Colin Kaepernick was a star quarterback in the National Football League when he decided to take a stand against police shootings of unarmed Black men in America. Even though it was unpopular, and ultimately caused Kaepernick to be blackballed, he had decided that enough was enough. Instead of standing up during the Star-Spangled Banner at the beginning of every football game, Kaepernick decided to take a knee instead.

Standing up for what you believe in can make the world a better place. Standing up can also increase your self-worth and bring you the happiness that you deserve. Being a voice for the oppressed can bring people together and make a real difference in your community. However, standing up is not always easy and it takes certain qualities to fight for what you believe in. you must have empathy, courage, and humility.

Having a strong foundation in your personal values is key. It's not easy to speak up, so you will need strong convictions not to be swayed when you take an unpopular position. Holding on to your principles may not be popular but making a difference in the world counts. Keep yourself informed and educate yourself on the issues that matter to you. The more informed you are, the more confident you will have when you put yourself on the line. Be sure not to be disrespectful or hostile.

It takes serious dedication and commitment to stand up and do what's right, but the world may be counting on you to do it. ∎

Today's Live Happy Practice

Have you seen an injustice that just rubs you the wrong way? Give some thought as to how you can take a stand the next time it happens.

DAY 319

Do More Things that Make You Forget to Check Your Phone

Americans check their phones 96 times a day! It means that people look at their phones about every ten minutes throughout the day. This is an interesting phenomenon when you consider that 9 out of 10 Americans say they get offended when someone they're speaking with starts looking at their phone.

Eighty percent of people check their phones within the first 10 minutes of waking up in the morning, and 83% panic when they can't find their phone. Some people even text a person in the same room instead of talking with them. And to make matters worse, nearly 20% of parents spend more time on their phone than with their children. Ironically, studies have shown that those who constantly check their phones find technology a significant source of stress.

But what can you do about it?

One simple way to curtail your cell phone addiction is to make a commitment to limit its use during dinner. In addition to dinner time, you might also try going offline at various times of day, like one hour before bedtime; or an hour or two in the evening to watch a movie with your spouse or children. Another thing you can do is to start the practice of leaving the phone in another room. That way, it minimizes the chance that you will check social media. Leaving your phone in another room also helps you avoid the constant reminder that someone is trying to get your attention. ∎

Today's Live Happy Practice

Break your phone addiction by trying some activities that take you away from your phone like taking a swim, looking at old family photos, reading a book, or playing a board game.

DAY 320

The Benefits of Smiling

Have you ever noticed that you feel better when you smile? That should come as no surprise because smiling comes with some real health benefits. When you smile, your brain releases tiny molecules known as neuropeptides, which help your body fight off stress. Even a fake smile can boost your mood and increase happiness.

The good news is that smiling not only benefits you, but it also affects those around you. Smiling creates an infectious loop of happiness because people can't help but to smile when they see someone else smile.

While there are real benefits of smiling in your personal life, smiling can also improve your performance on your job as well. That's because positive emotions tend to invigorate humans; which leads to positive effects on productivity. Smiling makes you happier, and when you are happy, your brain releases dopamine, which in turn, makes you more creative and efficient.

Smiling also makes you more approachable. When you smile or laugh, people are automatically attracted to you. This actually helps you develop and cultivate positive relationships. A warm smile is the universal language of kindness. When two people share a laugh or smile, it helps to establish social bonds and communicates that they are sharing something together. So, the next time you're feeling down, find something to smile about! ■

Today's Live Happy Practice

Think of something that makes you smile right now. Then take look around. Smile at someone else and see if they smiles back.

DAY 321

How to Make Better Decisions

Three inmates who had served two-thirds of their prison sentence appeared before a parole board that would ultimately decide their freedom. The first man appeared early in the morning around 8am. The second man appeared in late afternoon around 3pm, and the third man appeared after 4pm. Only one of the men were granted his freedom. Can you guess which one? Only the man who appeared early in the morning was set free. The decision was predictable but it had nothing to do with their ethnic background or the crime they had committed. Researchers found a pattern in the parole board's decisions. It was all about timing. They reviewed over 1,000 cases and found that prisoners who appeared early in the morning received parole about 70 percent of the time, while those who appeared late in the day were paroled less than 10 percent.

It was due to something called decision fatigue which refers to the deteriorating quality of decisions made by an individual after long sessions of decision making. In other words, the more decisions an individual makes, the worse their decisions become. Decision fatigue can cause a quarterback to make bad decisions late in the game, or cause executives to make poor choices after long bouts of decision making. It also explains why you make impulse purchases after a long day of shopping, or why you buy useless features after long hours of haggling over a new car purchase.

This happens because your mental energy runs low after long hours of decision making, and when that happens, you are less able to override basic desires and more likely to go with whatever is easiest. Simply recognizing that this happens can help you make better decisions. ∎

Today's Live Happy Practice

In order to fight decision fatigue and improve your decision making, try these two things; first, make a list of your priorities, and second, make your most difficult decisions early in the day.

DAY 322

How to Talk to Anyone

If you have ever been at a party or networking event and ran into an awkward silence, then you know how difficult it can sometimes be to generate conversation with people you don't know. But if you want to be comfortable in social situations, it is imperative that you know how to keep a conversation going.

Good conversations provide value on both a personal and professional level. In fact, great conversations may be more important than you think because the more you talk with someone, the more you bond with them. Conversations are the life-blood of any relationship, whither it's personal or business. One of the hallmarks of a good conversationalist is to ask open-ended questions. Open-ended questions require the other person to elaborate on their response. They also show that you value the other person's opinion.

One way to ensure that you have a good conversation is to use the IFR method. IFR stands for inquire, follow-up, and relate. Inquiring means that you ask a sincere question and then wait for a response. Following up means that you actually listen to the other person and then ask another question to get more information about what they just said. Finally, relating means that you share something about yourself. Having good conversations help you find common ground and engage the other person. This is beneficial even when you have different perspectives on life. ▮

Today's Live Happy Practice

Try using the "timeline" method in your next conversation. Think about the past, present, and future. Start the conversation in the present by discussing the event that brought you together. Then talk about what the person has done in the past, and their plans for the future.

DAY 323

The Benefits of Complimenting Others

One of the primary psychological needs of humans relates to their esteem and feeling of accomplishment. Esteem plays an important role in both you physical and emotional well-being. Thinking positive about yourself and being confident about abilities can help you identify your goals and move you closer to the fulfillment of your life's purpose. That's why compliments are such an important factor in your mental well-being. But you don't just benefit when you receive compliments, you benefit when you give them as well.

A well-placed compliment can make the other person feel valued and appreciated. Research has found that receiving a compliment actually stimulates the same part of the brain that is activated by receiving a monetary reward. Therein lies one of the first benefits of generously giving compliments. When you give a compliment a compliment, the other person is ingratiated to you the same as if you had just given them some money. This is an amazing way to win friends and influence people.

Giving compliments also helps you notice and appreciate what's good in the things and people around you. It also gives you a more optimistic look on life. Pay attention and be specific. Say something good about the other person's behavior or appearance. Tell them how smart or kind they are. You might also compliment their hair or their shoes. When it comes to giving compliments, make it rain! Shower them with compliments every day. You will be amazed at how well people will embrace you and want to interact with you. And as an added bonus, your relationship IQ will shoot through the roof!

Today's Live Happy Practice

If you want to practice giving good compliments, the first thing you must do is be sincere. Not all compliments land the same and most people can sniff out an insincere compliment. Practice the art of giving sincere compliments all day today.

DAY 324

The Art of Storytelling

Great storytellers come in all shapes and sizes. A great storyteller can captivate and inspire people for years to come. The storyteller's art can make the past seem mysterious and the future accessible. Images that were once incongruent may be juxtaposed in a link that renders them comparable. A great storyteller can spend a yarn in such a way as to compel the reader to imaging the story, compelling them to enjoy the illusion that they are actually witnessing the characters and events described in the story.

This is the effect on the brain when you read a vivid book written by a good storyteller. But reading and enjoying a book is not just a matter of pleasure; it is much more. There are benefits beyond enjoyment that offers benefits to both your physical and mental health. Therefore, if you want to improve your life you should read every day.

Reading literally strengthens your brain. Your brain is like a muscle that is being exercised every time you read. It contains a complex set of networks and circuits that grow stronger and more sophisticated when you read. Reading builds your vocabulary and it helps to slow age-related cognitive decline. Reading also reduces stress by lowering your blood pressure and heart rate. In fact, reading just thirty minutes is just as effective on reducing stress as yoga or humor. So be the best you can be by enjoying the art of storytelling through the magic of books. █

Today's Live Happy Practice

Enjoy the benefits of reading today. Pick up a good book, curl up under a warm blanket, grab a cup of hot cocoa, and let your brain be whisked away to your next awesome and magnificent adventure.

DAY 325

Keep Moving With the Cheese

Not too many things in life are predictable, but although it might sound like an oxymoron, change is one of the few things that is constant. Change is an interesting phenomena because it keeps happening despite the fact that it is generally the last thing most people want to happen. But why do we resist change so much? It may be because it is disruptive. It represents a loss of control, and the greater the change, the more we feel like something out of our control is being done to us. One of the best ways to deal with change is to embrace it. Embracing it means that you don't see it as adversity; instead, you think of it as an opportunity to improve yourself or to try new things.

In the book, *Who Moved My Cheese?*, four characters lived in a maze and loved cheese. The cheese is a metaphor for whatever you want in life, whether it be a job of a good relationship. One day in the story, the cheese was gone. Two of the characters wasted their energy complaining, while the other characters accepted that things had changed and went out to look for more cheese.

This is a good lesson for us to learn when we are faced with changing circumstances. We must stay positive and quickly adapt to the change. When we are flexible, we can adapt and move forward; however, when we resist, it leaves us paralyzed and with a negative attitude. When you think about it, you will recognize that change is inevitable and that no one can stay the same forever. So if you really want to be successful, be like the mice and change with the cheese.

> ### Today's Live Happy Practice
>
> If you have experienced an unexpected change in life, take some time to think about what happened. Then make a list of the things you can do to continue moving toward your goal.

DAY 326

The Benefits of Sharing Knowledge

Most companies want their employees to share knowledge because it leads to greater motivation and better performance. Ironically, many employees think just the opposite and refuse to share information. Often times they engage in something known as knowledge hoarding where they pretend that they don't know something; or they promise to share information and just never do it.

But why would a colleague be reluctant to share knowledge with their coworker? One of the most obvious reasons that employees hoard information is lack of trust. If they don't trust the company, they may believe that sharing what they know is the quickest way to put themselves out of a job. They also may hoard information because they are afraid of making a mistake. This often happens when the company's culture is punitive in nature.

Knowledge is a valuable resource and actively sharing it saves time and money for the organization. But employees can benefit from knowledge sharing as well. When you share information with others, it can strengthen professional ties and foster a reciprocal relationship where colleagues are eager to share with you in return. In addition, sharing what you know actually helps you understand and internalize your own knowledge. When you share, you look good and you feel good. So if you want to improve your chances of advancement, share your knowledge. ■

Today's Live Happy Practice

When information stays inside a person's head, it minimizes the impact; but whey it is shared and passed along to others, the information turns into an asset that everyone can draw from. Practice sharing your knowledge and see what happens.

DAY 327

The Power of Thank You

I'm reminded of the guy who sat in the bookstore for hours but didn't buy anything. He just sat there reading, but he never bought. He felt a little guilty for not buying and was a bit sheepish when he finally walked toward the exit. He was shocked and pleasantly surprised when one of our volunteers said, "Thank you."

At first he couldn't understand why she had thanked him, but after pondering on the subject, it hit him that she was thanking him for at least visiting the bookstore. Her attitude of gratitude influenced him to return the next day. Not only did he come back, but he brought a friend and they bought some books.

His story is a reminder that we should not reserve "thank you" for big events or special occasions. Saying "thank you" is a very simple way of expressing gratitude. It brings an abundance of happiness into your life because it helps you realize the good things around you. Just like the guy in the bookstore, when you say "thank you" to other people, they will feel more motivated and encouraged to do good things in the future. When you are grateful, you are more inclined to have a positive attitude and believe that things will work out in your favor; and the more grateful you are, the more successful you will be. ■

Today's Live Happy Practice

If you feel challenged to think of things to say "thank you" for, just think about all of the people who have supported you over the past year. Think about the good things you've received from your parents, spouse, or children. Look around and recognize the countless things to be grateful for and take the time to say "thank you".

DAY 328

Remember the Person

If you want to be successful, it is important to dress the part. One famous fashion mogul said that when a person dresses shabbily, people remember the dress; but when a person dresses impeccably, people remember the person. One of the benefits of dressing better is that you feel better both mentally and physically. You also have more confidence when you look good in your clothes. As an added benefit, people who are well-dressed are perceived as leaders. But it would be a mistake to think that being well-dressed is all about the clothes you wear; it's about your demeanor as well. How you carry yourself makes a difference. In fact, your behavior attracts more crowds than your looks. People will be attracted to you; and success will come your way because of your inner goodness and the pleasant behavior that you show toward others.

One of the things you can do to be good to other people is to stand with them and help them build a future instead of judging them by their past. Everyone has a past; but treating them with respect is a sign of support that signals you want the best for them. It is also important to act with integrity. Acting with integrity means that people will trust you because you tell the truth. It also means that you don't publicize negativity. Take a note from what your parents taught you, if you don't have anything good to say, don't say anything. Or better yet, take a page out of Kid President's book and remember that if you can't think of anything good to say, it means that you're not thinking hard enough. ∎

Today's Live Happy Practice

Take a look at what you put on and be sure to look your best every time you go out. But remember that your attitude is part of your dress. And never forget that your behavior is the quality that puts you in a good light regardless of your financial status or position in the community.

DAY 329

The Benefits of Listening Better

If you want to respect and understand other people better, you can do it by improving your listening skills. Most people think that listening is easy and does not require any effort. But the truth of the matter is that there is an art to listening well. There are many benefits of being a good listener; including increased likability, better relationships, and greater clarity.

Be sure to notice the things that are not said. Good listeners notice all kinds of behavior, like the other person's facial expressions, voice, and body language. If the person's face is tense, it could be a sign that they are uncomfortable about something you said. This could be a signal for you to back off the conversation and move in another direction. If the person suddenly crosses their arms, it could indicate that they are defensive or that they disagree with what you are saying.

If you want to be a good listener, don't just blurt things out. Instead, make a conscious decision whether to add input. Sometimes you may decide to just listen and other times it might be appropriate to ask follow-up questions. If you need a moment to think; take it. Don't be too eager to respond. It is also a good thing to know when it's wise to interrupt. Interrupting is usually thought of as rude behavior because it can make the other person feel that you are uninterested in what they are saying.

The bottom line is that your body language can add energy to the conversation. When you listen intently and express curiosity about what the other person is saying, you will experience the many benefits of being a good listener. ■

Today's Live Happy Practice

When you listen, try to avoid thinking about what you want to say when the other person is speaking. Thinking ahead often results in missing the other person's point and making inaccurate predictions about what they are about to say.

DAY 330

Slow Down for Success

It may sound counter intuitive, but sometimes slowing down can actually help you succeed faster. We live in a microwave society where everything must be done quickly. That is not to say that the microwave oven should be discarded and relegated to the recycle bin. When it comes to reheating food, the microwave is almost always superior. In addition, the microwave also reigns supreme when you're dealing with small dishes instead of large meals. So, while moving at the speed of the microwave may be good in some instances; slowing things down may be better when it comes to you physical and mental well-being.

The reason why slowing down can actually help accelerate your success and create the life you want is because slowing down helps you gain greater clarity. Moving fast doesn't get you where you want to be if you're moving in the wrong direction. When you slow down, you give yourself time to reflect and think clearly. Slowing down gives your mind the break it needs to absorb the deluge of information you get on a daily basis. This can help lower your mental stress and help you make better decisions. If you are always on overdrive, it makes it easier for your body to fatigue, increasing your chances of burnout.

As contradictory as it may seem, slowing down can actually help you work faster and more efficiently. By doing so, you will increase your chances of sustainability; thus bringing you one more step closer to achieving your goals. ■

Today's Live Happy Practice

Slow down and take a few minutes of quiet time each morning to reflect on the things you want to accomplish during the day. This will give you time to think about what isn't working and gives you the insight to refocus your energy in the right direction.

DAY 331

The Art of Doing One Thing at a Time

In the world that we live in, we seem to have too much to do and not enough time to do it. This could be a result of our infatuation with multitasking. However, multitasking could prove to be a bad strategy since studies show that it is less productive than doing one thing at a time. If you are a person who frequently engages in multitasking, you might consider rethinking that habit. You will get more done when you focus on one thing at a time because you will be able to concentrate better and pay closer attention to the details.

When you really think about it, what we call multitasking is actually task-switching. Since your brain has a limited capacity to focus on multiple things, whenever you multitask, your brain is really switching back and forth from one task to the other. This behavior slows down your productivity because you never really get into the zone of either task since you keep switching from one to the other. Therefore, it will take you longer to finish when you work on multiple projects simultaneously than if you had worked on each one separately.

Something as routine as driving can suffer when you multitask. One study found that drivers took longer to reach their destination when they chatted on the cellphone while they were driving. This means that multitasking is not all it's cracked up to be. It is best to stick with one thing once you get in the right mindset. When you get in a zone, that's when the magic happens and you are more likely to finish and get it done. ■

> ### Today's Live Happy Practice
> One of the best ways to improve your efficiency is to do things in batches. For example, try sending all of your emails at one time or paying all your bills on the same day for more efficiency.

DAY 332

The Benefits of Being Generous

Like most of you, my closet is always overflowing with things. When I say things are in my closet, I don't mean skeletons. I mean good things like suits and ties. And if I'm honest, I have more shirts and shoes that I really need, which brings me to the point. When it comes to things in our closets, most of you have more clothes than you know what to do with; and that's okay because God has blessed you with prosperity and abundance. I mention this because there's a lesson in your closet. The lesson is that your closet has a limited capacity to hold things; which means that if you want to put new things in, you have to take some of the old things out.

Life is much like that closet; you have to give if you want to receive. Whether you give money or time, acts of generosity are essential to a happy and fulfilled life. That's because one of the biggest benefactors of generosity is the one who is dishing it out. People who engage in high levels of generosity reap all kinds of rewards.

Generosity is a key ingredient in satisfaction with life. It turns out that people who give are twice as likely to be more satisfied with life than non-givers. Generous people tend to receive a boost in their social lives as well. Other people are generally more willing to do things for people who are generous, such as visiting them at the hospital or helping them move. Generous people benefit on an emotional level too. They tend to be more satisfied with what they have and are less likely to feel that having more will make them happy. So if you want to dramatically improve your life, give.

∎

Today's Live Happy Practice

Be generous with your time and money. Freely give love and compliments. It won't cost you a lot, but the benefits can be enormous.

DAY 333

The Importance of Doing Nothing

It's hard to do nothing! Most of the time our lives are so busy that when we do nothing, we are constantly fearful that we should be doing something. We have been conditioned to associate inactivity with laziness or failure.

One study took 700 people and asked them to sit in a room for up to 15 minutes and do nothing. Each participant was given access to a button that they could press if they wanted out before 15 minutes had passed. If they pressed the button, however, it would administer an electric shock. Almost 70 percent of men in the study chose to shock themselves rather than sit quietly in the room doing nothing.

This is a troubling trend because doing nothing is essential to maintaining a happy and balanced life. When you do nothing, you are actually rejuvenating your brain. When you are in this state; your brain is working to complete many unconscious tasks, including consolidating memories and reinforcing learning. As an added benefit, creativity thrives in stillness. When you step away from everything, your mind can wander and create innovative and unique ideas that were not possible when you're constantly focusing your attention on other specific tasks.

I want to encourage you not to feel obligated to do something in every minute of every day. And by doing nothing I don't mean sitting on the couch checking social media or talking on the phone. What I mean is turning everything off and doing absolutely nothing.

∎

Today's Live Happy Practice

Create a daily ritual of doing nothing. Try sitting on your porch and bask in the sun. Watch the squirrels play. If it's cold, curl up with a warm blanket and look out the window at the falling snow. Start a habit of spending 30 minutes every day doing nothing.

DAY 334

A Man of Refreshing Candor

Everyone says that they prefer candor, but most people tend to be defensive when they get it. We say we want people to be open and honest because that's the best way for us to improve. Really good ideas go unexplored when people are reluctant to speak their minds. But if you do decide to be frank in your communications, it doesn't mean that it's open season on disrespect. The best way to give candid feedback is to be positive. Stick with the facts and focus on the good of the other person. You should also assume the best intentions of the individual and refrain from scapegoating. But just as it is important to be able to give meaningful feedback with candor, it is equally important to be able to accept it. Critical feedback may be important to your growth but it is not always an easy pill to swallow. Here are a few tips that can help when you are on the receiving end of some tough love.

- Listen carefully. Be sure to listen carefully to what is being said. Resist the urge to interrupt and defend yourself.
- Ask follow-up questions. The best way to accept what is being said is to be clear about how the information can help you improve. Asking follow-up questions also brings you closer together because it signals to the other person that you actually care about their input.
- Recognize that it is not personal. Be sure to recognize that the feedback is not about you personally; it is about your behavior. You must dig deep and have a healthy self-worth in order to not get defensive. Be sure to keep the feedback in perspective.
- Take action. Once you receive the feedback, it is important to act on it; so create a plan and take action to improve. ∎

Today's Live Happy Practice

Reread the tips on receiving feedback and implement them in your life.

DAY 335

The Serious Pursuit of Play

Have you ever noticed how happy you feel when you pass a playground and hear the uninhibited giggles and screams of joy from children at play? When children are playing, they are developing communication and social skills. They are also testing new ideas, developing self-control, and learning how to make decisions. But the benefits of play don't just apply to children; they extend to adults as well. That's why adult play is so important.

Adult play is critical in the area of stress relief. It also helps to keep you young and energetic. Studies have shown that play improves memory and triggers growth in brain cells. Many adults overlook the importance of play because they believe that playing is for children. This is a mistake because adult play promotes freedom and escapism from a world filled with goals and responsibilities.

Sometimes it can be challenging to think of ways for adults to play, but there are many playful activities that adults can do. If you are physically fit, you can engage in rough-and-tumble play such as basketball, scavenger hunts, or swimming. Adults can also play checkers and chess or other board games like Monopoly or Clue. Then there's a myriad of card games like Uno or poker. Adults can also participate in imaginative play like coloring, drawing, or painting. And for added benefits, you might try storytelling, comedy, or improve classes. There are countless ways that adults can enjoy the benefits of play. If you want to engage, find out what works for you and have at it. ∎

Today's Live Happy Practice

Review the various ways that adults can play in today's inspiration. Identify one that works for you and commit to engaging in it today.

DAY 336

Living with Your True Self

Being your true self can sometimes be a challenge because, in childhood, you may have learned to adapt your behavior to align with others around you. This is particularly true of authority figures like parents or teachers. But as a happy and whole adult, it is important to shed the masks that may inhibit true expression and hold you back from the expression of your authentic self.

Being authentic liberates you and gives you the authority to rise to your highest potential. When you are true to yourself, you trust your own judgement and decisions. In addition, other people will trust you and they will respect your values and your beliefs. When you are authentic, it means that your actions and your beliefs line up with each other. You can experience total peace and happiness when your outward expressions align with your inner ideals. Being authentic to who you are means breaking through layers of learned behavior and borrowed beliefs. Authenticity alarms should sound in your brain when you engage in fake behavior or insincere actions in order to fit in or be accepted.

The good news is that true authenticity is yours to be had if you want it. All you need to do is drop the need to conform. You are not required to go along to get along so there is no need to conform your behavior to what everyone else is doing. A better approach is to connect with people who, themselves, are genuine, and who appreciate surrounding themselves with others who are genuine. These are the people who have outgrown the need to fake it and who are grateful for others who concur. ■

Today's Live Happy Practice

Examine the areas in your life where you know you are being inauthentic. Think about the things you say or do that does not represent your authentic self. Work on letting those things go.

DAY 337

Mr. T

You should never judge a book by its cover, and that goes for people too. The other day I stumbled across and interview with Mr. T and learned a whole lot about the man that I never knew. Although I liked some of his work, like when played the boxer named Clubber Lang in the movie *Rocky III*, I still thought of him as a one-dimensional cartoon character who walked around with a neck full of gold chains and Mohawk hair style. His catchphrase, "I pity the fool," didn't help to elevate him in my mind either. But when I saw him on the interview, my entire opinion about him changed. I realized that I was judging him without knowing much about him. I was intrigued, so I researched him by viewing documentaries, watching interviews, and reading books.

I learned that he was the youngest of 12 children who grew up in a three-room apartment in the projects on the Southside of Chicago. I learned that he wore the Mohawk as a powerful tribute to the Mandinka warrior in West Africa after reading about the tribe in National Geographic. I also learned that he spent his entire life working with sick children and encouraging young people to do what's right. Here's one piece of advice he gave, "You can't take people for granted. You can be with somebody every day and never really know them. So don't treat people like furniture. Don't treat a teammate like he's invisible because everybody is important on your team. Take the time to find out what people are about and you'll be glad you did. Listen to a friend, Mr. T." ■

> ### Today's Live Happy Practice
> Think of someone that you have developed preconceived notions about and judged without really knowing. Research or talk to the person to learn more about who they really are.

DAY 338

Forgiveness Does Not Change the Past, but It Does Enlarge the Future

Have someone ever done something to you that was simply unforgivable? The best thing you can do is forgive them anyhow. But in many cases, that is easier said than done. No matter how difficult it is to do, forgiveness is a worthwhile endeavor because when you forgive others, you set yourself free. There is a causal relationship between forgiveness and your health. It means that not forgiving others can cause harm to your body by releasing all the chemicals of a stress response.

Some people believe that you should forgive and forget. But while you may be able to forgive, it doesn't mean that your brain will forget what happened. Not forgiving ties you to the past, and while you can't change the past, there is no need to view your life through the lens of hostility, resentment, or anger.

Blaming others turns you into a victim, but forgiveness helps you move from being a victim to being valuable. The key is to move away from being fixated on the past event. One of the best things you can do is to find a way to impersonalize the hurt. When you don't take it personally, it helps your brain stop being attached to the incident. Learn from it. Don't condemn or blame, just try to understand the other person's behavior. After that, release it. This can free you from the past. It can also be a catalyst for you to help others who may have gone through a similar experience. ■

Today's Live Happy Practice

Think about someone who you have been unable to forgive. If you're going to forgive, it must be intentional so make a commitment to yourself to do it. Be sincere with yourself. Make a phone call or write a letter to the person. Set yourself free from the past and be at peace.

DAY 339

Taking the Blinders Off

If you've ever seen a horse strolling through the French Quarter in New Orleans, or pulling a wagon on State Street, you may have noticed that they always have blinders over their eyes. Horses can see nearly 360 degrees around them because of how their eyes are positioned on the sides of their head. It means that their eyes work similar to a motion detector, which causes them to be easily distracted nearly all the time. Therefore, they wear blinders so they can stay focused on the task at hand. The blinders also help the horse relax and pay more attention to what's in front of it.

When it comes to success in your life, your actions are very much influenced by your personal paradigms. Your paradigms are simply the way you see the world. Just like the blinders on a horse, your paradigms act as blinders and restrict what you actually see. All of your interactions are influenced by your paradigms; including your social, spiritual, and financial interactions. As you might imagine, your paradigms can limit your growth and success; therefore, if you want to be more successful, it is imperative that you shake off the old limiting paradigms and create new ones.

Essentially, a paradigm is a thought system that drives your habits. They can be difficult to change because they are built up over time based on the truth that you accept and repeated actions you take. But don't worry; even though a paradigm shift may not be easy, it is not impossible. If you do the things that line up with the good traits you want in the future, you can create new habits that reinforce new paradigms. ∎

Today's Live Happy Practice

In order to create new paradigms, think about the results you have been getting and compare it to the results you desire. Do the things that line up with the good traits you want in the future. Continue doing them until they become habits.

DAY 340

How to Be Proactive

There are basically two kinds of people in the world; those who are proactive and those who are reactive. People who are proactive plan ahead, but people who are reactive always seem to be a step behind. That could mean the difference between controlling your life instead of letting it control you. People who are reactive often feel stressed. On the other hand, people who are proactive are more relaxed because they don't feel as if they are living a life out of control.

Proactive people get things done on time and they don't get frustrated when unexpected things come their way. Since they are prepared, proactive people can receive feedback, which gives them the opportunity to make adjustments and revisions as they go along. This is a great way to elevate your progress and reflect on the outcomes that you desire.

When you are prepared in advance, challenges can be minimized, allowing you to stay cool and calm. If you want to be a proactive person, the most effective way to do it is to think about what you want to do and plan for it. ∎

Today's Live Happy Practice

Follow these steps to develop your plan:

- Defining the deliverables of your project.
- Break it into smaller, more manageable chunks.
- Determine what resources you will need.
- Estimate the duration and cost of the project.
- Create a measurement baseline to keep yourself on track.
- Develop your technical skills.
- Execute your plan.

DAY 341

How to Win and Get More Out of Life

Some people believe that in order to win, somebody's got to lose. But this is a fallacy because there is no shortage of anything in the universe. The idea that there is a lack of something is the result of a scarcity mindset. This type of thinking causes your brain to panic and make choices based on faulty information and incorrect assumptions.

Do you often worry that you don't have enough money or other tangible things? There is good news for you if you are obsessed about a lack of resources. The good news is that you can adopt an abundance mindset. One of the ways to do it is to engage in win-win thinking. Win-win thinking is like having your cake and eating it too. Win-win thinking is based on an abundance mentality; which is the belief that there is enough for everyone, and that one person's success doesn't diminish or threaten the success of someone else. People with an abundance mentality don't struggle and fight over who gets a bigger slice of the pie; instead, they use their energy and resources to bake more pies.

Thinking win-win requires optimism. It requires you to look beyond any constraints in resources and look for opportunities to work together. Everyone wins when you find a solution that benefits both sides. It is better to value cooperation over competition because there is plenty of resources to go around. ∎

Today's Live Happy Practice

Think about ways to manifest mutual advantages in your relationships. Pay attention to how good it feels when everyone wins. Be clear that there are plenty of positive benefits for all involved and continually be on the lookout for ways to engage where everyone wins.

DAY 342

Impossible is Just an Opinion

At the beginning of the year in 1969, the idea of going to the moon was impossible. But then on July 20 of that year, NASA sent two astronauts there and the dawn of the space-age became a reality. Before 1954, it was impossible for a human to run a mile in less than four minutes, and then on May 6 of that year, it happened.

The word "impossible" means that something cannot be done. The belief that something is impossible can have an impact on how people think and feel. It can also have a profound negative effect on their behavior. That's what happened with the moon landing and the four-mile run. It can be very difficult to see the possibilities when the prevailing thought is that something is impossible. But when you recognize that impossible is just an opinion, then doors fly open. That happens because, once you believe on the inside, you begin to see the possibilities on the outside.

Who said it's impossible to change careers at your age? Whoever it was, that was just their opinion. The truth is that there are always an endless amount of possibilities within your reach. You just have to believe it. If you want to make impossible things possible, you need to have a vision. Finding the possibilities is about finding ways to do things. Life is full of endless possibilities. All you have to do is believe. ■

Today's Live Happy Practice

Write your vision down. Look for opportunities and adopt an attitude of optimism. Commit to doing the thing that you always wanted to do and take action. Identify the roadblocks that may be holding you back and figure out how to get around them.

DAY 343

Stuck In the Middle

A soft rock song was released in the early 70s that was titled *Stuck in the Middle with You.* It is not entirely clear what the song is about but some pop commentators have speculated that it's about the paranoia one musician experienced when he was invited to a music industry cocktail party. Supposedly, the musician feels that he's stuck in the middle of a bunch of clowns and fakers.

Personally, I think the song is about something else. While it does appear that the musician is paranoid and unsure about being at the party, it seems to me that he's also suffering from indecision. While the character in the song does appear to be out of place at the party, his indecisive personality seems to go a lot deeper then just his concern about the festivities. He even had trouble making a decision about the chair he's sitting on.

Do you struggle with indecision? Is being indecisive keeping you stuck in a cycle of procrastination? Is not making a decision causing you to suffer from worry or fear? If indecision has you spending your wheels like you're stuck in the mud, it could be preventing you from reaching your goals. If you want to get unstuck, the first thing you need to do is commit to making a decision. Make a list of your options and evaluate each one. Systematically go through the list and eliminate the ones that you can. Consider the pros and cons of the remaining choices and choose the best option. ■

> ### Today's Live Happy Practice
> Whenever you find yourself delaying a decision, attach a deadline and stick to it. If you make a decision and it doesn't work out, remember that taking chances is just a part of success. Take a small step today. Don't wait for tomorrow, make a decision and start acting now.

DAY 344

How to Learn Everything Faster

You have heard the saying that knowledge is power. That is simply not true. Knowledge is the awareness or practical understanding of a subject. Power, on the other hand, is the ability to direct or influence the behavior of others. Basically, power is the ability to act on the knowledge you have. The limitation for most people is that they don't have the ability to act on the knowledge they possess. Therefore, knowledge is potential power; which means that the more you know, the better your chances of success. The bottom line is this; the faster you learn, the more success you can have. With that in mind, here are three things you can do to learn everything faster.

- Say it out loud. Many times when we learn something, we read or think about it silently. But research shows that saying the information out loud helps make it easier to remember. That's because the act of saying the word makes it more distinct and fixes it in your long-term memory.
- Take handwritten notes. Research has shown that you benefit more by handwriting your notes than you do by typing them. You will retain more when you rewrite the information in your own words. It is also a good idea to review and organize your notes directly after you take them.
- Teach someone else. Teaching the information to someone else helps you learn it better because, when you teach someone else, you have to go through the process of seeking out key points and organizing the information into a coherent structure. ▮

Today's Live Happy Practice

Being a quick learner can give you a greater advantage over your competition. Use the tips in today's inspiration to retain more and learn everything faster.

DAY 345

The Power of Finishing What You Start

Why is it so important to finish what you start? The answer to this question might seem obvious, but the benefits of finishing are more than just checking something off your to-do list. Finishing what you start gives you a sense of achievement and increases your confidence in your ability to win. When you finish things, you gain the trust and respect of people around you, which could prove to be a valuable asset for future projects. Other people are more apt to follow you when they know that you have a good track record of completing things.

It is typical behavior to feel enthusiastic at the beginning of a new project, but the key is to follow through even when you feel stuck. Your project may require more time and effort that you had originally thought. You may also experience a lack of resources, or maybe a decline of focus or will-power. All of these things could add up and cause you to lose focus, but it is imperative to stay on track in order to finish what you started.

You can improve your chances of finishing by breaking your project down into small steps. Be selective of what projects you take on. Only commit to those things that you care about and have some passion for. Your time is precious so you'll want to spend it wisely. Finally, be sure to budget your time and energy accordingly. Be realistic about how much time you can devote to the project, and be sure to plan for contingencies. ∎

Today's Live Happy Practice

One of the things you can do to improve your chances of finishing is to visualize the entire project up front. Make a mental note before you start. Get an idea in your mind of everything that needs to be done. Make a plan by writing down the resources you will need, including the people and the money. Do your homework up front by gathering the necessary data.

DAY 346

The Power of "No"

Some people consider "No" to be a negative word. But "No" doesn't always have to mean negativity. It would be a mistake to confuse the two because negativity is a mindset, while "No" is a choice. When you say "No," you are making a conscious decision not to be influenced by others. "No" can actually be a beautiful thing when it helps you remain true to your values.

Many times in life, other people will overwhelm you with requests. Some people will even demand things from you. In many of these instances, "No" is the appropriate response. But what makes "No" such a powerful word? It is because each of us individually have a limited amount of time and resources. It would be a mistake to waste your resources on things that you dislike or that are ridiculous or unhelpful.

Many times, you may have said "Yes" so often that you feel guilty when you don't. Have you ever found yourself in a situation where someone invited you to a function or event and you really didn't want to go? Did you feel bad about saying "No?" Did you say "Yes" out of a desire not to disappoint them? Or worse yet, did you come up with a fantastic lie just to get out of saying "No?"

Just because it's easier to say "Yes" doesn't mean that you should. Why should you disregard your own feelings or well-being in order to appease someone else? You should recognize that saying "No" does not make you a bad person and it doesn't signify a lack of moral character. ■

Today's Live Happy Practice

If you have trouble with the word "No," try thinking of other words to get your point across. For example, try saying "Not at this time," or "I'll pass on that." It lets the other person know that you decline the request but it may not seem as harsh as saying "No."

DAY 347

Smile

The pop star, Michael Jackson, was often quoted as saying that his favorite song was the song *Smile*, which was composed by the silent film star, Charlie Chaplin. In the song, the singer is telling everyone to cheer up because there is always a bright tomorrow as long as you just smile.

Michael Jackson had a good reason to like that song because there are some real-life benefits to smiling. Sometimes it may not be easy to smile, but in a stressful situation you will actually feel better if you do. When you smile, a host of tiny molecules are released in your brain. These molecules act to help fight off stress and boost your mood. When a smile forms on your face, it activates certain pathways to your brain that tricks your brain into a state of happiness, and this happens even if you fake a smile.

Smiling offers benefits in the work environment too. Happiness at work has been known to boost productivity, and it helps you make better decisions and be more creative.

Another good thing about smiling is that the benefits are not limited to you. Whenever you smile, other people around you can't help but smile back. That's great news because it means that smiling is infectious. And as an added benefit, other people are naturally attracted to people who smile. Smiling makes you look more youthful because the muscles used to smile tend to lift your face, similar to what happens when you get a facelift. So if you want to be happy and achieve more success, just smile. ∎

> ### Today's Live Happy Practice
> Take the waiting challenge. When you are waiting in a line or doctor's office, stop and smile at someone. Pay attention to see if the other person smiles back.

DAY 348

Qualities of a Good Friend

There is a real connection between health and friendship. Good friendships are not always easy to build or maintain, but they are well worth the effort. Friends can help you celebrate when times are good and provide support when things are bad. Humans need to belong and, outside of your family, your friendships are the best way to fulfill that need.

As you grow as an individual and gain more responsibilities, your friendships can sometimes suffer. A demanding job, children, or aging parents can sometimes prevent you from spending the time you need to maintain your friendships. But be assured, if your friends are as valuable and considerate as you think, then they will understand your situation. And if they don't, it could be a sign that you have outgrown the relationship.

That being said, if you want to nurture a good friendship, you must be a good friend in return. Let the other person know that you care about them. You can accomplish this by being kind. Your kindness and gratitude toward your friend will go a long way toward strengthening your bond. Be sure to listen to them. Ask about what's going on in their life. Be responsible and dependable with your friend. You should also be trustworthy. That means keeping information private when they share with you in confidence. Be sure to value and nurture your friendship. And remember, in order to have a good friend, you must first show yourself friendly. ∎

Today's Live Happy Practice

If you need to end a friendship that you have outgrown, begin to slowly fade it out. Do it in a non-confrontational way and remain civil. Gradually decrease the amount of time you spend with them. Don't call them as frequently, and if they're abusive in any way, just cut them off all together.

DAY 349

How Chivalry Died

Along with chivalry comes a mixed bag of opinions. In the beginning, chivalry referred to the ideal qualities of a knight, including courtesy, generosity, and valor. In modern times it came to represent the courteous behavior of men toward women; like holding doors or offering a jacket when it's cold.

Today, it seems that chivalry is a sexist behavior because it assumes that women are weak and in need of protection from men. It perpetuates gender inequality and some people actually perceive a chivalrous act as a put-down to women.

But why should men refrain from acts of kindness toward women if it's something that makes them happy? It almost becomes a catch-22. If a man holds the door open for a woman, he's being sexist; but if he doesn't hold the door, he's being rude. So what's a guy to do?

I say that when it comes to chivalry, it's better to err on the side of doing it. Although it may not be true in all cases, most women would not rebuff a well meant gesture from a gentleman offered in kindness. Most women would appreciate it if a man chose to stand in a crowded room to offer their seat. And what wife would complain about her husband dropping her off at the door of the mall when it's raining?

Although some women might find it obnoxious, the act of chivalry is really just a selfless act of respect and generosity. It's also okay for women to offer chivalry to men if they choose to do so. After all, what's fair is fair. You may not be able to control how another person feels about your acts of generosity, but that doesn't mean that you shouldn't offer. ∎

Today's Live Happy Practice

Let's bring chivalry back! Practice being polite and courteous toward women wherever you go.

The Mark of Maturity

Have you ever encountered a person who you'd rather not interact with because they were too immature? You know the person I'm referring to. The one who won't own their mistakes, or who is overly defensive about everything.

Many people assume that maturity comes with age, but that may not necessarily be the case. It may be hard to believe, but maturity is not a function of getting older. Instead, it's about how you behave and interact with the world around you. Here are several characteristics of a mature individual, regardless of age.

- The ability to accept criticism. Mature people know how to accept criticism gracefully. Immature people's first reaction is to defend themselves. But mature people resist the urge to do that. Instead, they take a moment to process what is being said. The mature thing to do is thank the person for their feedback and learn from it.
- The ability to keep long-term commitments. Honoring your commitments means being on time and keeping promises. If a commitment cannot be honored, mature people notify the other person early. When mature people promise things, they do it, and if they don't intend to show up, they say "No" up front.
- The ability to seek wisdom. Mature people are able to learn as they go. They are teachable and are inclined to seek wisdom before acting. They never presume that they have all the answers and they are not ashamed to seed guidance form someone with more experience. ∎

Today's Live Happy Practice

Review the characteristics of a mature individual and reflect on your own behavior. Are you a mature individual?

DAY 351

The Power of Dreams

Everyone dreams! Dreaming happens during the deepest part of sleep. Most of the time, you won't remember your dreams, but you may wake up and indulge in the activity that you were dreaming about. For instance, if you were hungry in your dream, you may wake up and head to the fridge.

There is a lot we don't know about dreams because dreaming is such a complex phenomenon. Some people believe that dreams are a prediction of the future and others believe that they are memories from past lives. Sigmund Freud believed that dreams were expressions of repressed sexual desires, and Carl Jung felt that they were shaped energy or inchoate thoughts released deep in the subconscious.

But aside from the act of dreaming while you sleep, many people will have dreams that emanate from their imagination during waking hours. Successful people have the ability to turn these types of dreams into plans. Essentially, these entrepreneurs have the vision to turn their dreams into practice that can literally change the course of their lives. These dreams can be very powerful because they allow you to draw on your talents and gifts, thus giving you direction to shape your actions for the future. Your dreams can provide you with big things to aim for. They can increase your potential and tap into the power of your creativity and imagination. The greater your dreams, the greater your potential to think outside the box of your current limitations. ∎

Today's Live Happy Practice

Think about the dreams you have for yourself that have never manifested themselves in your life. Prioritize the dream and put a plan to it to give it direction. Don't be afraid to dream big and allow your dreams to give your life purpose, direction, and meaning.

DAY 352

Focus on Growth

Being successful is often a function of being able to solve problems and develop solutions to situations as they arise. This is how you learn and grow. Focusing on growth is about having faith in yourself and your abilities. When you focus on growth, you force yourself to break through your own personal limitations. In order to stretch yourself and grow, you must set ambitions goals so that you inspire yourself to new heights. One way to do this is to expand your network of people. It's great to network inside your current space, but you can expand your thinking exponentially by networking with successful people outside your current sphere of influence.

If you want to grow, you have to think bigger. Whatever your income goals are, you must double it. It doesn't matter what area of your life you are working on, you need to multiply what you want. There's no need to live below your potential because your dreams are not big enough. Since you have to plan anyway, you might as well plan big. Sometimes people have the tendency to play it safe. But by playing it safe, you may be thinking too small. Having a bigger goal does not necessarily mean working harder. It means implementing a different strategy or developing a creative approach to achieve what you want. Great ideas and hard work does not guarantee success; nothing can do that. But it is a guarantee that you will have a significantly better chance of success by thinking big than you will by thinking small. ■

Today's Live Happy Practice

Think about your big plans in life. What's preventing you from achieving them? If you don't have the skills you need, figure out a way to get them. Keep in mind that the size of your success is determined by the size of your beliefs.

DAY 353

Get Uncomfortable

It is probably a good idea not to live a life overwhelmed with stress, but it may not be so great to eliminate stress altogether. Some people look at stress as a dirty word, but a little bit of healthy stress may be just the thing you need to push you out of your comfort zone and into extreme success and happiness.

If you want to grow and get better, you have to experience a little discomfort. In fact, staying in a comfortable place too long can be detrimental to your success. Being uncomfortable requires you to look at situations in a different way; which is how you grow and get better.

Getting better can happen in a number of ways. First, you can get better by conquering your fears. Since discomfort is a form of fear, learning to accept it and develop new ways of dealing with it is most beneficial. Meeting your challenges head on, even in the face of fear and discomfort, will make you a stronger person. One of the biggest sources of discomfort stems from the fact that we cannot control certain situations. That's what causes fear to set in. But if you want to achieve greater success, you must stay positive and be creative. Once you move outside of your comfortable you will likely move into the fear zone. But if you remain diligent and keep moving forward, you will soon enter the growth zone, and that's where the magic happens. ■

Today's Live Happy Practice

If you want to grow, embrace your discomfort. Strive to push yourself. It may even be beneficial to seek out discomfort. Look for things that push you to stretch. Pick something that's hard and just do a little. Start slow and continue working at it until you master the thing. The key is to start. Once you get going, you will be surprised at how much you can accomplish.

DAY 354

What it Means to Have a Clear Vision

Have you ever been driving your car when all of a sudden you ran into a heavy rain storm or a snow blizzard that was so thick that you couldn't even see the car in front of you? One of the worse feelings you can have is when your visibility suddenly disappears. It can cause panic and give you the feeling of sheer dread. That loss of vision can be devastating because there is no way for you to know what's going on up ahead.

The same thing happens to your goals when you don't have a vision; they just disappear. The benefits of a clear vision statement can be enormous in helping you get where you're trying to go. It gives you a sense of direction and helps you focus on what's important. You can move forward faster and make better decisions when you have a clear vision. If you can see where you're supposed to go, it makes it easier to know when you're off course. You can stop and ask questions and you can make any necessary adjustments. A clear vision can also be motivating and inspiring; which are equally important in continuing the forward motion toward your goals. Creating a vision for yourself requires time and thoughtful reflection. You need to consider your values and ideals, and be open to explore the possibilities that exist for your life. Once you create a clear vision for yourself and develop a plan to execute it, anything is possible. ∎

Today's Live Happy Practice

One way to create your vision is to work backwards. Think about your life with the end in mind. What do you want your life to look like five, ten, or twenty years from now? What things do you need to learn and what beliefs do you need to change now, to get the results you want in the future? Write your plan down and then set about acquiring the knowledge and skills you need to get where you want to be.

Time Shifting

Do you remember the days before the video cassette recorder (VCR)? Before this technology was invented, the only way to watch a television program was to be at home sitting in front of your television set when it was broadcast. Now all you have to do is record and play back. This is known as time shifting and it helps you do two things at one time.

The concept went mainstream in 1966 when it was depicted on an episode of *I Dream of Jeannie*. Jeannie's master, Major Nelson, wanted to watch a football game and at the same time, he wanted to make a trip to the supermarket. So Jeannie magically paused the live broadcast so that major Nelson could do both.

Times were much simpler then; and slower. In today's society, things move fast. It is imperative to do things quick. We all live under a serious time crunch. Hundreds of tasks every day. It seems that no one has enough time in a day. But if you can master the art of time shifting, you might be able to benefit from switching between hyper productivity and an awareness of the world around you. The point is that the increased speed at which you live your life actually makes your awareness of time move faster. The result is that the future arrives much quicker. But if you can practice time shifting, you can slow down and focus your attention on the present moment. Think of it as taking a break and saving time. You can accomplish this by just doing nothing. Don't check your phone. Don't watch TV. Just sit quietly and notice the birds and the trees. Take a deep breath and simply relax. Try this as often as you like and appreciate how time seems to slow down. ▮

Today's Live Happy Practice

Try time shifting by being spontaneous. Pick a day where you make absolutely no plans. Just go out and see where the day takes you. Leave your schedule behind and just explore. Notice how time seems to slow down since you are not on a fixed schedule.

DAY 356

The Benefits of ZZZs

Most of us have so many things to do that it's hard to find time to sleep. Many times we sacrifice sleep in order to fit everything in, but this could be a mistake since sleep is vital to your well-being. Your body repairs itself while you sleep, and sleeping has a clear impact on your mood and your performance. As it turns out, research indicates that sleep is an important factor in your happiness. When you don't get enough sleep, it can impair your reasoning and problem-solving skills. But a sufficient amount of sleep leads to a healthier heart and a sharper brain. Try these tips if you find yourself having trouble sleeping.

- Reduce blue light. The blue light from your electronic devices like phones and computers make it more difficult for you to sleep, so it's best to turn off the TV and other electronics a couple hours before going to bed.
- Limit caffeine intake. Caffeine tends to stimulate your nervous system and may make it more difficult for your body to relax. Therefore, it is better to consume drinks like coffee early in the day. Caffeine can stay in your blood for up to eight hours so it can interfere with your sleep if you consume it too close to bedtime.
- Go to sleep at the same time. Your body is naturally equipped to align itself with sunrise and sunset. This is referred to as circadian rhythms. Going to sleep and waking up at predictable times help you sleep better, but irregular sleep patterns can throw off these rhythms and result in poor sleep habits. ∎

Today's Live Happy Practice

If you have trouble sleeping, try relaxing before you go to bed. You can listen to soft music or meditate just prior to getting in bed. Reading a book or taking a hot bath may also help you relax and improve your sleep patterns.

DAY 357

Find Joy in the Little Things

Most of the time we are moving so fast that we fail to notice the sunset. Too often we miss the birds singing and the color of the leaves on the trees. But it is the small things that can have a dramatic impact on our lives and our happiness. Many times we take the small things for granted because we desire the big things, like getting a promotion or buying a new car. But the truth is that life is made up of the little things. It is a great feeling when you complete your next task or accomplish your next goal. But it can be equally satisfying to cuddle under a warm blanket when it's cold or breathe the crisp morning air in the fall.

In the movie *Click* (2006), Adam Sandler plays a workaholic architect who acquires a remote control that allows him to control reality. He uses the remote to fast forward through all the little things in life so he can get to the big ones. Eventually the remote control learns his preferences and begins to fast forward through the little things automatically, causing him to skip large chunks of time, thus missing years of his life.

While the movie was by no means a blockbuster; it did contain a profound message for those who were paying attention. The takeaway is that life is made up of the little things and if you ignore them, you will be left with a handful of big days. ∎

> ### Today's Live Happy Practice
> Take the time to look at the stars and express gratitude for each moment, no matter how small. Be aware of the details and notice the little pieces of beauty in everything around you.

DAY 358

Out-of-Control Junk Drawer

When was the last time you looked inside your junk drawer? You know the drawer I'm talking about. Everybody has one. It's the drawer that's piled up with junk; which by definition, is junk. Lots of people will tell you how to organize the drawer, but that is an impossible task. It's impossible because once you clean and purge all the junk, it's no longer a drawer full of junk. Don't get me wrong, I'm not advocating for junky junk drawers; they probably should be cleaned. After all, why should you take up valuable space with junk?

Just like you ought to declutter useless things from that drawer, it can also be beneficial to declutter your life. Decluttering may sound like a big project but it does not have to be. You can take 15 or 20 minutes to tidy up one room or one closet. That small increment of time can have big benefits to your sense of well-being. Decluttering you space can be energizing. It can help you feel a sense of accomplishment. Organizing and decluttering your space can also help to reduce your anxiety level because people often experience a sense of calm when their space is free of clutter.

But when you declutter, you must beware the urge to wax nostalgic. It can be very tempting to hang on to everything that reminds you of something. Try to determine what is truly important and get rid of everything else. If you're having trouble tidying up your place, start small. Just pick one drawer or one closet and start there. ▮

Today's Live Happy Practice

One of the easiest things you can do to declutter is to dump the duplicates. That means getting rid of all the things that you have too many of. A good rule of thumb is get rid of an item whenever you buy a new version of that same thing.

DAY 359

One Yes

Sometimes you're driving along minding your own business when all of a sudden, out of nowhere, something appears to block your path. These roadblocks can sidetrack your progress and stand in the way of your success. But if you want more out of life, it is important to identify the roadblocks and find a path around them. Roadblocks can manifest themselves in many different ways. For example, your progress may be impeded because you have no clear vision for what you want to do and how to get there; or you may suffer from procrastination or a lack of motivation.

If you want to push through the roadblocks that pop up, you might try accepting the ONE YES challenge. The challenge encourages you to choose one roadblock and work on it. The quicker you identify the impediments trying to block your road to success, the sooner you can reach your personal goals.

One of the most critical things you must do when you encounter a roadblock is to believe in yourself. When you have confidence in your own ability to succeed, it will be that much easier to work through any challenges that might present themselves. It also helps to know your priorities. If you want to continue your forward motion, you need to be committed to your objectives and pursue them without wavering.

Roadblocks do not have to mean the end of your plans. There are going to be little bumps on the road on every successful journey. The key to finishing well is to ensure that those little twists and turns don't deter you away from the finish line. ■

Today's Live Happy Practice

In order to maneuver around any roadblock, it helps to enlist the help of others when possible. Spend some time today thinking about who you might get on your team, or who you might approach as a mentor or coach.

DAY 360

How to Be a Good Observer

Maya Angelou said that you can't us up creativity because the more you use, the more you have. I think that she was correct. Everyone can generate bold and creative ideas if they put their mind to it. The best way to become a good thinker and to create new ideas is the free yourself from the mundane and average thoughts that keep popping into your brain. Great ideas don't just happen. If you want to think out of the box, you must get your brain thinking in new ways. You can do this by observing the world around you. If you can develop your ability to perceive your surroundings, you will have a constant supply of inspiration for new thoughts.

Have you ever been driving home from work and planned to make a quick stop at the grocery store, but all of a sudden when you looked up you were pulling the car into your garage? This happens because your brain is so familiar with the route home that it switches on autopilot. The human brain is designed to switch off when it is doing routine tasks. That means that we do them without really thinking about them.

Your brain functioning on autopilot may be beneficial in some instances, but not so much when it comes to observing the world. The same routine and familiar places can cause your mind to kick into autopilot and you can miss all the important details that help your creative juices flow. If you want to be more creative and bold in your thinking, you will need to hone your powers of observation; which in turn, will help you change your perspective and see the possibilities in everything around you. ∎

Today's Live Happy Practice

You can improve your powers of observation by cutting out distractions like cell phones and laptops. Be intentional. Look at everything through the lens of curiosity.

DAY 361

How to Stop Putting Things Off

Have you ever had a big project due at school or an important report due at work and then, all of a sudden, you got a burning desire to clean your whole house? If you frequently find yourself putting off critical actions or delaying making important decisions, you may be a procrastinator.

Procrastination can interfere with your happiness because it can impact your ability to successfully pursue your goals. If you're not careful, procrastination could even increase your stress and lead to other physical and mental challenges.

But why do people do it? Most people think that procrastination is simply a lack of self-control or laziness; however, the issue is much more complex than that. In many instances, procrastination can stem from anxiety, fear, or other negative emotions. The fact of the matter is that procrastination has nothing to do with laziness. After all, a lazy person would not set out to clean their entire house. Procrastination is an active process where you choose to do something other than the task you should be doing. On the other hand, laziness is the inactive process of ignoring the task altogether.

The good news is that procrastination doesn't have to take over your life. You can overcome it by recognizing that you are doing it. After that, create a to-so list or schedule and follow it. Break the task down into bite-sized chunks and do one thing at a time. Minimize distractions and your home free. ∎

Today's Live Happy Practice

Since procrastination is about emotions, if you want to overcome it, you must forgive yourself for doing it. Don't beat yourself up. When you forgive yourself, it helps you feel more positive. After that, commit to the task and promise yourself a reward when it's done.

DAY 362

Incredibly Curious People

I find it very interesting that we are all born inquisitive, but from the very beginning of life, everyone seems to want to kill our curiosity. Parents want their children to stop climbing on things and stop touching things. Teachers want children to read a book and memorize things for a test instead of allowing them to explore and think what they want about the text. Society itself seems to have little tolerance for any deviations from the norms and standards it has established.

This is an interesting observation because, while we seem to want to crush curiosity, curiosity is the very thing we need to succeed. But if society has been arresting your innate curiosity, what can you do to ensure that it does not zap you of your much needed inquisitiveness?

One thing you can do to maintain your curiosity is to listen without judgement. You should resist the urge to size people up or make assumptions as to what they are all about. Instead, try focusing on exploring who they are and expressing empathy toward them. This will help you learn, as well as cultivate great relationships. Another thing you can do is continually ask questions. Try to find out the who, what, and why of things. The moment you start finding things out, you will naturally become more inquisitive and intentional about learning. ∎

Today's Live Happy Practice

If you want to increase your curiosity exponentially, don't be afraid to be wrong. You will be amazed at how freeing it is to not have to be guarded all the time. Liberate yourself from having to be right and you will never stop learning.

DAY 363

The Joy of Crossword Puzzles

The crossword puzzle was invented as a diversion to the bleak realities of war. In fact, the first crossword puzzle was introduced in December 1913 on the eve of World War I. The first published brainteaser was call a Word-Cross puzzle, but due to a typographical error, the title was inverted and printed as Cross-Word puzzle. The mix-up stuck and, today, crossword puzzles are the most popular word game in the world.

Crossword puzzles are fun to play, but it would be a mistake to think that their only virtue is to provide an enjoyable way to pass the time on a lazy Sunday afternoon. On the contrary, there are many benefits to regularly solving crossword puzzles. For one, they are good for brain health and have been shown to help alleviate dementia and delay memory loss. In one amazing study, researchers found that people who regularly solved crossword puzzles had the brain strength of someone 10 years younger than themselves.

Another benefit of working crossword puzzles is that it helps strengthen social bonds. This happens when you collaborate with people of different ages and backgrounds to solve the squares. Crossword puzzles can also help you relieve stress and boost your mood. Working puzzles gives you the opportunity to relax and get more quiet time. When you focus on the puzzle, your brain actually times out the world around you and focuses on the game of solving the clues. This type of activity can make you calmer and happier; and what's not to like about that? ■

Today's Live Happy Practice

If you want to experience the benefits of solving crossword puzzles, you can purchase a puzzle book at your local convenience store or work one online for free. Try it, you might like it.

DAY 364

Holiday Traditions

I always loved the holidays when I was growing up and I still do. Everyone is always happy and in a good mood, and there's nothing better than the sweet aromas wafting from the kitchen and up my nostrils. I can remember the sounds of a holiday parade on TV or sports in the background. But it really doesn't matter what else is going on in the world around you, the thing that makes the holidays so memorable is the rituals and customs that the family regularly engages in. It's those family traditions that makes the holidays stand out; and it's the rituals that give you the memories that will stick with you for a lifetime. Here are some things you can do this year if you want to create a new holiday tradition for your family.

- Tell one thing you're thankful for. Go around the table and have each person say one thing that they are thankful for this year. You will be amazed at how many blessings your family has received and you will be grateful that they recognize it.
- Pass around a journal. Instead of saying it out loud, simply pass around a journal and ask each person to write one thing they are thankful for. At the end, read the list aloud.
- Bless a family. Try starting a tradition where each member of your family purchase one thing to donate to another family. Find a less fortunate family and bless them with the items.
- Wear matching pajamas. Have the entire family spend a night at your house and ask everyone to wear the same pajamas, or at least the same color. Everyone can bring a blanket or sleeping bag and just go for it.

Today's Live Happy Practice

Pick one of the tips above and initiate a new holiday tradition for your family this year.

DAY 365

Be Good to Yourself

Being good to yourself is vital for both your physical and mental well-being, but often times, your busy schedule may not allow time for self-care. Self-care is simply the act of appreciating and taking care of yourself. It means that you have a high regard for your own well-being and happiness. It means accepting yourself for who you are, and not being overwhelmed or disappointed in minor setbacks or failures. When you care for yourself and hold yourself in high esteem you are more likely to make healthy choices.

If you want to practice self-care, you can start by treating yourself like you are worth it. Take care of your body like it is a precious commodity, because it is. Initiate a healthy diet and incorporate exercise into your daily routine. Whatever you do, it doesn't have to be big. Doing little things can make a big difference.

Here's one final tip for engaging in self-care; be sure to have a sense of humor. You will feel a lot better about yourself when you don't take yourself too seriously. If you make a mistake, don't beat yourself up, just learn from it. If you find a flaw in yourself, fix it. And if your plan is not going the way you like, change it.

Whatever you do, treat yourself right. Be kind to yourself and have a high regard for your own well-being and that of others. And above all… Live Happy! ■

Today's Live Happy Practice

One of the best things you can do to care for yourself is surround yourself with positive people. Also, be sure to always engage in positive self-talk because your internal voice can either make or break you, so always say good things to yourself.

NOTES

NOTES

NOTES

NOTES

ABOUT THE AUTHOR

Dr. Derrick B. Wells is one of the foremost authorities on spiritual principles, mind potential, and high performance. He's a spiritual leader and corporate CEO whose platform has reached and served the underserved. Going from a street kid to a successful leader, teacher, speaker, and clergyman, Derrick's call and courage have inspired learners worldwide and helped facilitate untold breakthroughs. Whether through his writings, lecturing internationally, or coaching, he continues to be a stand for the personal empowerment of those he believes can learn the habits that lead to wealth, manifest their untapped talents, and unleash their limitless potential.

As Founder and CEO of *Live Happy Network LLC*—Derrick has developed countless workshops and training programs that have transformed the lives of men and women through his educational business. The results have helped to improve the life trajectory of people throughout the country and across the world. He shares practical, creative, inspirational messages weekly with his global *Temple Talks* Facebook Group. Dr. Wells also gives leadership to Christ Universal Temple, one of the largest New Thought spiritual communities in the world.

Derrick is an award-winning author of four books. His fifth book, *Live Happy*, released in 2021 is a blueprint to better. *Live Happy* continues Derrick's commitment to ensuring those who engage him have a clear and practical road map for personal success, direct from the life experiences of its beloved author. *Live Happy* is the eagerly anticipated follow-up to Derrick's *Guidelines For A Master*.

Derrick lives, works, and plays in the greater metropolitan Chicagoland area.

To find out more about Derrick's *Designing the Life You Deserve E-Course*, *Play Bigger, Coaching Programs*, and audio and video programs, or to inquire about hiring him as a speaker, trainer, or consultant, you can contact his office at:

Live Happy Network, P.O. Box 877, Flossmoor, IL 60422
E-mail: livehappy@DerrickBWells.com
Web site: www.DerrickBWells.com
Social media: @DerrickBWells

Live Happy

Made in the USA
Las Vegas, NV
14 December 2024

14032275R00208